Socializing Epistemology

Studies in Epistemology and Cognitive Theory

General Editor: Paul K. Moser, Loyola University of Chicago

A Useful Inheritance: Evolutionary Aspects of the Theory of Knowledge
by Nicholas Rescher, University of Pittsburgh

Practical Reasoning: Goal-directed, Knowledge-based, Action-guiding Argumentation
by Douglas N. Walton, University of Winnipeg

Epistemology's Paradox: Is a Theory of Knowledge Possible?
by Stephen Cade Hetherington, University of New South Wales

The Intellectual Virtues and the Life of the Mind
by Jonathan L. Kvanvig, Texas A & M University

Blind Realism: An Essay on Human Knowledge and Natural Science
by Robert Almeder, Georgia State University

Epistemic Virtue and Doxastic Responsibility
by James A. Montmarquet, Tennessee State University

Rationality, Morality, and Self-interest: Essays Honoring Mark Carl Overvold
edited by John Heil, Davidson College

The Problem of the Criterion
by Robert P. Amico, Saint Bonaventure University

Socializing Epistemology: The Social Dimensions of Knowledge
edited by Frederick F. Schmitt, University of Illinois at Urbana-Champaign

Socializing Epistemology

The Social Dimensions of Knowledge

EDITED BY

Frederick F. Schmitt

ROWMAN & LITTLEFIELD PUBLISHERS, INC.

ROWMAN & LITTLEFIELD PUBLISHERS, INC.

Published in the United States of America
by Rowman & Littlefield Publishers, Inc.
4720 Boston Way, Lanham, Maryland 20706

3 Henrietta Street, London WC2E 8LU, England

British Cataloging in Publication Information Available

Library of Congress Cataloging-in-Publication Data

Socializing epistemology : the social dimensions of knowledge / edited by Frederick F. Schmitt.
p. cm. — (Studies in epistemology and cognitive theory)
Includes bibliographical references and index.
1. Social epistemology. I. Schmitt, Frederick F., 1951–
II. Series.
BD175.S623 1994 121—dc20 94–11232 CIP

ISBN 0–8476–7958–6 (cloth : alk. paper)
ISBN 0–8476–7959–4 (pbk. : alk. paper)

Printed in the United States of America

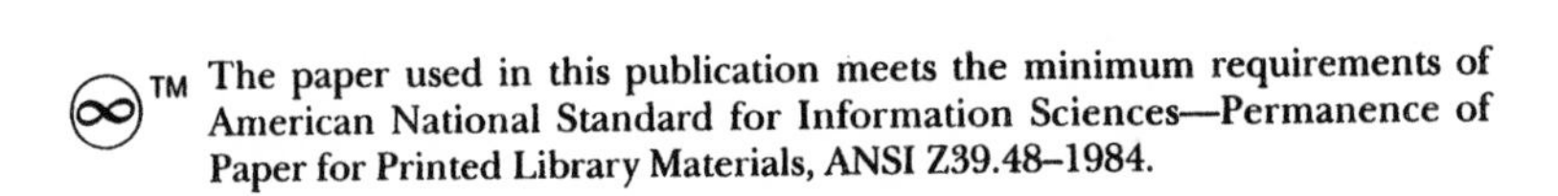
The paper used in this publication meets the minimum requirements of American National Standard for Information Sciences—Permanence of Paper for Printed Library Materials, ANSI Z39.48–1984.

For my mother, Elizabeth B. Schmitt,

my father, Frederick F. Schmitt,

and

my son, Nathaniel

Contents

Acknowledgments ix

1 Socializing Epistemology: An Introduction through Two Sample Issues, *Frederick F. Schmitt* 1

2 Belief-forming Practices and the Social, *William P. Alston* 29

3 Egoism in Epistemology, *Richard Foley* 53

4 Speaking of Ghosts, *C. A. J. Coady* 75

5 A Conservative Approach to Social Epistemology, *Hilary Kornblith* 93

6 Contrasting Conceptions of Social Epistemology, *Philip Kitcher* 111

7 The Fate of Knowledge in Social Theories of Science *Helen E. Longino* 135

8 Good Arguments, *Richard Feldman* 159

9 Accuracy in Journalism: An Economic Approach, *James C. Cox and Alvin I. Goldman* 189

10 A More Social Epistemology, *Miriam Solomon* 217

11 Remarks on Collective Belief, *Margaret Gilbert* 235

12 The Justification of Group Beliefs, *Frederick F. Schmitt* 257

Socializing Epistemology: A Bibliography, *Frederick F. Schmitt and James Spellman* 289

Index 311

Contributors 313

Acknowledgments

I would like to thank Paul Moser, our adventurous series editor, and Jonathan Sisk of Rowman and Littlefield for making this volume possible. Jim Spellman gave excellent editorial assistance. His philosophical criticisms made a notable improvement in my contributions to the volume. And we worked together on the bibliography. I would also like to thank Glenna Cilento who, despite difficult personal circumstances, never fell short of her usual superb secretarial work and typesetting.

1

Socializing Epistemology: An Introduction through Two Sample Issues

Frederick F. Schmitt

Social epistemology is the conceptual and normative study of the relevance of social relations, roles, interests, and institutions to knowledge. Thus it differs from the sociology of knowledge, which is an empirical study of the contingent social conditions or causes of knowledge or of what passes for knowledge in a society, a study initiated by Karl Mannheim. Social epistemology centers on the question whether knowledge is to be understood individualistically or socially. I have yet to find an informative general characterization of what it is for knowledge to be individualistic or social. Rather, there is a loosely related family of disputes, each concerning a different kind of knowledge or a different way in which knowledge might be social.

HISTORY

Epistemology has traditionally ascribed a secondary epistemic status to beliefs indebted to testimony (call these "testimonial beliefs"), as well as to expert authority, consensus, common sense, and received wisdom, or it has denied them any status at all. Plato, Bacon, Descartes, Locke, and Hume, despite great differences, shared a conception of knowledge or justified belief as cognition that results from a proper method or from the proper use of certain faculties, where a proper method or use aims at the true, explanatory, coherent, or stable thought of the knower. Social relations were assigned one of three roles. They could *support* a proper method by making its use materially possible, or by inspiring (but not justifying) new theories and new observations (Bacon). Social factors could *extend* an individual's faculty of perception by supplementing it, through testimony, with what is perceived by others (Hume). Or they could *prevent* us from acquiring knowledge, either by bequeathing improper methods through common sense and received wisdom (Bacon, Descartes), or by preempting proper methods through interference with reason.

The history of social epistemology is largely unexplored, with the exception of the history of thought about testimony, which we owe to the pioneering work of C. A. J. Coady (1992), from whom I borrow liberally in what follows. Plato, Aristotle, and their medieval heirs excluded testimonial beliefs from knowledge. One explanation for their doing so is that they sharply distinguished knowledge from opinion, knowledge being the deliverance of reason—of intuition, demonstration, and (for some philosophers) perception—and opinion being nondemonstrative, including (for some) belief on faith and testimony. Thus, Aquinas (1945, 1987) assimilated testimonial beliefs to faith (though he elevated both above mere opinion). However, this explanation of the secondary status of testimonial beliefs is incomplete without an account of the grounds on which intuition is counted on the side of reason and testimony is not. If it is said that reason yields certainty, then we must ask why it was common in medieval thought to put received opinion and authority on the side of reason. At any rate, testimony was recognized as useful and reliable (i.e., tending to lead to true beliefs). From this vantage, Aquinas and Hume agree at least roughly on the reliability and usefulness of testimony and differ mainly in whether such reliability makes testimony justifying.

In the seventeenth century, two trends forced a rethinking of the place of social relations in knowledge. One was the emergence of the new science, with its break from Aristotelian and common sense pictures of the physical world. For Bacon (1857-59, IV *Novum Organum*, para. 41, 43, 52, 59-60) and Descartes (1984, II *Meditations I*), common opinion (Bacon's "idols of the tribe" and "idols of the market"), as well as received philosophy ("idols of the theater"), were an impediment to proper method. They could be overcome only by reason and experience in the new science. A second trend, consequent upon the new science, was a remapping of the distinction between knowledge and opinion. Reason could no longer be assigned the whole burden of knowledge if the new science was to count as knowledge; perception had to be admitted as well. Yet Descartes's effort to employ reason to tame perception and render its contribution to knowledge consistent with the requirement of certainty did not carry conviction. Thus the distinction between probability, on the one hand, and knowledge or epistemic justification, on the other, eventually had to be rejected, or else, as with Hume, knowledge or justification itself demoted. It is no accident that Hume was among the first self-consciously to assign testimonial belief a high epistemic status, assimilating it to perceptual belief.

Reid (1969, 1975) also assimilated testimonial belief to perceptual belief, but he assimilated it to belief whose justification derives from a primary source rather than to belief deriving from perception. In offering this alternative to Hume, Reid not only broke with the traditional assignment of a secondary status to beliefs indebted to social relations. He also made the status of social factors a topic of controversy. In doing so he founded social epistemology as a significant, self-conscious philosophical subject.

Subsequent epistemology challenged both the secondary status of beliefs indebted to social relations, and the assignment of nonsocial cognitive aims to the proper method. For example, Peirce (1955) understood the proper method as aiming at consensus. And Nietzsche suggested that knowledge has a noncognitive social aim—the needs and preservation of a community or "herd." Here Nietzsche intends an explanation of the importance of knowledge in human life, rather than an analysis of the concept of knowledge.

The vast bulk of work in social epistemology in the twentieth century has been done by analytic philosophers since Thomas Kuhn (1970) proposed that the great scientific revolutions involve shifts from one paradigm to another incommensurable paradigm—incommensurable in the sense that the two cannot be compared on the basis of observations or experimental results because these observations are theory laden. Science does not progress by the accumulation of accepted observations and theories. From this vantage, it is tempting to think of scientific revolutions as taking on more the character of social changes in attitudes than choices between theories in light of the same evidence (though it is doubtful that Kuhn ever intended such a view).

Since 1980, social epistemology has taken its inspiration from two sources. Sociologists of knowledge—especially those associated with the "strong programme" in the sociology of science (Barnes 1977)—and feminist philosophers of science (Harding 1986) have argued that social interests interfere with methods directed toward truth or empirical adequacy, and some have proposed that knowledge should be conceived, not as belief in accordance with proper methods—at least not with methods that aim at truth—but instead as belief in accordance with social interests. This work has prompted epistemologists to take seriously the idea that knowledge is a matter of consensus or accordance with a multiplicity of perspectives. The other inspiration of recent work in social epistemology is naturalistic epistemology (Quine 1969a). If, as naturalistic epistemology proposes, knowledge is belief that results from natural propensities, it is reasonable to ask whether knowledge does not also extend to belief that results from socially endowed propensities, whether or not the latter are thought of as natural. Hilary Kornblith makes this point forcefully in his contribution to this volume.

Social epistemology may be divided into three branches: the role of social factors in individual knowledge; the organization of the cognitive labor of individuals and groups of individuals; and the nature of collective knowledge. It is impossible in this introduction to review all significant recent contributions to these branches. I will therefore concentrate on the first, illustrating it with the topic of testimony, the topic most extensively covered in classical texts and in recent literature. (Parallel issues arise for common sense and received opinion.) I choose testimony because I regard it as the most fundamental test of epistemological individualism. If individualism concerning testimony is defensible, then epistemology will remain in an important sense individualistic. And if it is not defensible, epistemology will have to be profoundly social, whatever may happen on other topics. Since testimony is covered in only two of the articles in this anthology—those by Richard Foley and C. A. J. Coady—I feel a review of the issue is in order. I will then discuss social constructivism about knowledge, a topic that spans the several branches of social epistemology.

CONDITIONS OF INDIVIDUAL KNOWLEDGE: TESTIMONIAL JUSTIFICATION

Our first topic is whether the conditions of individual knowledge or justification are in any way social. It is obvious, and would be admitted by everyone, that systems of epistemic evaluation are social: we learn epistemic terms, concepts, and conditions from others; epistemic evaluation is mostly evaluation of the cognitive states of other individuals; and such evaluation is possible only because there are social systems of reinforcement that facilitate it. It is less obvious, but also true, that certain items that figure centrally in epistemic evaluation are social—e.g., cognitive belief-forming processes are exercised by many individuals and are evaluated across their entire output. See William Alston's contribution to this volume for further discussion. It is also clear that the system of epistemic evaluation serves certain social purposes—e.g., facilitating the flow of information across individuals, consensus among members of society, and the coordination of behavior by enabling us to anticipate future events. What is quite controversial is the claim that any of these social elements appears in the conditions of knowledge or justification themselves.

Thought about the epistemic status of testimonial belief may lead to just that conclusion. We may begin with the question whether testimony is a primary source of knowledge or merely derivative from another source, such as perception. *Strong individualism* denies that any testimonial beliefs are justified; all beliefs must be justified first-hand. (Locke [1959] endorsed a version of this view that applies to knowledge rather than justified belief.) This view is hard to countenance; it excludes my knowledge of my own name, birthdate, who my parents are, what town I live in, and the proposition that a cloudless sky is generally blue. A more attractive view is *weak individualism*, endorsed by Hume (1975) and arguably the dominant view of testimony since the eighteenth century. On this view, testimonial beliefs may be justified, but always on the basis of nontestimonial beliefs.

There are three versions of weak individualism. It will suffice for now to mention the most popular, the *inductive* version, on which a testimonial belief is justified on the basis of the belief that the testimony is trustworthy or reliable, and this in turn is justified by induction from a first-hand observed correlation between testimonial belief of this sort and the truth of the propositions testified to. I will argue that there is currently on the table no convincing motivation for weak individualism. I will also argue that there are currently no convincing objections to the inductive version of the view. And I will say something about what must be done to settle the issue.

Let us begin with the motivation for weak individualism. Ideally we would locate a motivation for the view capable of explaining its historical dominance. The history we have so far canvassed may explain why the role of testimony in knowledge shifted from exclusion in Aquinas to inclusion in Hume, but it does not explain the particular form of that inclusion—one that relegates testimonial beliefs to a secondary status. For it adverts to the relation between knowledge and opinion and the association of knowledge with reason and certainty; and, even for Descartes, testimony is no more doubtful than perception in its naive use (though for Descartes it may be that there is no way to rectify testimony through reason, as there is a way to rectify naive perception). Why, then, must testimony be based on perception? Of course one can explain the secondary status of testimonial beliefs by pointing to the dominance of individualism in modern thought. More specifically, one might appeal to an ideal of cognitive autonomy—that individuals should always think things through for themselves. If cognitive autonomy requires that one rely in reasoning only on beliefs that are not testimonial, then it entails weak individualism (at least, on the assumption that justification is a matter of living up to cognitive ideals). But this is hardly an *independent* motivation for weak individualism. The latter goes hand in hand with cognitive autonomy.

I can think of six possible motivations for weak individualism:

The Egocentric Project. Most contemporary epistemologists would no doubt trace the motivation for weak individualism to the egocentric epistemological project of Descartes and his followers. In this project, the subject is asked to attend systematically to his or her own system of beliefs. There are perhaps two versions of the project. In the *radical* version undertaken by Descartes, the subject's aim is to rebuild the system of beliefs from scratch. The point of rebuilding the system from scratch is to enable the subject to eliminate the possibility of erroneous beliefs. In the *moderate* version of the egocentric project, the subject's aim is instead to put the system of beliefs in proper order, relying on some or all beliefs in the system to do so. (Reflective equilibrium theories of justification are sometimes designed to fit the kind of justification defined by the moderate project.) On either version of the project, the beliefs that emerge at the end of the project count as knowledge or as justified beliefs.

How might weak individualism be motivated by appeal to the egocentric project? Let us consider the radical project first. I doubt whether the radical project really entails weak individualism, but we need not decide whether it does. For if it does, the most plausible reason would be that the justified beliefs that emerge at the end of the project must be justified on the basis of whatever beliefs are justified in the course of the project. And the latter beliefs must be justified on the basis of no beliefs at all—hence on a nontestimonial basis. The trouble with this motivation is that it undermines *perception* as a primary source of justification if it undermines testimony, and so it cannot be used to motivate anything like Hume's view of testimony, on which there is an asymmetry between testimony and perception. One might respond that perceptual beliefs could satisfy the requirement here by being justified on the basis of perceptual impressions rather than beliefs. But if so, we must ask whether testimonial beliefs could not also have primary justification on the basis of testimony. It is not obvious that justification on the basis of testimony is justification on the basis of a *belief.*

The moderate project is actually a more promising source for weak individualism than the radical project. The moderate project employs some favored initial beliefs we already possess. Now, on one version, the justified beliefs at the end of the project are justified on the basis of these initial beliefs, and the latter are in turn justified in whatever way we take them to be prior to the project. This version has no prospect of motivating weak individualism, since whether testimonially justified beliefs must be based on nontestimonial beliefs depends on whether they are excluded from a favored status, and the project does not by itself tell us which beliefs have a favored status. The moderate project may, however, be amended so that the initial beliefs do not inherit their justification from any prior justification they may have, but acquire it within the project. For example, coherentist and reflective equilibrium versions of the project propose that we begin with what we already believe and make our beliefs coherent; justification then depends on coherence. This will entail weak individualism if any belief, to be coherent, must be based on nontestimonial beliefs alone. But I can see no ground in this version of the project alone for the latter requirement. Even if a belief must be justified on the basis of nontestimonial beliefs, it does not follow that it must be justified on these alone. Coherentism may yet motivate some kind of individualism—I will say more on this later—but it does not motivate weak individualism.

Add to all this the point that no reason has been offered for embarking on an *egocentric* rather than a social project of revising our beliefs. Why should we not work together to put our beliefs in order? One might say that disagreements among us will prevent resolution. But these disagreements will be there after we have egocentrically put our houses in order, and they will quite soon unsettle those houses. Of course, the choice of a social project would not necessarily exclude weak individualism. Whether it does depends on whether in working together with you I must rely on you as something more than a source of inspiration and doubt. Must I rely on your testimony to justify my beliefs without my possessing your reasons? It seems quite clear that I need *some* help from others, and perhaps I need help even to know what I actually believe. (How do I know what I think until I see what I say—to someone?) Thus, it remains an open question whether I can put my house in significantly better order than it is now in without relying on the testimony of others for justification.

The Antiskeptical Project. What we have said about the motivation from the egocentric project carries over to a motivation from an antiskeptical project. One might suppose that answering skepticism requires starting from one's own experience, hence first-hand knowledge. For in calling into question the existence of the physical world, skepticism also calls into question the existence of other persons, and thus my beliefs cannot ultimately be justified on the basis of testimony. But of course skepticism is raised in the first place by asking an individual to establish the reliability of his or her beliefs given only the resources of his or her own experience. The task might have been different: to establish the reliability of his or her beliefs given the testimony of others to their experience. It might be objected that skepticism disallows whatever the subject may doubt and thus disallows reliance on the reported experience of others. But it seems that individuals can doubt their own experiences. Perhaps it can't seem to me that I am in pain unless I am. But then I can doubt that things seem to me a certain way. Of course, the antiskeptical project has no hope of answering skepticism unless doubt leaves some resources—e.g., whatever must be assumed if the skeptical challenge is raised, or whatever must be true in the demon situation or other possible situation designed to generate doubt. But it is not clear that this creates an asymmetry between my own experience and the reports of others.

The Deontic Conception of Justification and Accessibility Internalism. The deontic conception of justification might motivate a view akin to weak individualism: that one cannot be justified on the basis of reasons possessed by others. According to the deontic conception of justification, *deontic* concepts like "ought" and "permissible" apply to beliefs, and justification is epistemically permissible belief (see Alston 1989a for criticism). From this it may be inferred that a subject must be able to avoid a belief when it is unjustified. For "ought" implies "can," and thus impermissible belief must be belief the subject can avoid. But then the subject cannot be justified on the basis of reasons possessed by others. For one cannot avoid an unjustified belief if the reasons that make it justified are possessed by others. For one can avoid an unjustified belief when there are no such reasons only if one can tell whether there are such reasons. But one cannot in every case of justified belief tell whether there are such reasons, since one does not always have access to the reasons possessed by others. Consequently, one cannot be justified on the basis of reasons possessed by others. This does not quite argue for weak individualism but rather the negation of one of the alternatives to it (namely, transindividual reasons—see below). Nevertheless, it will do for the moment.

This appeal to the deontic conception of justification assumes a most implausible asymmetry between our access to our own reasons and those of others. Surely no one is always able to tell, in every instance in which a belief might be justified, whether he or she possesses the reasons that make the belief justified, and people are often able to tell whether others possess reasons. The motivation might gain some plausibility if we turn from the requirement that subjects be able to tell whether they possess a reason to the accessibility internalist requirement that they be able to tell this *by reflection alone*. There is some chance that a subject will be able to tell whether she possesses a reason by reflection alone, at least on some occasions, but there is no chance that a subject will be able to tell by reflection alone whether others do. I see some prospect of an asymmetry here. But what this motivation makes up for in support of asymmetry it loses in the diminished plausibility of the requirement. In the end, an appeal to internalism is no stronger than an appeal to the deontic conception of justification. Moreover, the asymmetry here will not rule out alternatives to weak individualism that do not entail that testimonial belief is based on another subject's reasons. As I remark below, accessibility internalism is consistent with at least one alternative to weak individualism.

Naturally vs. Artificially Obtained Reliability. Another possible motivation for weak individualism may lie in the view that testimony differs from perception and induction in requiring surveillance to make it likely that the subject will form reliable testimonial beliefs. Worries about the reliability of testimony are clearly at the heart of early modern ambivalence about whether to allow it as a source of knowledge. Now, perceptual and inductive beliefs tend to be, within their customary domain of everyday life, *naturally* reliable—i.e., reliable in the absence of the subject's assessment of their reliability. Testimonial beliefs, it might be said, differ in being unlikely (or at least less likely) to be reliable in the absence of guiding justified beliefs about their reliability. For this reason, it might be proposed, testimony yields a justified belief only if the subject is justified in believing the testimony reliable. This motivation connects weak individualism with the traditional idea that social factors tend to interfere with cognition by reducing its reliability. Testimony, on this motivation, is a social factor, reliance on which tends to make beliefs unreliable. To correct this tendency the subject must verify the reliability of testimony by relying on nontestimonial beliefs.

No doubt Descartes regarded testimony as generally unreliable, but he also regarded sense perception as generally unreliable. For Descartes, our common ways of thinking depend on a mistaken teleological metaphysics, the antidote to which is a systematic doubt from which Cartesian metaphysics is supposed to emerge. But what if Descartes had not rejected our naive metaphysics? Then it seems he would have had no basis for rejecting the natural reliability of either testimony or perception.

Anyone who accepts naive metaphysics ought to give in to the natural reliability of testimony. Testimonial beliefs seem to be naturally reliable in nearly as broad a range of circumstances as perceptual and inductive beliefs. Let us waive here doubts about the reliability of naturally occurring perceptual and inductive beliefs (e.g., doubts raised by the work of Kahneman and Tversky concerning inductive and probabilistic beliefs). On any view, perception and induction are naturally reliable in some everyday circumstances and not in others. And it seems that testimonial beliefs are naturally reliable in nearly as broad a range of circumstances as perceptual and inductive beliefs. It is true that in the circumstances in which testimonial beliefs are not naturally reliable, we may have to rely on previous testimony to arrive at justified beliefs in their reliability. But we would equally have to rely on previous perceptual or inductive beliefs to judge the reliability of a perceptual or inductive belief when it is not naturally reliable—a Humean point. There is no prospect of motivating weak individualism by insisting that testimonial beliefs are less often naturally reliable than perceptual or inductive beliefs.

Necessity of First-hand Justification. On any view, testimonial justification is parasitic on *someone's* first-hand justification—if not the subject's, then the testifier's. Hence there is an incentive to encourage first-hand justification, and one way to do this is to identify justification with first-hand justification. But of course if it is impossible or even difficult to pursue first-hand justification without second-hand justification, then the incentive for first-hand justification must be tempered with an acceptance of second-hand justification.

Familiarity of the Reduction. A reduction would subsume testimonial justification under well understood epistemic phenomena—inference from nontestimonially justified beliefs. (This is perhaps more attractive for the inductive version of weak individualism than for other versions.) Add to this optimism about reduction, and one can see why philosophers would rest content with weak individualism. But such optimism can never have been warranted, for reasons I will give below.

We have canvassed possible motivations for weak individualism and found all wanting. Let us now turn to objections to the view. These must be launched against specific versions of weak individualism, of which there are three. The first two parallel the analogical argument for other minds and face some of the same obstacles as that argument.

1. On the *inductive* version, already introduced above, a testimonial belief is justified on the basis of the nontestimonially justified belief that the testimony is reliable, and the latter belief is in turn inductively justified on the basis of first-hand observed correlations between testimony and the truth of the testimonial propositions.

Let me treat the most serious objections to this version. First, it is quite obvious that the testimonial beliefs of small children cannot result from these inductive inferences, since they lack beliefs about the reliability of testimony and also lack the premises from which reliability might be inductively inferred. Yet we do attribute justification to children's testimonial beliefs (Reid 1975; Plantinga 1993). This objection may be fortified by tying testimony to language learning. The claim would be that language learning requires the learner to believe the testimony of the teacher; yet such beliefs are acquired before there can be a nontestimonial basis for an induction to the reliability of the testifier. To this objection it may be replied that our attributions of justification to the beliefs of small children are too tenuous to carry much weight. Moreover, it is not obvious that language teaching is testimony or even that learning the meaning of terms involves acquiring propositional knowledge, as opposed to acquiring the skill of using the language.

Second, Coady (1992) has argued that if a testimonial belief is to be justified on the basis of an induction from nontestimonial beliefs, it must be possible for us to discover that testimony is unreliable. Otherwise testimony would be guaranteed reliable. Yet we cannot conceive of testifiers whose reports are not generally reliable. For one thing, statements that are generally false would not count as *reports* of states of affairs or events (by the definition of "report") and would therefore not count as testimony (by the definition of "testimony"). For another thing, reports must, by charity, be interpreted in such a way as to make them generally true.

Waiving the question whether reports and hence testimony must generally be true (and granting the principle of charity assumed here), there are still two grounds for doubting this objection to the inductive version. In the first place, it is not *generally* true that a belief can be justified by induction only if it is possible for us to discover that beliefs of the sort are unreliable. It is not possible to discover that analytic beliefs are false and hence unreliable (if the reference class of beliefs in terms of which the reliability of these beliefs is defined includes only beliefs of this sort); yet one can be justified by induction in believing that all bachelors are unmarried. Of course the problem remains that such an induction would be pointless when there is a much better argument for reliability by appeal to analyticity. This brings me to the second response to Coady. Even if there is an a priori argument for the general truth of testimony, it does not follow that any testimony is sufficiently reliable for purposes of justification in any instance. That would follow if the epistemically relevant reference class of testimony were all instances of testimony, and a reliability greater than one-half were sufficient for justification. But neither of these assumptions is plausible.

Third, the final and most serious objection to the inductive version is this. We rely on testimony for most of the beliefs that would have to serve as the nontestimonial basis of the induction to the reliability of testimony. No individual has checked more than a few testimonial reports. It is indeed practically impossible to check more than a tiny percentage of these reports. The basis for an induction is therefore too slim to provide much justification. (See Coady 1992 for an argument that an attempt to justify testimony by inference to the best explanation faces the same objection: the basis for the inference is infected with testimony.)

It is no easy matter to judge the force of this objection. The proponent of the inductive version may respond by appeal to a nonenumerative view of induction. Some inductions—e.g., to the color of birds of a species, or the melting temperature of a metal—justify their generalizations on the basis of very few instances. This may happen because there is a necessary relation between the properties observed (color and belonging to the species). If there is such a relation between a testimonial utterance and its probable truth, then the objection to the inductive version will fail. One might think this response takes leave of induction altogether. But it takes some enumeration to establish which properties are projectible (the species, a certain sex of the species, adult vs. immature, etc.). And in any case the justification of the reliability of testimony is not a priori—it depends on a contingent correlation observed by someone. Thus, judging the merits of the inductive version turns on the question whether human beings are constituted socially so as to believe and speak the truth, and on how the matter of constitution relates to inductive justification. These are vexed questions, and on the latter there is less philosophical work than one might suppose. We are very far from being able to settle the plausibility of the inductive version and thus of weak individualism. Further progress must await an account of induction that addresses the relevant questions.

Analogous to the third objection to the inductive version is an objection on the basis of *expert* testimony (Schmitt 1987a). Unfortunately, this objection faces a response analogous to the response to the third objection. (See Coady 1992 amd Goldman 1991a for further responses to this objection.)

2. Let us turn now to the second, *a priori* version of weak individualism. This version appeals to an epistemic parity between my own beliefs and those of others. The idea that my own beliefs are no more justified than those of others is ancient. Sextus Empiricus uses it to urge *epoche* in the *Outlines of Pyrrhonism* (1933): I ought to suspend judgment when others disagree with me. The a priori version of weak individualism depends on the contrapositive argument as follows:

> If I am to be justified in my own beliefs, I must have reason to trust them—i.e., I am justified in believing them reliable.
> But I have no more reason a priori to trust my own beliefs than I do those of others.
> But if I have reason to trust the beliefs of others, then I am justified in my testimonial beliefs.
> Consequently, I am justified in my testimonial beliefs.

Of course this argument does not yet distinguish between justified and unjustified testimonial beliefs, but this distinction may be introduced by allowing testimonial justification to be defeated by the subject's prior testimonial and nontestimonial justification. (Richard Foley employs a parity argument like this in his contribution to this volume, though in the service of a nonindividualistic account of justification.)

One objection to the a priori version is that it assumes a priori that I am justified in my beliefs. But what is the basis for this assumption? Is there any reason a priori to prefer the parity argument to its skeptical contrapositive? To argue a priori that all my beliefs are justified, the a priorist might appeal to a principle of *negative coherence*: any belief for which there is no defeater is prima facie justified (at least initially). But surely this principle is less plausible than a direct social principle on which testimonial belief is justified (see Reid's principle of testimony below). We would do better to adopt a social principle and abandon weak individualism. The a priorist can make progress here only against a strong individualist who accepts negative coherence. But the best reason for strong individualism is a doubt about the reliability of testimony, and that doubt depends on a reliabilist account of justification inconsistent with negative coherence. If this is right, then the a priorist who appeals to negative coherence is tilting at windmills.

Turning now from the a priori status of the parity argument to the plausibility of the argument itself, one might object that it trades on an ambiguity in "trust." What is plausible is that I must trust others in the same sense in which I trust myself. But when I trust myself, I am justified in believing that my beliefs are reliable in the sense of "reliable" relevant to *my* beliefs' being justified. Thus, when I trust others, I must be justified in believing that *their* beliefs are reliable in the sense relevant to *their* beliefs' being justified. It does not follow that I am justified in believing that their beliefs are reliable in the sense relevant to the justification of *my* testimonial belief. For I can very well recognize that a testifier's belief *p* is justified without thereby acquiring testimonial justification for believing *p*. It might be replied that this can happen only if I possess some defeater for *p*. But it is far from obvious that in the absence of any defeater I am justified on the basis of testimony. More generally, I may trust others to form beliefs that are justified for them. But whether I can become justified by adopting those beliefs depends on whether my epistemic position is relevantly similar to that of the testifiers—whether I have the features that make their beliefs justified. And there is no reason a priori to suppose that I do. Certainly that conclusion does not follow from the view that a priori I have no more reason to trust my own beliefs than those of others. The a priori version should therefore be rejected.

3. On a final version of weak individualism, a testimonial belief is justified by its *coherence* with nontestimonially justified beliefs (and with other already justified testimonial beliefs). The difficulty with this version is that the objection to the inductive version, if good, shows that there is little coherence between any given testimonial belief and the nontestimonially justified beliefs that might form the basis of an induction to the reliability of testimony. There is little *inductive* coherence. And the same objection shows that the nontestimonially justified beliefs are very impoverished. So it is doubtful that they together cohere or that any given testimonial belief will cohere with them to the degree necessary for justification. The proponent of the coherence version might turn to the view that testimonial beliefs are justified by the coherence of all beliefs together, testimonial as well as nontestimonial. But this is no longer a version of weak individualism, since testimonial beliefs are no longer justified on the basis of nontestimonially justified beliefs alone. To be sure, the coherence version still counts as a version of individualism. But since we currently have no idea how all these beliefs are supposed to cohere, it seems we lack even an attenuated individualistic account of the justification of testimonial beliefs. Moreover, the coherence theory suffers from implausibility. For it entails a symmetry of justification where there is none. Suppose a historian finds a manuscript attributable to Lincoln that sheds light on the extent to which Lincoln may be

credited with freeing the slaves. That Lincoln authored this manuscript intuitively provides much more reason to assign him a large role in freeing the slaves than the latter provides the former. Yet coherentism entails that, in certain circumstances, these propositions are equally justified, since they receive their justification from their mutual coherence. Coherentism is thus less plausible than a nonindividualistic view that ascribes justification to the proposition that Lincoln authored the manuscript to Lincoln's own testimony in the manuscript itself.

We have raised objections to the three versions of weak individualism, but the outcome is in doubt. In light of all this, it seems appropriate to take seriously the following alternatives to weak individualism:

1. *Primary Prima Facie Justification*: Reid urged that we treat testimonial justification as underived from perception and analogous to it. Such justification is governed by a first principle, "That there is a certain regard due to human testimony in matters of fact, and even to human authority in matters of opinion" (1969, p. 640). We are able to conform to this principle because we are endowed innately with certain dispositions: veracity, which disposes us to tell the truth; and credulity, which disposes us to believe what is said. For Reid, first principles cannot be directly proved, but they may be supported by appeal to such features as common assent, conformity to language and the human constitution, and practical necessity (see Coady 1992 for an excellent discussion). In appealing to these features to establish first principles, Reid may have had in mind the view that first principles characterize the proper functioning of cognition (as Plantinga 1993 has suggested). Or Reid may have had in mind that they characterize its reliable functioning (1969, p. 328).

The degree of justification of testimonial beliefs characterized by first principles is, initially, quite low ("a certain regard"). Nevertheless, this degree of justification is sufficient for justification simpliciter; otherwise the objection to weak individualism will carry over to Reid's view. Testimonial beliefs are initially basically justified. Thus, small children may be justified in them. Testimonial beliefs have only prima facie justification: their justification may be defeated by that of nontestimonial beliefs, as well as by testimonial beliefs already justified. Reid's principles of prima facie justification are, however, crucially different from those recently proposed by Chisholm and Pollock, in two respects. For Reid, first principles do not in general express necessary truths, either synthetic or analytic. The justification of testimonial beliefs might not have been characterized by the first principle above, and indeed we might not have been justified in our testimonial beliefs if we had been differently constituted and governed by other practical necessities than we are. Nor, for Reid, do first principles in general define any concept.

The availability of an alternative to individualism that exploits primary prima facie justification may permit the nonindividualist to embrace accessibility internalism (contrary to Webb 1993). Whether this kind of nonindividualism can be internalist depends on the exact form of the principle. There are more and less social, hence external ways to formulate the principle. The more social formulation is, "If someone testifies to *S* that *p*, then *S* is prima facie justified in believing *p*." This formulation is inconsistent with accessibility internalism, since we are not able to tell by reflection alone whether its antecedent is satisfied. But if the principle says, "If it seems to *S* that someone testifies to *S* that *p*, then *S* is prima facie justified in believing *p*," this is quite consistent with accessibility internalism—or at least makes no more trouble for accessibility internalism than a perceptual principle. Note that the justification licensed by this principle is not justification on the basis of a "seems" belief. Nor does the principle have to be understood to license justification on the basis of there seeming to be testimony. It may differ from principles of perceptual justification on which perceptual beliefs are justified on the basis of seeming. In short, an accessibility internalist could add a testimonial principle of justification to the list. (But see my contribution to this volume for doubts about internalist accounts of *group* justification.)

2. *Reliabilism*: An externalist alternative to individualism is the view that testimonial beliefs are justified in virtue of resulting from reliable belief-forming processes. We might understand the belief-forming processes solipsistically, as cognitive processes strictly within individual cognizers (though exercised by different cognizers on different occasions). If we understand the processes this way, then we must decide between a more and a less social way of individuating them—individuating in terms of the individual's *representation* of the testimony, or in terms of the actual testimony itself. On the other hand, we might understand the belief-forming processes to be *social* cognitive processes involving the cognition of the testifier as well as the testifiee (and perhaps the testimonial communication itself). If we understand the processes this other way, then the reliability approach to testimonial justification is consistent with the following view.

3. *Transindividual Reasons*: A third alternative to individualism relies on *transindividual reasons*—the testimonial belief *p* is justified by reasons for *p* possessed by the testifier. On this approach, a testimonial

belief is justified only if there is an actual testifier who possesses reasons for the belief. We may understand what it is for the testimony to be justified by the testifier's reasons in two ways. The testimonial belief may be justified inferentially, as on Hume's view, but on the basis of the *testifier*'s reasons. Or the testimonial justification may be assimilated to the justification provided by memory, at least on one view of memory: just as beliefs justified on the basis of memory might be said to owe their justification (albeit noninferential) to the reasons for which they are originally believed, even when these reasons have been forgotten by the subject, so testimonial beliefs might be said to owe their justification noninferentially to the testifier's reasons, even though these are not possessed by the subject.

All of these accounts—primary prima facie justification, reliability, and transindividual reasons—embroil us in the large task of describing the transindividual structure of testimonial justification. It must be determined whether testimonial justification requires that the testifier be justified in believing the testimonial proposition or that the testimony be delivered in any particular way. And there will remain many unsettled questions even after deciding between the accounts—e.g., whether in certain circumstances knowledge requires first-hand knowledge and whether the subject must sometimes contribute a certain amount of original justification for testimonial beliefs (Schmitt 1987a).

It has not been my purpose to judge the prospects of these accounts. We will not be able to do that until we have detailed versions of the accounts. As things now stand, we do not even have a detailed version of weak individualism, even though it is the historically dominant view of testimony! My purpose has been to inquire into the issues, explore what needs to be done to settle a few of them, and label the alternatives.

CONDITIONS OF INDIVIDUAL KNOWLEDGE: OTHER MATTERS

Testimony is only one topic, albeit a pivotal one, affecting the conditions of individual knowledge and justification. It is worth mentioning one other topic that affects the conditions of individual knowledge before moving beyond individual knowledge. One might argue that the concept of knowledge has a social content by appeal to the social functions of the concept. Not all social functions of a concept go into its content. The concept of mountain may have a social function, but it has no social content. Nevertheless, if the social function of the concept of knowledge turns out to be a social *epistemic* function, there may be considerable plausibility in inferring a social content. Thus, Edward Craig (1990) has proposed that the concept of knowledge derives from the notion of a good informant (see Schmitt 1992b for criticism). For a second example, Alston (1989c) has proposed that we have the concept of justification because of its applicability to or in the practice of justifying propositions in dialogue, and at least one feature of the concept of justification derives from this applicability: a weak requirement of the accessibility of reasons (see Schmitt 1992a for criticism). Along these lines, one might try to argue for the stronger view that a subject is justified in believing a proposition (or in making a claim) just when she is able to justify a proposition to an audience—or just when she is able to hold her own in a conversation in which the proposition comes in for criticism. (Admittedly, that view is rather hard to defend, since we ascribe justification to inarticulate people.) These are only a few of the ways in which the conditions of knowledge might acquire a social content.

THE ORGANIZATION OF COGNITIVE LABOR

Human society is possible only if individuals coordinate and institutionalize their inquiry in such a way as to obtain knowledge. Though this is a matter of great importance, traditional epistemology has offered little advice for organizing cognitive labor. I will list here some little explored questions about this matter.

1. When should individuals relay to others information they possess that is relevant to a given inquiry, and when should they refrain from doing so? Alvin Goldman (1991a) has argued for *epistemic paternalism*: it is sometimes epistemically appropriate for individuals to withhold relevant information from others who must judge an issue.

2. What role do good arguments play in the business of conveying information and producing knowledge? Goldman (1994) has offered an account of good argumentation which evaluates arguments with regard to their promulgation of true beliefs. In his contribution to this volume, Richard Feldman proposes an epistemological person-relative alternative to Goldman's veritistic speaker- and audience-relative view.

3. What is the best arrangement of social incentives to encourage individuals to relay true or useful information to others and to pick up such information? In this volume, James Cox and Alvin Goldman advance our thinking on this question with an economic model of accuracy in journalism.

4. Do the social interests of individuals (e.g., ambition for professional credit) steer individual research and belief-formation in such a way as to enhance the prospects of true belief? Goldman and Moshe Shaked (1991) have employed an economic model to give an affirmative answer to this question.

5. Are the prospects of group knowledge enhanced when individuals pursue lines of inquiry that are unpromising or based on implausible theories? Philip Kitcher (1990) has argued for an affirmative answer: group cognition is sometimes better off (according to a decision-theoretic calculation) when individuals pursue diverse lines of inquiry even if the individuals who pursue them must hold irrational attitudes. In this volume, Miriam Solomon also argues for an affirmative answer to the question by showing how biases induced by the organization of cognitive labor itself—by individuals' professional preoccupations and perspectives—may enhance the prospects of rational group belief.

One might wonder what implications the answers to these questions have for the place of social factors in individual knowledge. Do the answers listed above imply that the conditions of individual knowledge are social? They do not. On the contrary, these answers assume an individualistic account of individual knowledge. For example, Kitcher and Solomon both assume that individual rational theory choice is a matter of conforming to textbook conditions of theory choice. Nevertheless, their views do have an important consequence for individual rationality: individualistic individual rationality has less value for science than one might suppose. This does not show that science does not need individual rationality; it may still need as much rationality as individuals can give. But we are led to reduce the esteem we lavish on individual rationality.

COLLECTIVE KNOWLEDGE

There is another question that does speak to whether the conditions of individual rationality are social rather than individual: are the goals of proper method to be understood individualistically? In traditional epistemology, it was often a matter of indifference whether the proper methods which produce knowledge are aimed at true *individual* belief or at *common, group, communal*, or *impersonal* belief ("it is believed that *p*"). Moreover, it was often obscure whether the knowledge so defined was *individual* or *collective*. Traditional theories of knowledge, both foundationalist and coherentist, were often most plausible as accounts of communal knowledge, since the resources needed to meet the specified conditions went well beyond those possessed by any individual. Reflection on the exact nature of the aim of proper method might reveal whether the conditions of individual knowledge are individualistic or whether, alternatively, individual knowledge is less significant than we think.

Peirce (1955, p. 12) addressed the question whether the aims of proper method are individualistic or social. While he retained the traditional view that proper belief is belief that results from a proper method of inquiry, he argued that the aim of proper method is consensus. For the aim of fixing individual belief can be fulfilled only if the beliefs of others are fixed as well, since a divergence with the beliefs of others will induce doubt. But if a proper method must aim at consensus, one might think it would require the coordinated effort of numerous individuals; a lone individual could not employ such a method. Whether this is so, however, depends on whether we think of a proper method as one that includes what could, under suitable circumstances, convince others (e.g., evidence), or instead includes all the resources needed to convince others (e.g., communication). The latter would undermine the significance of individual knowledge, but the former would not.

Even if we resist the Peircean demotion of individual knowledge, there remains the question how group and individual knowledge are related. For that, I will have to refer the reader to the chapters here by Miriam Solomon, Margaret Gilbert, and myself.

THE SOCIAL CONSTRUCTION OF KNOWLEDGE

Knowledge may be said to be socially constructed in at least three senses:

1. One claim is that the propositional *content* of knowledge is social. Joseph Rouse (1987) has argued for this claim by appeal to the view that

> (a) the content of scientific theories must be understood in terms of particular actual experiments.

By the "content" of scientific theories, I mean what these theories say, or what is preserved in meaning-preserving paraphrase. (Rouse does not actually use the term "content," and it is possible he would reject this way of putting his proposal; but if his proposal does not concern content in this sense, I do not know what it does concern—see below for further discussion.) Thesis (a) is part of a general picture of scientific knowledge as local rather than global. (Another part of this picture is thesis (b) discussed below.)

Thesis (a) is in turn supported by the claim that the phenomena to which scientific laws strictly apply do not exist in nature but are created in laboratories. Here "created" means "caused to exist" in the ordinary sense, rather than constituted in properties and existence by human thoughts and actions—though Rouse also holds phenomena to be so constituted. The laws, then, taken strictly, generalize only over manufactured phenomena. Rouse does not, however, mean to deny that the laws may be taken less strictly, so that they generalize beyond manufactured phenomena. Understood in this way, they apply to items in nature. But this less strict construal, Rouse appears to say, is possible only because the laws are supplemented with standard ways of replicating the manufactured phenomena in new circumstances. Such standardization makes possible generalization over phenomena in nature that were not in fact manufactured, but might have been manufactured in a standard way.

Now, Rouse's apparent claim that scientific laws generalize only over manufactured or manufacturable phenomena is most implausible. But Rouse need not make this claim, and it is quite possible that he has a different view in mind, one which avoids a restriction to these phenomena. The view that he may have in mind is that scientific laws have the analogical content "Natural phenomena are like the manufactured phenomena." The content of such laws no longer restricts the phenomena over which theories generalize to those that could or would be standardly manufactured, and it no longer says anything about how we are related to the laboratory phenomena. Yet it still adverts to experiments, which are no less (and, unfortunately for Rouse, no more) social here than under the "standard replication" interpretation.

I am inclined to agree with Rouse's claim that scientific theories must be understood in terms of particular experiments and in social terms, but I take this quite differently from the way he does. First, I see no ground for thesis (a) and I am inclined to doubt the thesis itself. Rouse's case for thesis (a) is unconvincing. For the claim that the laws specified by theories strictly apply only to manufactured phenomena is implausible. It is true that *explicit formulations* of scientific laws often fail to specify the possible effects of all the parameters held fixed in laboratories—parameters which vary in nature and render the formulations inaccurate. These formulations are true, if at all, only of laboratory phenomena. But it hardly follows that scientific theories fail to specify laws that apply to phenomena in nature other than those that might be produced in a standard way. One could think so only if one assumed that scientific laws are specified by their explicit formulations alone. But laws are specified by these formulations only in the context of additional theoretical explanations of the possible effects of fixed parameters and by hints for future research on these effects. There is no case here for the claim that theories specify laws that strictly apply only to manufactured phenomena. Nor do I see a case for the claim that theories specify laws that apply to phenomena in nature only by referring to a resemblance between the manufactured and the natural phenomena. Theoretical explanations of the effects of fixed variables and hints for future research *may* amount to such a reference, but they need not. And in cases in which there is a reference to resemblance, the theory may specify the degree and respect of the resemblance, and such a specification may be equivalent to the specification of a property other than resemblance, eliminating the need to refer to the manufactured phenomena. Nor, even if a reference to resemblance turned out to be universal, would it follow that the *content* of scientific theories must be understood in terms of this resemblance, as opposed to the *conditions of reference* of the terms of the theory to phenomena.

Despite my objections to Rouse's case for thesis (a), I am inclined to accept a claim akin to his thesis: that the terms of scientific theories *refer* to phenomena in virtue of a relation the terms bear to manufactured phenomena, and that scientific laws are specified in virtue of this relation. But this is merely the old Kripke-Putnam line that natural kind terms get their extensions by adverting to paradigmatic examples of the kind: an item belongs to the extension of a natural kind term in virtue of its resemblance to a paradigmatic example of the kind. I am also inclined to accept that the conditions of reference are social; for reference involves a causal relation between the use of the term and a baptism of the term in the presence of manufactured phenomena, and this causal relation is a social relation involving the social institution of language transmission. But again, this is more of the old Kripke-Putnam line. Thus, I am inclined to agree that we can crank the conclusion that the conditions of reference of scientific terms are social out of what is plausible in Rouse's thesis (a), but this conclusion bears little resemblance to what Rouse had hoped for.

Perhaps I should emphasize here that a social account of the conditions of reference of scientific terms does not entail a social account of the content of scientific theories. It leaves open that the content of scientific theories is quite different from that of, say, statements about hammers (to use an example of Rouse's). Plausibly, the term "hammer" is defined in terms of social factors, since to be a hammer is to play a certain role in human society. But it is not similarly plausible that a term like "electron" is defined in terms of social relations. The most that is plausible is that the conditions of reference of "electron" are social. The latter proposition does not entail, as thesis (a) does, the implausible consequence that nothing would be an electron if human beings did not exist (though, let it be noted, thesis (a) does not entail that the things that are electrons would not exist if human beings did not exist). That the conditions of reference of "electron" are social entails only the plausible consequence that the term "electron" would not refer to anything if human beings did not have social relations.

Perhaps Rouse would deny the distinction between the conditions of meaning of the theories and the content of the theories; but if content is what is preserved in successful paraphrase, it cannot be conflated with the conditions of meaning. Clearly, even if the conditions of meaning of all statements are social, there is still an intuitive difference between statements whose *content* is social ("This is a hammer") and statements whose content is not social ("This is a frog"). To undermine this difference, it would take more than the point that the conditions of meaning are social. Rouse would have to undermine the very distinction between the conditions of meaning and the content of theories, and this he doesn't even attempt to do.

Rouse might try to defend the claim that scientific theories have social content by appeal to a social constructivism about the manufactured phenomena themselves: they have their features in virtue of their role in human society. But even if the phenomena are socially constructed in Rouse's sense, and even if the theories have the content "Natural phenomena are like particular manufactured phenomena," it does not follow that the terms of a theory are defined in terms of the social factors that do the constructing, any more than it follows from the fact that buildings are constructed with bulldozers that the term "building" is defined in terms of bulldozers. One might contest the analogy with buildings on the ground that the construction in the case of buildings is only causal, not constitutional. One might insist that if what is constructed are the conditions of existence and individuation and the properties of the phenomena, then these must go into the content of statements about the phenomena. But this is far from obvious. If content is whatever is preserved in successful paraphrase, and paraphrase sticks to the colloquial, and the natives are completely unaware of any conditions of existence or individuation that are constructed, then these conditions do not go into the content. Appeal to the present social constructivism does not help.

2. Another form of social constructivism, again defended most forcefully by Rouse, is that the *conditions of knowledge* are social. For

> (b) the standards of knowledge to which scientific theories are held are determined by particular theoretical and experimental activities.

This is another part of Rouse's insistence that science is local rather than global. The basis for (b) is that research opportunities are determined by local conditions, and these research opportunities in turn determine, not merely how scientific theories are generated and accepted, and which scientific discoveries are made, but also which theories amount to scientific knowledge. Thus the *conditions* of scientific knowledge must advert to research opportunities. For the requirements of the future use of a theory as a basis for further research will determine the degree of support required of the theory. The degree of support required of a theory is thus relative to its future use in research. But its future use depends on the opportunities for research on future occasions. Thus, the conditions of scientific knowledge must advert to social factors. There is work by Bruno Latour and Steven Woolgar (1979) and by Latour (1987) that supports this thesis: the epistemic status of a scientific statement is relative to its "modalities" (or embeddings in other statements). I am afraid that the force of this claim has been overlooked by philosophers because Latour and Woolgar prefer to speak, tendentiously, of the construction of scientific facts rather than the epistemic status of scientific statements.

I am inclined to regard thesis (b) as true and important, and I believe that Rouse makes a good case for it. But I would urge caution in drawing social consequences from the thesis. Even if future use in research, hence opportunities for research, determine the degree of support required of a scientific theory for it to be knowledge, it does not follow that what *endows* a theory with the degree of support it has is also determined by the opportunities for research. The argument shows only that the degree of support required is determined by social factors. Here social factors enter the conditions of scientific knowledge in a relatively superficial way.

3. A third version of social constructivism holds that scientific knowledge is socially constructed in the sense that it is generally *caused* by social, economic, and political interests—a claim made most forcefully by proponents of the "strong programme" in the sociology of scientific knowledge (Barnes 1977). This causal claim is offered in opposition to the "rationalist" view that scientific theory choices are caused by textbook

rational reasoning (i.e., conformity of the theory to observations and theoretical desiderata like simplicity), except where social factors interfere. I will not attempt to judge the merits of the sociologists' causal claim. There are excellent critical reviews in J. R. Brown (1989) and Roth (1987). What I wish to address here is whether the causal claim has any *epistemological* implications. Might the causal claim entail that scientific theory choices are not textbook rational, or that rational theory choices are not textbook rational choices but rather socially interested choices?

I believe that the sociologists could bring epistemologists surprising news in this quarter, up to a point. The arguments for the causal claim are either *a priori* or *empirical.* The a priori arguments appeal to such matters as the underdetermination of theories by observations and the theory-ladenness of criteria—matters which are supposed to show that rational considerations cannot decide between theories, so that social considerations must enter in. Thus, to the extent that the causal claim is supported by an a priori argument, it depends on a certain account of rational theory choice (or at least of textbook rational choice). Thus, sociology could *not* bring news to epistemology from this quarter. All the arguing is done *before* any sociology enters the picture.

The empirical argument for the causal claim, on the other hand, is an inductive argument from case studies: interests cause theory choices in particular cases, hence generally do. This is not an argument that depends entirely on prior epistemology. We may ask, then, whether such an argument could lead to the conclusion that actual theory choices are generally nonrational.

The answer is: not by itself. To reach the conclusion that actual theory choices are generally nonrational, an inverse correlation between interested theory choices and rational choices would have to be established. But we could establish such a correlation only if we *already* knew which theory choices are rational—something sociology does not by itself tell us. The most that sociology could show is that *either* actual theory choices are generally nonrational, *or* rational theory choices are really interested rather than textbook rational. That disjunctive conclusion would be an important and distressing epistemological result, but it falls short of the claim that sociology could show the nonrationality of actual theory choices. See Philip Kitcher's contribution to this volume for further reflection on the epistemological consequences of recent sociology of science.

To decide between these alternatives, we would need to take a stand on the outcome of applying correct philosophical method to the question of the rationality of theory choice. If, for example, "naturalism" is the correct method, then actual theory choices will generally be rational. For according to naturalism, we determine which choices are rational by extracting the conditions of rationality from the actual choices. In this case we should embrace the new theory that rational choices are interested. If, on the other hand, wide reflective equilibrium is the correct method, then we might conclude that actual choices are generally nonrational.

If we embrace the conclusion that actual choices are generally nonrational, our degree of pessimism will turn on the details of the sociological findings about interests. If interests do not inevitably cause theory choices, we may ask how to eliminate their effects. If, on the other hand, they *do* inevitably cause theory choices, then we may ask whether there is any hope of *reducing* their effects. For example, one might hope that opposing interests would reduce each other's detrimental effects on textbook rationality. This hope has led some to a multiperspectival or consensus theory of rational choice: the rational theory choice is the choice that is accepted from each of various perspectives representing opposing interests. Helen Longino (1990) offers a sophisticated version of this view, as she does in her contribution to this volume. But I am not sure that the multiperspectival or consensus theory is coherent. For it presupposes the epistemological claim that it is desirable to reduce the effects of interests on textbook rational theory choices (together with the rationalist claim that interests merely interfere with textbook rationality, so that their effects can be alleviated). Yet the epistemological claim seems plausible only on the assumption of a textbook theory of rational choice—a theory inconsistent with the multiperspectival theory. It would take a lot of work to sort out the issues here, but I am inclined initially to suspect that a multiperspectival view can be motivated by the claim that interests cause theory choices only if it is taken as derivative from the textbook theory and is proposed, not as a theory of rational choice, but as a procedure for ameliorating the interference of interests with textbook rationality.

One might be tempted, after reaching skepticism, to give up on rationality and epistemic evaluation altogether and turn to social and political criticism of science instead. But I can see no way to make this approach coherent. If interests prevent us from getting straight about electrons, they will also prevent us from getting straight about interests. Skepticism about science mandates skepticism about social science. In short, well-founded social and political criticism of science—and I'm all for it—presupposes that science makes disinterested choices. There is no way to abandon rationality and epistemic criticism in favor of social and political criticism.

Thus, I am inclined to think that if interests inevitably prevent textbook rationality, we are in a deep skeptical ditch. But it's too early to lose any sleep over the matter. Sociology has yet to provide much evidence for the claim of inevitable interference or, for that matter, the causal claim. Of the three versions of social constructivism, the third, causal version now enjoys the least support.

All three versions of social constructivism suggest important respects in which group or communal knowledge is social, beyond the requirement of a joint account of group knowledge. The second version, concerning the conditions of knowledge, seems best supported. The first version lacks support, while the third is an empirical claim for which there is currently little evidence. We may add to the second version, as a plausible stronger claim about the sociality of rational group belief, Miriam Solomon's view of rational group belief in her contribution to this volume.[1]

Note

1. I would like to thank Jim Spellman for insightful comments and Richard Foley for illuminating correspondence about the parity argument.

2

Belief-forming Practices and the Social

William P. Alston

I

The social enters epistemology in a variety of guises.[1] For one thing, it provides distinctively social subject matters. Instead of the epistemologist addressing herself to the beliefs and knowledge of individual cognitive subjects, as has been most usual in the discipline, she can study what *we* (the members of a certain social group) know or believe. Or she can consider the knowledge "stored" or "embodied" in certain institutions, disciplines, or organizations. There are also socially established (transmitted, sanctioned) procedures and methods that are directed to the acquisition of knowledge or rational (justified) belief, and hence have epistemic import.

In this chapter I will look at none of these, but rather at social influences on individual cognition. This is a rich field of investigation that has been mined extensively by the sociologist and the social psychologist. I have neither of those specialties, however. I am writing as a philosopher, concerned with epistemology. Hence, in line with the terms of my calling I shall be concentrating on the conditions under which beliefs enjoy one or another epistemic status, realize one or another "epistemic desideratum"[2]—being rational or justified, or qualifying as knowledge, to take the examples that have figured most prominently in epistemology. Actually, I will be considering not only what it takes to enjoy one of these statuses, but also how we can tell when this is the case. And, in line with the theme of this book, I will be exploring the ways in which the social bears on one or another of these problem areas.

II

My first point will have to do, not with epistemic assessment, but rather with the way in which social practices bulk large in our actual cognitive activity, more especially in the formation, preservation, and evaluation of beliefs.[3] It seems clear that our belief-forming activities are mostly carried out in accordance with patterns that are not only widely distributed in a society but also transmitted, reinforced, and sanctioned through socialization. I will begin by sketching a conception of social practices of belief formation and evaluation (call them *doxastic practices)* that I have developed with help from Wittgenstein (1969) and that I have expounded more fully in Alston (1989b, 1991, ch. 4).

The concept to start with is that of a belief-forming (doxastic) disposition (habit / mechanism / process / ...). A human psyche has at its disposal a number of more or less fixed dispositions to go from an input of a certain kind (beliefs and/or experiences, usually) to a belief output. Such a disposition / habit / mechanism / ... can be thought of as the "realization" of a function that yields a belief content related in a certain way to relevant features of the input. If the input is the belief pair [John is an athlete \ Athletes are usually muscular], a familiar function will yield the belief [John is likely to be muscular]. If the input is a sense experience as of something red, then a familiar function will yield the belief that something red is in front of one.

So long as we are describing and analyzing doxastic mechanisms we are confined to individual psychology; we are studying the internal cognitive structure and processes of individual human beings. It is logically possible that all this could go on within an individual psyche in total isolation from social interaction. But only logically possible. We have to ask where these mechanisms came from, how they came to be entrenched in individual psyches, why this or that person forms beliefs in these ways rather than others. Innate endowment undoubtedly plays a role. It seems clear that innate mechanisms play a large role in transforming the chaos of sensory stimulation into organized percepts—a visual field, for example, that is inhabited by houses, trees, cows, and the like. But that cannot be the whole story. The most obvious reason for this is that the concepts that provide content for one's doxastic outputs are not themselves innate, at least for the most part. We learn from our socialization to recognize items in the environment as trees, as almond trees, as dachshunds and terriers, as parents and siblings, and so on. Without the information flow, the encouragement, the sanctioning, the modelling of social interaction, we would never acquire the particular belief-forming dispositions that fill our psyches to the bursting point. Our doxastic mechanisms are thoroughly social—socially transmitted, socially reinforced and monitored, socially shared.[4]

Alvin Goldman (1986, pp. 92-93) makes a distinction between basic, unlearned *processes* and acquired *methods* that are encoded or stored as recipes, algorithms, or heuristics. He regards perceptual belief formation and simple forms of inferential belief-formation as processes. In a footnote, Goldman admits that what he counts as processes may not all be completely independent of learning of any kind, and that since "a fully satisfactory formulation of the process method distinction . . . has eluded me, . . . I shall rely throughout on an informal grasp of this distinction" (p. 92, n. 11). Taking the distinction intuitively, it seems fairly obvious that methods have a social side to them. But what I have been pointing out is that the same is to be said for what Goldman counts as processes. To repeat the main point, the mere fact that learned concepts are involved in any belief formation, and that concept acquisition invariably involves socialization, is enough to show that even perceptual and simple inferential belief formation have a social aspect.

Particular doxastic mechanisms can be of various widths. The input type could be something as narrow as a certain determinate configuration of specific sensory qualia and the output type as narrow as a belief to the effect that that person is Susie Jones. Or there might be a very wide function that takes inputs of the type *an experience of the sort S would take as a case of X's appearing ϕ to S* and yields outputs of the correlated type *a belief of the form "X is ϕ."* Analogous distinctions can be made between inferential mechanisms.

Just what mechanisms we have, and how wide or narrow these are, is, at least in principle, a question for cognitive psychology, however far that discipline may be from being able to tackle it adequately at present. I think we will find a more appropriate target for our investigation into the social side of the epistemology of individual belief if we think in terms of large families of doxastic mechanisms that are bound together by marked similarity in input, output, and/or function. I call these families *doxastic practices*. Thus the group of doxastic mechanisms that take as inputs sensory experience, plus background beliefs where these are involved, and yield as outputs beliefs about the immediate physical environment, we may term the *sense perceptual* doxastic practice ("SP" for short). Mechanisms that respond to the apparently obvious truth of propositions we may term the *rational intuition* doxastic practice. There is a variety of inferential practices that take belief inputs and that differ in the nature of the function. (Each form of inference determines a belief-forming function.) There is no one right way to divide the territory up into such families. Instead of proceeding on the basis of a general sense perceptual practice, we could distinguish a visual practice, an auditory practice, and so on. For purposes of this essay it will be convenient to think in terms of broad practices, typified by SP and the deductive inferential practice.[5]

Here are some major features of doxastic practices.

1. Doxastic practices have an evaluative side, as well as being ways of forming beliefs. SP, for example, involves distinctive procedures and criteria for assessing and correcting perceptual beliefs—in terms of conditions of observation, the condition of sense organs, the testimony of other observers, the nature of the environment, and so on. These procedures and criteria are drawn from a background picture of sense perception and the settings in which it is exercised, and, more generally, of the physical world as a whole. There is every reason to count the background belief system that underlies the evaluative procedures as a part of the doxastic practice.

2. Doxastic practices do not, in general, function independently of each other. I will give just two examples of this: inferential practices are beholden to other practices for their doxastic inputs; again, the background belief system attached to SP was not built up by the use of SP alone, but also required the use of memory and reasoning of various sorts.

3. A point emphasized by Wittgenstein is that doxastic practices are acquired and engaged in long before one is explicitly aware of them and subjects them to critical reflection. When one arrives at the age of reflection, one finds oneself ineluctably involved in their exercise. Practice precedes theory; if it didn't, the latter would be impossible.

4. Doxastic practices are pursued in a wider context of practices. We learn to form perceptual beliefs in the course of learning to deal with perceived objects in the pursuit of our ends. The practice of forming beliefs about other persons is intimately connected with interpersonal behavior.

III

If the above is even close to being correct, social structures, interrelations, and processes impinge in crucial ways on individual activities of belief formation and evaluation. But so far this is all (social) cognitive psychology of an armchair variety. I have been sketching what I take to be certain broad features of the ways in which we do actually form, preserve, modify, and evaluate beliefs. But epistemology, as a philosophical enterprise, is essentially (though not exclusively) evaluative. We want to know, not just how we in fact form beliefs, but what is the (a) rational, justified, warranted way of doing so. Again, we want to know what belief-forming practices are *reliable*—will (would) yield a preponderance of true beliefs over suitably numerous and varied occasions of their exercise. Do social considerations have any place in these inquiries?

If I were to carry on this discussion in terms like "rational" and "justified," I would have to enter into the continuing controversy over how those terms are properly understood.[6] If I were to do so, I would have no time for the main theme of the chapter. Hence I will cut the Gordian knot by turning my back on the question of how to understand "justified" or "rational" and concentrate on reliability. (I will deviate from this policy only briefly.) If you think that a belief's being justified or rationally held requires that it be reliably formed (preserved), then you will take this discussion to have a crucial bearing on those issues. Even if you do not, you will, presumably, recognize that since it is of the utmost importance that our beliefs should be true, it is of commensurate importance that our belief-forming practices be reliable. To nail down that point, I will give a very brief account of how I understand the reliability of belief formation.

To call a doxastic practice "reliable" is to judge that it will or would yield mostly true beliefs. But over what range of exercises? All those so far? That would be to identify reliability with a favorable track record, but that can't be right. An unreliable practice might have happened to yield truths on the few occasions of its use. Anyone can get lucky! Indeed, we cannot identify reliability with a favorable record over all past, present, and future exercises. A practice or an instrument that is never employed might be quite reliable in that it would yield mostly true beliefs in the long run. To call a practice reliable is to speak about the kind of record it *would* pile up over a suitable number of uses, suitably varied. Moreover, these uses must be in the kinds of situations we typically encounter. The fact that SP would not be a reliable source of belief in unusually deceptive environments or in cases of direct brain stimulation does not show that it is not reliable. So a doxastic practice is reliable provided *it would yield mostly true beliefs in a sufficiently large and varied run of exercises in situations of the sorts we typically encounter*. An actual favorable track record is crucial evidence for a judgment of reliability just to the extent that it is a good indication of that.

Although reliability is, of course, a matter of degree, I shall simplify the discussion by proceeding in terms of an absolute distinction between "reliable" and "unreliable." You can think of a reliable practice as one that falls above some minimum degree of reliability.

IV

Against this background I can turn to the central question of this essay: how, if at all, the social has to be taken into account in assessing the reliability of doxastic practices. To have a concrete focus for the discussion, I will continue to concentrate on the broad practice I have been calling "SP."

First, I will consider the most objective question in this area—whether there are social requirements for a doxastic practice's *being* reliable. Is it a necessary condition of such reliability that certain social facts obtain?

One might think that the answer to this question is obviously negative.[7] Even if, as I have been contending, we have the doxastic practices we have because of social factors, those or any other social factors are powerless to bring it about that one of these practices is reliable. It is, clearly, a social fact that a given practice is *taken to be* reliable in a given society, or that there are socially accepted and sanctioned standards of rationality according to which it is rational to take the practice to be reliable. But none of this makes it the case that the practice is, in fact, reliable. For a doxastic practice to be reliable is for it to have a tendency to yield a preponderance of true beliefs.[8] (Call this a "verific tendency.") And social facts have no power to determine whether that is so. If examining the entrails of sacred beasts to predict the future is not suited to engender correct predictions, then no social arrangements can make it the case that it is reliable.[9]

However, on further reflection we can see that the case for a negative answer is based on too narrow a view of what counts as a social fact. Certainly, social facts of the sorts just mentioned are not to any degree constitutive of the reliability of a doxastic practice. But let's take a closer look at what is so constitutive. It is the fact that the practice has, as we put it above, a verific propensity. That is, there is something about that way (or family of ways) of forming beliefs, in the situations in which we typically find ourselves, which can be depended on to bring it about that mostly true beliefs are produced. But since we are restricting what we are calling "doxastic practices" to *social practices* in a strong sense of the term (practices that are not only widely engaged in in the society, but also socially transmitted and sanctioned), the fact that such a practice is reliable (has the propensity in question) *is itself a social fact.* And hence in that way what makes a practice reliable is a social fact. The social is crucial, after all, to whether a doxastic practice is reliable.

One may dismiss this point as boringly trivial. If the only sense in which the social is constitutive of the reliability of a doxastic practice is that the practice is itself social, that doesn't amount to any distinctively social entanglement with reliability. The same point could be made about the attribution to doxastic practices of any property whatever. In response, I agree that this constitutes a minimal relevance of the social. Later I will distinguish "grades of social involvement" (by analogy with Quine's "grades of modal involvement"), and this one will figure as the lowest grade. But I deny that it is without significance. However, I will postpone any attempt to display its epistemological significance until I come to the next topic, whether social considerations enter into reasons for supposing doxastic practices to be reliable.

In making the above point, I am not, of course, denying that there can be idiosyncratic practices of belief formation, confined to one individual. The exercise of such practices, and their reliability or unreliability, are not social facts, even though the same property of reliability can be attributed to them. This is another way of bringing out the point that the social character of what makes a doxastic practice (in my restricted sense) reliable stems from what a doxastic practice is, rather than from what reliability is. But while recognizing this, I would also add that any such idiosyncratic practice is secondary, derivative from the individual's mastery of, and participation in, social belief-forming practices. It is only after learning to do it in the socially accepted ways that one has the resources to devise deviant belief-forming practices of one's own.

V

So much for the (minimal) way in which the social is *constitutive* of the reliability of doxastic practices. Now I turn to the ways in which considerations of the social are involved in determining whether a given doxastic practice is reliable. In deciding whether SP is reliable, is it relevant to take into account the social entanglements of SP? This moves us from the "ontological" issue as to what constitutes reliability, what it *is*, to the epistemological question of what reasons (considerations, evidence, grounds, bases) are relevant to making a judgment as to whether something is reliable. Let's use the term *criteria* as a catchall term for the latter, and ask whether there are social criteria for the reliability of doxastic practices.

First let's ask what would be the most direct and conclusive reason for taking a doxastic practice to be reliable. Since reliability consists of a verific propensity, and since propensities are dispositions to issue manifestations of certain sorts (perhaps under certain conditions), the most direct check on *X*'s possession of a propensity is to put *X* through its paces and determine the proportion of productions of the relevant sort. Thus the most direct and conclusive basis for taking a doxastic practice to be reliable is to examine a representative sample of its doxastic outputs and determine the proportion of truths in that sample. We determine its track record over a suitable spread of employments. And exactly the same kind of procedure would issue in the most direct and conclusive basis for judging a practice to be unreliable, if the sample contains mostly false beliefs.

It is clear right away that this track record criterion is social in exactly the same way as what *constitutes* the reliability of a doxastic practice. It is a social criterion just because doxastic practices are social. In examining a suitable sample of exercises of the practice we are examining a social fact, because the exercise of a social practice is, ipso facto, a social activity. But, again, it would seem that it is only in this minimal sense that this is a social criterion. Exactly the same procedure would be used on an idiosyncratic practice to get the most direct and conclusive evidence for its reliability. We would check a representative sample of outputs for truth value, and make the judgment on the basis of that. Again, the social character of the criterion comes from the subject of the attribution, rather than from what is being attributed.

VI

If the truth values of the outputs of doxastic practices were generally and unproblematically available to us, we could conclude our discussion at this point, having established that the criteria of reliability are social only in the most minimal way. But that condition is not satisfied, and hence we are forced to go beyond the most direct criteria of reliability. For one thing, we simply don't know the truth values of many beliefs. This is often the case in science, religion, history, and other spheres in which we form beliefs about matters that are far from being obvious. But I want to concentrate my attention on a difficulty with the track record approach that would remain even if all our beliefs had truth values that are as obvious to us as is (or seems to be) the case with simple perceptual beliefs. That difficulty has to do with what I call "epistemic circularity," a kind of circularity that is paradigmatically exemplified by giving an argument for the reliability of a doxastic practice, some of the premises of which were acquired by the use of that very practice. Although such an argument would not (necessarily) exhibit the basic kind of logical circularity (the conclusion does not appear among the premises), nevertheless it is circular in a way. For in taking some of our premises from that practice (supposing them to be true), we are, as we might say, making a "practical" presupposition of the reliability of that practice, assuming it, in practice, to be reliable. If I give a "track record" argument for the reliability of SP, I will enumerate a number of its outputs and point out that at least most of them are true. For example, one output of my SP was that my car was in the driveway when I came home this afternoon. But how do I know (many of) these outputs are true. The claim that the argument is "epistemically circular" is just the claim that I cannot know they are true without relying on (the reliability of) sense perception, the very point the argument is concerned to establish. I will now make a few remarks in support of that claim.

Elsewhere (Alston 1993b), I support the thesis that we cannot determine the truth values of outputs of SP (perceptual beliefs) without relying on SP itself (taking it to be reliable) in doing so by pointing out that SP is our only basic cognitive access to the physical world. In calling it our only *basic* cognitive access, I mean that any other access will depend on using SP and taking it, at least in practice, to be reliable. Let me spell this out a bit by considering a sample of the ways we have for determining the truth value of a perceptual belief about the external environment. Consider a perceptual belief that there is a birch tree in my front yard. What ways do we have for determining whether this is true other than by just taking another look at the area and determining whether a birch tree is there to be seen?

First, there are memories of previously seeing a birch tree there. But obviously this is no more trustworthy than those past perceptions that are remembered. Second, we can use general regularities to infer the presence of a birch tree from other facts. Thus I might find some leaves in my front yard of the sort that only fall from birch trees. Here we presumably know about the leaves from perception, or from one of the other approaches we are considering that presuppose perception. Moreover our evidence for the generalization connecting leaves like that with birch trees will itself rest on observation. Third, we might make use of instruments—in this case, fairly simple ones like a camera. Let's say we have photographs of the front yard showing a birch tree. Here we must rely on SP both for knowing what is in the photograph and for supposing that the photograph gives an accurate representation of my front yard. Fourth, in other cases we might rely on higher level theories, as when the presence of another planet was inferred from deviations in the expected orbit of observed planets. Here we rely on SP both for the observation of the known planets and for evidence for the theories used in the inference. It seems that we have no way of assigning a truth value to a particular perceptual belief except by assuming or presupposing the reliability of SP.

Thus we cannot use the ideally direct method of assessing the reliability of SP without relying on SP (assuming its reliability) in doing so. Any argument for the reliability of SP from its "track record" is infected with epistemic circularity. And the same difficulty infects the attempt to use the next most direct approach to assessing the reliability of a doxastic practice—looking for something we have sufficient reasons for regarding as a reliable indication of a certain kind of track record. To take an analogy, in order to tell whether a liquid is an acid, we are not forced to do a full-dress chemical analysis in each case. A litmus paper test will be sufficient, since we have good reason for thinking that a certain outcome of this test is a reliable indication of acidity. But if the direct test suffers from epistemic circularity, so does this slightly more indirect procedure. To have reasons for regarding the secondary reason as conclusive, someone at some point had to have used the primary reason (a track record) as the basis for attributions of the property. Otherwise, we could never have compiled sufficient reasons for regarding the secondary indications as relevant. And so epistemic circularity will come in further back in the reasoning.

Spurred by a more or less explicit recognition of this situation, a variety of philosophers have sought to establish the reliability of SP and other basic doxastic practices (memory, inductive reasoning, deductive reasoning) by more indirect arguments. There is a variety of (supposedly) a priori arguments that seek to show that denying the reliability of SP is contradictory, incoherent, unintelligible, or self-defeating in some other way. In a more empirical vein, thinkers have sought to show that our sense experience is best explained by a "standard" theory that is such as to assert or imply the reliability of SP. In an earlier book (Alston 1993b) I consider a large number of such arguments—all the most promising ones known to me—and conclude that all those that are not disqualified in other ways suffer from epistemic circularity, sometimes in ways that appear only on close scrutiny. Since

I cannot go into all that here, I must refer you to the book. Although in that work I restrict the detailed examination to SP, I suggest that a like judgment is warranted for all our most basic practices of belief-formation.

Furthermore, even if I am mistaken about SP (or about some other basic doxastic practice), and it can be shown to be reliable without incurring epistemic circularity, we are still not out of the woods. Suppose that we can establish the reliability of SP by using only rational intuition and deductive reasoning. What about those practices? Consider rational intuition. Can we mount a noncircular proof of its reliability? If we can't, we have the same problem at a second remove. If we can, then if that proof depends on using SP we are involved in a very small circle. If we do not have to use SP, let's consider one of the practices we do use. Can we give a noncircular proof of its reliability? If not, our original problem has been postponed to this point. And so on. We are faced with the familiar dilemma of continuing the regress or falling into circularity. Whatever the possibilities of a noncircular proof of reliability for one or another practice, if we pursue the question far enough we will either (a) encounter one or more practices for which a noncircular proof cannot be given, or (b) be caught up in circularity, or (c) be launched on an infinite regress. Since the number of basic doxastic practices is quite small for human beings, we can ignore (c); and for the same reason, any circle involved will be a small one.

Suppose I am right about all this. We would seem to be confronted with a desperate situation. We are unable to give any otherwise cogent argument for the reliability of any of our most familiar doxastic practices, including those in which we repose the greatest confidence, without running into circularity somewhere. Then what attitude are we to take to the matter? Shall we "kill the bearer of bad news," avert our gaze, and strive to carry on as if everything is rosy? Or shall we fall into despair?

To be sure, I have argued in "Epistemic Circularity" (Alston 1989a) that it is possible for an epistemically circular argument to be used to show that a doxastic practice is reliable. The basic point is that, on a theory of epistemic justification I have defended, one doesn't have to be justified in supposing SP to be reliable in order to be justified in various perceptual beliefs. It is only necessary that SP *be* reliable. Hence I may be justified in the perceptual premises of an argument for the reliability of SP without having to be antecedently justified in supposing SP to be reliable. Hence the argument could bring me to become justified in accepting the principle that SP is reliable.

But though the epistemic circularity of an argument does not by itself prevent the argument from being used to show that a given doxastic practice is reliable, the fact remains that this showing (justification) will have been successfully carried out only if the practice *is* in fact reliable. The argument, if otherwise in order, will show that SP is reliable only if SP *is* reliable. But that is what we set out to determine. Being assured that the practice is reliable if it is reliable does not really advance us in the original quest.

A good way of making this point is to note that reliance on epistemically circular arguments would seem not to distinguish between doxastic practices it is, and those it is not, reasonable to regard as reliable. For any doxastic practice, if sufficiently self-consistent in its output, can be shown to be reliable *if* it is reliable. Just take each output twice, once as candidate output and once as showing that output to be true. That will give us a track record for reliability that will show the practice to be reliable if it *is* reliable. Consider crystal ball gazing. We look into the ball and form the belief that Clinton will be reelected in 1996. The same look assures us that this belief is true (since it assures us that Clinton will be reelected in 1996). In that way we can compile a remarkable track record for the practice, and infer that it is reliable. And if the practice *is* reliable, we will, on the conception of justification I am assuming, be justified in the premises of the argument (each of which says that a certain output of the practice is true); and hence the argument will establish the reliability of crystal ball gazing.[10] Thus simply being able to show that practice *P* is reliable, if it is reliable, is not of any help in separating the sheep from the goats. We are still faced with an epistemological crisis.

However, that is not the end of the story of epistemically circular arguments. Not all such arguments fall under the ban against maximally simple track record arguments for being equally available for any doxastic practice whatever. There are epistemically circular arguments that will help us to discriminate between practices, since they cannot automatically be used for any practice. To illustrate this consider the following ways in which SP supports its own claims. First, by engaging in SP and allied memory and inferential practices we are enabled to make predictions many of which turn out to be correct; and thereby we are able to anticipate and, to some considerable extent, control the course of events. Second, by relying on SP and associated practices we are able to establish facts about the operation of sense perception that show both that it is a reliable source of belief and why it is reliable. Our scientific account of perceptual processes shows how it is that sense experience serves as a sensitive indicator of certain kinds of facts about the environment of the perceiver.

These results are by no means trivial. It cannot be assumed that any practice whatever will yield comparable fruits. It is quite conceivable that we should not have attained this kind or degree of success at prediction and control by relying on the output of SP; and it is equally conceivable that this output should not have put us in a position to acquire enough understanding of the workings of perception to see why it can be relied on. To be sure, an argument from these fruits to the reliability of SP is still infected with epistemic circularity. Apart from reliance on SP we have no way of knowing the outcome of our attempts at prediction and control, and no way of confirming our suppositions about the workings of perception. Nevertheless this is not the trivial epistemically circular support that necessarily extends to every practice, the automatic confirmation of each output by itself. Many doxastic practices, like crystal ball gazing, do not show anything analogous to the above results. Since SP supports itself in ways it conceivably might not, and in ways other practices do not, its claims to reliability are thereby strengthened; and if crystal ball gazing lacks any comparable self-support, its claims suffer by comparison. Analogous points can be made concerning memory, introspection, rational intuition, and various kinds of reasoning. For example, the claims of rational intuition and deductive reasoning can be supported by considering the impressive and fruitful systems of mathematics and logic built up by their use.

VII

It is against the background just sketched that I want to discuss the question of whether, when we go beyond track record arguments, social considerations play any role in arriving at an assessment of doxastic practices for reliability. Not, of course, whether anyone can use such considerations in coming to make a judgment on this point, but whether it is reasonable, appropriate, warranted to do so. Do social factors have any weight in deciding whether to regard SP, for example, as a reliable way of forming beliefs? In discussing this I will be assuming that any strong reasons for taking SP to be reliable will exhibit epistemic circularity, that is, will rely at some point(s) on what we take ourselves to have learned through perception.

In (Alston 1989b; 1991, ch. 4), I reacted to the challenge of epistemic circularity by giving up on attempts to show that SP is in fact reliable (or even to provide strong reasons for this where these reasons fall short of "showing" it) and resorted instead to a "practical rationality" argument that runs as follows. Since we cannot establish the reliability of any doxastic practice without running into epistemic circularity, either in the argument for that conclusion or somewhere on a regress of the sort indicated in the last section, there is no reasonable alternative to sticking with the socially established practices we find ourselves firmly involved in. Given that total suspension of belief is not a human possibility, the alternative would be to find replacements for one or more of our present practices. But what would be the point of that? We would no more be able to establish the reliability of these newcomers without epistemic circularity than we are with our present repertoire; hence we would have gained nothing. Even if we could carry out the shift, we would have made an enormous effort for no discernible benefits at all. The only rational course is to stick with what we have. Moreover, although the argument so far says nothing about reliability but only that it is rational to engage in the practices, I argued that, in showing that to be rational, one has also shown it to be rational to take the practices to be reliable. For it can't be rational to engage in a *belief-forming* practice without its being rational to suppose oneself to be forming mostly true beliefs.

I made a sharp distinction between this argument for the "practical rationality" of taking a doxastic practice to be reliable, and an argument for the conclusion that the practice *is* reliable, an argument that seeks to provide a "truth-conducive" reason for that conclusion, one that indicates the conclusion to be at least likely to be true, one that raises the probability of the conclusion substantially. I did not take my practical rationality argument to provide any indication that the claim of reliability is, or is likely to be, *true*. I represented practical rationality as a fallback position. Since we cannot show that even our most deeply entrenched doxastic practices are reliable, the best we can do is to show that it is practically rational to regard them as such. As for significant self-support of the sort mentioned above, that was brought in only as a reinforcement of the judgment of practical rationality, rather than as an independent reason for supposing it to be true that the practice is in fact reliable.

I hasten to add that the policy I was arguing to be "practically rational" need not be so unreservedly conservative as the above exposition makes it appear. It leaves us free to abandon an established doxastic practice (if it is psychologically possible to do so) for good and sufficient reason. Such reason would be forthcoming if the practice yielded massive and persistent inconsistency in its output. I say "massive and persistent" because the odd inconsistency such as we find even in the most respectable practices like SP should not be taken as disqualifying. We are, after all, fallible creatures. Again, a practice is disqualified if its outputs come into massive contradiction with those of a more firmly established practice.[11] I suggested that various doxastic practices of divination that were socially established at one time have fallen by the wayside for these sorts of reasons.[12]

I now think that I overreacted to the problem of epistemic circularity. One indication of that is the fact, which I did acknowledge (Alston 1991, ch. 4), that the practical rationality argument is itself epistemically circular, at least in application to SP. Remember that an essential premise for that argument is that SP is a firmly socially established doxastic practice. How could one know (be justified in believing) this without using evidence gathered by observation? One can't know this by rational intuition or introspection. Thus this argument too suffers from epistemic circularity. It may seem that it does not if we restrict our attention to the conclusion that it is practically rational to engage in SP and to take it to be reliable. For although it seems clear that I am, in practice, assuming the reliability of SP when I accept its outputs as premises in arguments, it is not at all clear that I am assuming that *it is practically rational to engage in it and to take it to be reliable* when I accept its outputs as premises. But we must remember that the practical rationality of taking SP to be reliable is taken in turn to be a reason for so taking it. (Not a reason—at least not a sufficient reason—for supposing SP to *be* reliable, but a reason for *taking* it to be reliable.) Thus the ultimate conclusion of the argument really is that SP is reliable; and it is this that we are assuming, in practice, in using SP outputs as premises (or as support for premises).

But if the practical rationality argument itself is epistemically circular, we have lost our main motivation to abandon the attempt to show SP to be reliable, and content ourselves with practical rationality. For it was only epistemic circularity that precipitated that abandonment, and if we are going to rely on an epistemically circular argument anyway, we may as well go with the more ambitious ones that seek to show it to be true that SP is reliable. At least, that holds for the ones that I have put under the rubric of "significant self-support." The mere track record arguments still fall under the ban of being equally available for any doxastic practice whatever, no matter how disreputable.

Therefore, I suggest that we look at significant epistemically circular arguments that are directly for the reliability of SP and consider what place social considerations can have in them. And we should not concentrate exclusively on reasons for a positive judgment of reliability. Since we are interested in the relevance of the social for the issue of reliability, we should be equally concerned with the question of whether social considerations rightfully enter into reasons for taking doxastic practices to be unreliable.

VIII

We may as well begin with (non-track-record) arguments for unreliability, since they can be dispatched quickly. The ways of showing unreliability that were mentioned above had to do with massive inconsistency—either within the output of a single practice, or between the outputs of different practices. Still sticking with the case of SP, these arguments need not be epistemically circular, so long as one is evaluating one's own SP. I can check my own perceptual beliefs for consistency, and I can investigate whether there is massive inconsistency between my perceptual beliefs and beliefs of mine that stem from other sources, without relying on sense perception to do so. Rational reflection on what I know about my own beliefs will suffice.[13] But when it is a social practice that is under investigation, one obviously needs sense perception to learn what other people's beliefs are, so as to determine the incidence of inconsistency. Hence we are still confronted with epistemic circularity.

It would seem that the social involvement here is of the same minimal sort we noted with respect to the track record argument for reliability or unreliability. These reasons for unreliability are social in character just because, and only because, the practice we are evaluating is social. The social doesn't come in because of what it takes to show *unreliability* in particular, as is shown by the fact that the same argument for unreliability, directed to one's own case, makes no use of social considerations. We have not yet moved beyond the lowest grade of social involvement.

Let's turn next to the argument from the fruits of SP, mentioned above as an example of significant self-support. By engaging in SP, along with associated memory and inferential practices, we are able to discover dependable natural regularities, and construct impressive scientific theories of underlying structures and mechanisms, that enable us to anticipate and control the course of events to a considerable extent. And how would we be able to do this unless SP were not, by and large, providing us with true beliefs about what we perceive? These results put our attribution of reliability to SP in a stronger epistemic position than it would be if such outcomes were not forthcoming.

Another mode of significant self-support for SP we noted consists in the way in which, by engaging in SP and associated practices, we have been able to learn a great deal about the physics, physiology, and psychology of perception. That not only gives us reason for supposing that perception is a generally reliable source of information about the environment, but it gives us insight into how this is effected. These achievements also make a significant addition to our grounds for supposing SP to be reliable. For if it were not reliable, why should the picture of things we build up on its basis cohere so well with the supposition of its reliability?

How are these arguments related to the social? They, naturally, exhibit the lowest grade of social involvement we have seen to attach unavoidably to any reasons for attributing anything to a social practice. They appeal to the results of the *social* exercise of SP, and therefore, to that extent at least, appeal to social facts. But there is a heavier social involvement here. We do specifically argue from social features of the practices under consideration. We cannot argue from the successes of science and technology without appealing to the results of social mechanisms of cooperative inquiry and transmission of information, and without taking into account the development and use of scientific expertise. These are respects in which science is essentially a social phenomenon. In arguments that appeal to scientific success we are perforce appealing to the results of the use of social processes and mechanisms of the sorts just mentioned. Hence these arguments really do trade on social features of inquiry as a belief-forming (and knowledge-producing) practice. This is a second grade of social involvement, appealing to results that are possible only because of social features of cognitive practices.

In derogation of this point, it might be said that what is crucial for the argument is that reliance on SP and other doxastic practices has had these results. *In fact*, these results have been obtained by the use of social mechanisms of cooperative inquiry, transmission of knowledge, and so on. But isn't it possible that a super-scientist, perhaps a super-human scientist, could have achieved all this on his own? Isn't it even logically possible that such a super-scientist could have developed, cognitively and otherwise, without any socialization? And if that were the case, wouldn't we have basically the same argument for the reliability of SP as the one I have offered? And doesn't that show that these arguments do not *essentially* depend on appeal to anything social? There would be such an essential dependence only if the results to which appeal was made were themselves essentially social. Indeed, the results in question are social in character. The predictive capacities and control of nature are themselves socially shared and socially exercised, just as much as the activities that made them possible. But, again, they are not essentially social. They could, in principle, be enjoyed and exercised by an isolated individual. They are not intrinsically social results, in the way social organizations or political institutions or athletic competitions are essentially social phenomena. An argument that appealed to results like those would depend essentially on social considerations in a way this argument does not.

In a way, I don't want to contest any of this. My second grade of social involvement is not the strongest possible one, as my interlocutor has just pointed out. But I do take issue with the implication that this second grade of social involvement does not significantly go beyond the first. The fact remains that the arguments under consideration appeal to results that, so far as I can see, are really possible only for human beings who make use of social mechanisms and processes like those mentioned. The objector's contentions depend heavily on assertions of what is *logically* possible for cognitive subjects generally. But the arguments specifically deal with what has resulted from human scientific activity, which is in fact heavily social and probably is necessarily so for any subjects that would qualify as human. Therefore, it seems clear that the argument introduces social factors in a very important way, one that goes considerably beyond merely trading on the fact that the doxastic practice we are evaluating is a social practice.

My next topic is the practical rationality argument mentioned earlier. Or rather, since I am now supposing it to be possible to give significant epistemically circular arguments for the truth of the thesis that SP is a reliable practice, I want to look at the main feature of SP, and other established doxastic practices, appealed to in that practical rationality argument, viz., their social establishment. If we can use social establishment to support an attribution of reliability, I take it that no one would deny that the argument is essentially based on distinctively social considerations. Let's say that such an argument exhibits a third grade of social involvement, one in which the central focus of the appeal is on something that is essentially social.

The issue here would not be whether the argument is clearly an appeal to social considerations, but whether it holds any promise of supporting the claim to reliability. Why should we suppose that the social establishment of a doxastic practice provides any reason whatever for supposing it to be reliable? Doesn't the supposition that it does open us up to the worst kind of arbitrariness and relativism? Are we to take every form of magic and divination, no matter how primitive and unenlightened, as a reliable way of forming beliefs, just because it is ineluctably enmeshed in the fabric of the society?

Not so fast. I certainly did not suggest treating social establishment as a conclusive, or even a strong, reason for the attribution of reliability. The suggestion was only that it might add some weight to the case. This accretion would have to be minor enough to be outweighed by whatever reasons we have for denying that various superstitious magical practices are reliable ways of forming beliefs. Let's see what can be said in support of so weak a claim.

I will refrain from arguing that it is practically rational to take any firmly socially established doxastic practice as reliable until we have sufficient reasons for unreliability. For I am now considering only reasons for taking it to be *true* that a practice is reliable. What I will say is this. One explanation for the social entrenchment of a doxastic practice is that it is doing a pretty good job of delivering accurate information. If it were failing badly at that, this would be likely to show up sooner or later, in which case, given the supreme importance to us of true beliefs, it would be abandoned, perhaps only gradually. Hence if a doxastic practice continues to be socially entrenched over a long period, that is some reason for thinking it to be at least fairly reliable.

There are, of course, other possible explanations of the social establishment of a doxastic practice. The beliefs it yields may satisfy deep human needs, as Freud supposed that religious beliefs do. It may be in the interest of some power elite that the beliefs it yields be generally shared. And there are other possibilities. Since reliability is not the only explanation with some antecedent plausibility, social establishment does not constitute a very strong reason for reliability. But since reliability does constitute one explanation that would account nicely for the phenomenon, that phenomenon does give some reason for supposing that explanation to obtain.

Objections to this position often depend on confusing a doxastic practice (which involves some distinctive input to belief-forming mechanisms, as well as, sometimes, a distinctive type of output) with a theory or a theoretical orientation or a conceptual scheme. The most popular candidates for socially established but unreliable practices would seem to be astrology and psychoanalysis. But these do not qualify as doxastic practices as I am using the term. They are both theories, together with practices (not of forming beliefs but of doing more "practical" things) based on the theory. I am not aware that either makes use of any distinctive inputs to belief-forming processes. They both involve empirical evidence, theoretical speculation, explanation, and other modes of reasoning. Thus, as far as doxastic practices are concerned, they fall into the fairly diverse ballpark that we may term "scientific theorizing." They may be good or bad specimens of that, but they do not constitute separate doxastic practices.

Let me once more emphasize that I am not suggesting that social establishment is a conclusive, or even a very strong reason for an imputation of reliability. Much less am I suggesting that every socially established doxastic practice is reliable. We can think of numerous examples of doxastic practices of magic and divination that do involve distinctive inputs (what one "sees" in a crystal ball, dreams, experiences when under the influence of drugs, etc.) that have been established for a considerable time in one or another society, but which we have good reason to regard as unreliable, and which gradually lost their hold because of that. Moreover, even where we don't have sufficient evidence of unreliability (from internal inconsistency or inconsistency with the output of SP or whatever), social establishment by itself would be insufficient to make it reasonable to consider the practice to be reliable. This would have to be combined with reasons of other sorts that we have been considering.

Be all that as it may, the argument from social establishment does exhibit a high grade of social involvement. The basic appeal is to a fact that is essentially social in character. Unless my discussion has been badly skewed, it is noteworthy that the self-support that is most strongly social in character is relatively weak, compared with some less deeply social modes of self-support. There may be a moral here.

IX

To sum up, we have distinguished three "grades of social involvement" of reasons for the reliability or unreliability of doxastic practices.

1. Since the practices being evaluated are themselves social, reasons for their reliability or unreliability, at least those reasons that have to do with characteristics of the practices, will themselves be social facts.

2. Some reasons bring in results that were arrived at by essentially social processes.

3. Some reasons consist wholly in facts that are clearly social in character.

Putting all this together, it amounts to a considerable case for the relevance of social facts to the epistemic evaluation of individual beliefs. To be sure, as we have noted, by no means all epistemologists agree that the reliability of the practice (mechanism, process) that gave rise to a belief has a bearing on whether that belief is justified. But, as I briefly indicated, there are reasons to reject that position. And, in any event, most epistemologists will acknowledge that reliability of mode of formation is an epistemic desideratum. Or if a given theorist would withhold the term "epistemic" in this connection, he will at least admit that it is a *cognitive* desideratum, something that is desirable from the standpoint of the aims of cognition. Therefore I suggest that the considerations of this chapter exhibit some ways in which social considerations are relevant to the epistemic status and assessment of individual beliefs.

Notes

1. For an illuminating survey of the territory, see Goldman (1992).

2. See Alston (1993a) for an explanation and deployment of this concept.

3. Our psychological activity with respect to beliefs involves not only forming (acquiring) a belief, but also its subsequent fate. The belief may be stored in a more or less accessible form, connected with others in various ways, modified, and/or deleted. To simplify this discussion I will leave all that out of explicit account and focus exclusively on the acquisition stage (in addition to higher-level evaluation). I don't believe that any of the issues I will be discussing are affected by this partiality.

4. It is also worthy of note that some psychologists think that socialization is needed to train and encourage, or even to force, small children to distinguish between fantasy and perceived reality, and to accord the latter the attention it needs if they are to make their way in life.

5. The term "practice" will be misleading if it is taken to be restricted to voluntary activity, for I do not suppose belief formation to be voluntary. (See "The Deontological Conception of Epistemic Justification" in Alston 1989a.) I am using "practice" in such a way that it stretches over psychological processes as well as voluntary action.

6. For a presentation of some of the main issues, see "Concepts of Epistemic Justification" and "Internalism and Externalism in Epistemology" in Alston (1989a), and Alston (1993a).

7. Eleonore Stump has made clear to me the need to make explicit that when I speak of a "necessary condition" of reliability I am thinking of a condition that is conceptually or otherwise logically necessary, not a condition that is necessary because of contingent facts about what sorts of things there are in the world or what causal order obtains with respect to them. No doubt, there are social conditions that are necessary for the reliability of our doxastic practices in that latter sense. For example, as she pointed out to me, we could have social practices of conditioning children in ways that would make various belief-forming practices highly unreliable. The (social) fact that we do not proceed in this way is thus necessary in the weaker sense for the reliability of those practices.

8. This is short for the more complex formulation given above.

9. In laying down these judgments I am making an assumption that had best be made explicit. I am assuming a "realistic" conception of truth, according to which whether a proposition is true is solely a function of whether what the proposition is about is as it is said to be in the proposition. The truth value of the proposition that sugar is sweet hangs solely on whether sugar *is* sweet. It is not in any way constituted by whether the acceptance of the proposition meets social (or other) standards for being rational, justified, or warranted. Nor is the truth of the proposition a matter of social consensus or what "one's peers will let one get away with." If I were to work with one of these nonrealist conceptions of truth, it would be a different story; I would not be able to assert with such confidence that the reliability of a doxastic practice is not a function of any social facts. But by "true" here I mean *true*.

10. Note that I restricted the claim that any doxastic practice can be shown, by a track record argument, to be reliable if it is reliable, to those that "are sufficiently self-consistent in their output." To be sure, the procedure sketched can be used even for radically inconsistent practices. We can still "establish" the truth of each output, one by one, by using each output twice, once as testee and once as tester. The reason for excluding sufficiently inconsistent practices from the claim is that the inconsistency, if radical enough, will suffice by itself to establish the unreliability of the practice, and thereby negate any appearance of positive support given by the track record argument. I am indebted to the editor of this volume for alerting me to the complexities of this situation.

11. See Alston (1991, pp. 171-172) for an account of what being more firmly established comes to.

12. It will be noticed that I part company with Wittgenstein in supposing that there can be reasons for or against taking a basic doxastic practice to be reliable.

For Wittgenstein there is no perspective, either within the practice or outside it, from which such questions can be raised.

13. I don't mean to suggest that one's grasp of one's own beliefs is infallible, only that one can do well enough here without the use of sense perception. Nor does my point presuppose the denial of the widely accepted view that I couldn't have the ability to get knowledge about my own beliefs and other psychological states unless I also had the ability to get perceptual knowledge. That may or may not be true, but my position here doesn't commit me one way or the other.

3

Egoism in Epistemology

Richard Foley

When you tell me that something is the case, there are two kinds of questions for me to face. First, there are questions about your sincerity. Do you really believe what you are telling me, or are you saying this to mislead me, and how can I tell the difference? Second, there are questions that presuppose I can reliably determine whether or not you really believe what you are telling me and that then go on to ask, how, if at all, your opinion should affect my opinion. Is the fact that you believe a proposition sufficient in itself to give me a reason to believe it as well, or does your believing it give me a reason to believe it only if I have some independent reason to think you are a reliable judge of its truth?

Questions of the second sort raise the issue of testimony stripped of worries about sincerity. The issue is how I am to make use of the information that you believe some claim. Alternatively, if we prefer to do epistemology in terms of degrees of belief rather than beliefs *simpliciter*, the issue is whether your believing the claim with a higher (or lower) degree of confidence than I do gives me a reason to have more (or less) confidence in it.

It is questions of this second sort that I will be examining. A way to dramatize these questions is to suppose that I have found a diary in which you have constructed an extensive list of what you believe. Of course, no list could capture everything you believe. So, lots of propositions that you believe will not be on the list, and let's suppose that among the omitted ones are those that would provide me with personal information about you. As a result, I am able to infer from the diary little or nothing about your background, history, training, abilities, and circumstances. Moreover, I have no other information about you from any other source. Under these conditions, how if at all should I adjust my opinions in the light of your opinions?

Let's also stipulate that all of the opinions listed in the diary are stable, in the sense that you would be willing to stand behind them on reflection. Stipulating this helps avoid some needless problems, since, even in my own case, mere opinion counts for little when questions of rationality are at stake. There are some propositions that I believe only because I haven't given them much thought. If I were to reflect on them, I wouldn't be willing to stand behind them. These opinions are the doxastic counterparts of whims. Not all of my opinions are like this, of course. Some are more stable and hence more suitable than doxastic whims for deliberations about what else to believe. And so it may be with the opinions of others. Perhaps I should take them seriously only if they are stable.

There are variations of the above scenario that are also worth exploring. In the original scenario I know nothing about the diarist other than what the entries in the diary allow me to infer, and they only provide me minimal information. But we can imagine scenarios in which I am given limited additional information about the diarist, and we can then ask whether this information should make a difference in how I regard the opinions listed in the diary. For example, would it make a difference if I knew that the diarist was a contemporary, as opposed to someone who lived in a different age?

I will have things to say about some scenarios of this sort, but for now I want to concentrate on the original scenario, since it is the one that raises most clearly the issue of whether it is reasonable to grant fundamental authority to the opinions of others. Fundamental authority is to be contrasted both with derivative authority and with what Allan Gibbard has aptly called "Socratic influence" (Gibbard 1990, pp. 174-175).

Suppose you get me to believe a claim through a series of well-thought-out questions and instructions. Afterwards, I understand what you understand, and hence believe what you believe. The rationality of my believing this claim is not dependent upon your believing it, since I now understand on my own why it is true. As I use the terms, you have exercised *influence* over me, but not *authority*. Of course, there isn't always a sharp line dividing the two. In many cases, influence and authority are mutually reinforcing and hence hard to distinguish. Still, there is a difference, and epistemologically it's a significant one. Crudely put, it's the difference between my taking your word for something and my not doing so.

But even when I'm prepared to take your word about some claim, I need not be granting you fundamental authority. I may be prepared to take your word only because I have independent reasons—i.e., reasons that don't derive from your believing the claim—for thinking that you are reliable with respect to claims of this type. If so, I'm granting you derivative authority. It is authority generated from my reasons for thinking that your information, abilities, or circumstances put you in an especially good position to evaluate the claim.

Authority, whether derivative or fundamental, can exercise its influence directly or indirectly. If you say "*p*" and I trust you and thereby come to believe *p* myself, then your authority over me has been direct. On the other hand, if you recommend method *M* to me and if as a result I adopt *M* which then leads me to believe *p*, then your authority over me with respect to *M* has been direct but with respect to *p* it has been indirect. For the sake of simplicity, I will be discussing only direct authority, although I do think that the theses I'll be arguing for apply to indirect authority as well.

One of these theses is that it is reasonable, at least for most of us most of the time, to grant fundamental authority to the opinions of others. There should be no real controversy about whether we are influenced by others. We clearly are. Nor should there be much controversy about whether it is reasonable for us to be influenced by others. Everyone except a few skeptics will admit that this often is reasonable. The interesting question is, what makes it reasonable for us to be influenced by others? I will be maintaining that it can be reasonable for us to grant fundamental authority to others. Hence, it can be reasonable for us to be influenced by others even when we have no special information indicating that they are reliable.

The contrary position is that fundamental authority is always bogus. Thus, every instance of rational authority is an instance of derivative authority. I will be calling this position *epistemic* egoism. The epistemic egoist grants no fundamental authority to others. In and of itself, the fact that someone else believes a claim gives me no reason whatsoever to believe it.

Egoists can grant derivative authority to others. If I am the egoist, for example, I can grant you derivative authority with respect to an issue if I have reasons to think you are reliable about issues of this sort. The most straightforward way for me to have such reasons is by being acquainted with your track record. If by my lights that record is a good one, I will have reasons, all else being equal, to count your current opinion as credible. So, if you tell me that *p* is true and I don't yet have my own opinion about *p*, I should be inclined to take your word. Your believing *p* gives me a reason to believe *p*. In a nice phrase, Phillip Kitcher has called this "earned authority" (Kitcher 1992).

Not all derivative authority is earned authority. Even if I have no knowledge of your track record, I as an egoist can have reasons to trust your opinions. You may have had training that gives you expertise, or you may have special access to relevant information, or you may just have thought a good deal about the issue. These kinds of considerations, and others like them, can make it reasonable for me to grant you authority, albeit not authority that is earned on the basis of your track record. Earned authority derives from your past opinions being calibrated with the truth as I see it. Unearned but derivative authority derives from some other source that attests to your reliability.

Epistemic egoists who grant derivative authority to others are in a position analogous to ethical egoists who act altruistically. It can be consistent for ethical egoists to promote the interests of others, since doing so might have instrumental value for them. It can even be a general rule for egoists that they ought to promote the interests of others. Doing so might make it appear as if they are altruistically motivated, and in the long run this may best serve their self-interests. Similarly, it can be in the self-interest of ethical egoists to promote the interests of others even in cases when in the short run this imposes enormous sacrifices on them, since the long-run benefits might outweigh the short-term hardships.

There are epistemic counterparts for each of these. It can be consistent for epistemic egoists to defer to others on an issue, since it might be reasonable for them to believe that others are in a better position to evaluate the issue. Likewise, egoists can make deference to others their regular practice once they have reasons to think that others have expertise that they lack. Egoists can defer to others even on issues that they otherwise felt very sure of.

So, epistemic egoists need not appear intellectually arrogant. On the contrary, they can appear unassuming. It is no easier to identify epistemic egoists from their intellectual behavior than it is to identify ethical egoists from their moral behavior. What separates ethical egoists from non-egoists is their attitude toward the goals, desires, and needs of others. Ethical egoists value the satisfaction of the interests of other people only as a means to satisfying their own interests, whereas non-egoists value the satisfaction of the interests of at least some other people for its own sake. Correspondingly, epistemic egoists are distinguished from non-egoists by their attitude toward intellectual authority. Non-egoists grant fundamental intellectual authority to at least some other people. Egoists do not. They grant only derivative authority to other people.

Epistemic egoism is not a fictitious position. Some of the most influential epistemologists have been egoists—John Locke, for example. His egoism grew out of his ethics. He thought that just as we have an obligation to conform our behavior to moral standards, so too we have an obligation to conform our opinions to epistemic standards. Fulfilling this intellectual obligation requires that we think critically about the operations of our own intellectual faculties and that we trust only those faculties that we have reasons to regard as reliable. Similarly, we ought not to trust uncritically the faculties of others. We have an obligation to think things through for ourselves rather than deferring to commonly held opinions.[1] Indeed, Locke so emphasized the importance of intellectual self-reliance that he even expressed doubts about granting derivative authority to the opinions of others, much less fundamental authority.[2]

David Hume was also an epistemic egoist. However, unlike Locke, he emphasized the usefulness of derivative authority. He appreciated the extent to which we rely on the opinions of others, but he also insisted that it is reasonable for us to rely on these opinions only to the degree that we have reasons for thinking that they are reliable. Hume's empiricism led him to add that these reasons must come in the form of observations.[3]

There are also influential figures in the history of epistemology who rejected epistemic egoism. Thomas Reid was perhaps the most forthright about doing so. He insisted upon the reasonableness of our natural attitudes of trust both in our own intellectual faculties and those of others. According to Reid, it is reasonable, all else being equal, for us to take someone else's word for something even if we know little if anything about the reliability of the person. Testimony, or at least sincere testimony, is *prima facie* credible. Indeed, Reid thought that if our natural attitudes of trust, first in ourselves and second in others, were not reasonable, the inevitable result would be skepticism. There would be little that we could rationally believe (Reid 1975, VI, xxiv).

Each of these positions, the egoism of Locke and Hume and the non-egoism of Reid, has its characteristic advantages but also its characteristic drawbacks. Egoism will be attractive to those who treasure independence of mind and who correspondingly worry about the temptations of group-think. Its drawback is that it threatens to cut us off from expertise and information that others have and we lack. It's not just that relying on the expertise and information of others enables us to pursue our intellectual projects more rapidly, although this is true enough. It's also that a good many of our intellectual projects are so complex that it would be altogether impossible for us to conduct them alone. To the degree we take egoism seriously, there is a threat that we will be deprived of the benefits of these joint projects. After all, many people with expertise and information that we lack are people about whom we know little. Hence, there may be little or no basis for us to grant them derivative authority.

The non-egoist eliminates this threat by acknowledging that, in intellectual matters as in other matters, we are thoroughly social beings. Our opinions are massively influenced by others about whom, often enough, we know little. Despite this lack of familiarity, we can reasonably make use of their expertise and information, since it is reasonable for us to grant fundamental authority to them. The drawback of this position is that intellectual authority has a potentially chilling effect on intellectual innovation. Insofar as credulity is a necessary condition of rationality, it becomes more difficult for individuals to criticize the opinions of others in a radical but rational way. The stronger the intellectual authority of others, the less room there is for rational rebellion.

An adequate account of intellectual authority must find a way of avoiding the potential drawbacks of both egoism and non-egoism. We need an explanation of how it can be reasonable for us to rely on the expertise and information of people about whom we know little, and the explanation has to leave room for the possibility of our radically but rationally disagreeing with the opinions of our contemporaries. For the moment, however, I'm going to set aside this problem and focus instead on what turns out to be a related issue—namely, intellectual trust in oneself.

Fundamental trust in one's own intellectual faculties is an unavoidable part of any nonskeptical intellectual life. Regardless of how we make use of our intellectual faculties, we are not going to find non-question-begging guarantees that our ways of proceeding are reliable. But if so, all our intellectual projects must involve an element of intellectual faith in ourselves. In particular, we must have faith in those intellectual faculties and procedures that are so fundamental that we cannot defend them without making use of them.

Those who cannot accommodate themselves to this reality—i.e., those who refuse to be satisfied with anything short of non-question-begging guarantees of their own reliability—are forced to be skeptics. Although there is nothing inherently incoherent about being a skeptic, the fact of the matter is that most of us are not. By and large we are prepared to trust our own intellectual faculties even if we cannot provide non-question-begging assurances of their reliability. Moreover, it can be reasonable for us to have this kind of trust in our faculties. Rationality doesn't require us to have non-question-begging guarantees of our reliability (Foley 1993).

But if we reasonably have fundamental trust in our own intellectual faculties, can we coherently withhold such trust from others? In other words, can we coherently be egoists? There are degrees of epistemic egoism. Those who invariably give more weight to their own views than the views of others can plausibly be said to be egoists, but in what follows I will be concerned with radical egoism. For radical egoists, the opinions of others count for nothing per se. They grant fundamental authority to no one other than themselves. The question is whether this is a coherent position. If they grant fundamental authority to themselves, can they legitimately deny it to others?

In thinking about this question, it is important to resist the notion that epistemic egoism is inevitable, since we have no choice but to make up our own minds about who is reliable. No one else can do this for us. It then might seem a small step to conclude that in making up our minds about who is reliable, we are in effect granting, or refusing to grant, derivative authority to others. Thus, what at first glance might seem to be fundamental authority is really derivative authority.

For example, suppose I yield to you on an issue. Then, according to this way of thinking, I must have decided that you are more reliable about this issue than I am. Or if I haven't explicitly thought about this question, I at least haven't decided that you are unreliable, whereas I could have (at least in normal cases). In either event, I am responsible for having deferred to you.

This is the kind of inescapable responsibility that existentialists and managerial types drone on about, the former with their talk of our being condemned to be free and the latter with their ditty, "you can delegate authority but not responsibility." On this view, there is no, and can be no, authority that excuses me from responsibility for my own opinions. It is I who bestow authority, if only by omission.

But even if all of this is correct, it misses the interesting epistemological question. Grant for the sake of argument that insofar as I defer to the opinions of others, there has been at least an implicit decision on my part to do so, and thus I am responsible for having granted them authority. Nevertheless, this leaves unanswered the question of whether I am compelled on pain of irrationality to grant them this authority, given that I trust my own intellectual faculties. What makes epistemic egoism an interesting position is that it answers no to this question. Egoists are prepared to assert that there is nothing incoherent about having fundamental trust in my own intellectual faculties while not having such trust in that of others.

Attempts to trivialize epistemic egoism are analogous to attempts to trivialize ethical egoism. In the ethical case, the strategy is to try to show that we are all egoists. Those who appear to be altruistically motivated—parents, lovers, friends, even the Mother Teresa's and Albert Schweitzer's of the world—are really egoistically motivated. After all, Mother Teresa wouldn't be motivated to relieve the suffering of others unless this were something she desired. So, if she succeeds in reducing the suffering of others, she is satisfying one of her desires. Happiness, it is argued, is essentially a matter of having one's desires satisfied. Thus, Mother Teresa is acting in a way that, if successful, will make her happy. The conclusion, then, is supposed to be that her motivation is no different in kind from that of the most ingratiating used car dealer. They are both motivated by an end the achievement of which would make them personally happy.

There is much that could be said, and has been said, about arguments of this sort; but for purposes here the important point is that they fail to address the central ethical question, which is whether the desires and goals of others should count for something in our decisions about what to do. Even if it is true that we are motivated to act benevolently only when we have a desire that the desires, goals, and needs of others be satisfied—a desire whose satisfaction, like any other, brings us a kind of contentment—this leaves unanswered the question of whether it would be wrong or incoherent or irrational for us not to have some such desire. Is there something incoherent about our not having this desire insofar as we take our own desires and goals seriously in making decisions? Likewise, is there something incoherent about our not having this desire insofar as we want others to take our goals and desires seriously in their decisions?

Similarly, even if it is granted that when we intellectually defer to others, we are implicitly making a decision that grants them authority, this leaves unanswered the central epistemic question, which is whether it would be incoherent for us not to grant some such authority to others, given that we trust our own intellectual faculties. We trust our own faculties even though we cannot give a non-question-begging defense of their reliability. But if we trust ourselves in this way, aren't we rationally compelled to trust others by and large? Egoists say no, and non-egoists say yes.

However, egoists and non-egoists need not disagree on all matters concerning testimony. For example, both can agree that if the opinions of others are to give me a reason to alter my opinions, I must rationally believe that they have those opinions. In effect, what this means is that non-egoists as well as egoists can admit that there is a significant difference in the way that first-person and third-person opinions help shape what it is rational for me to believe. If I am deliberating on my own, without consulting the opinions of others, it's ordinarily not necessary for me to have rational beliefs about what my beliefs are. For me to believe *p* rationally on the basis of *q*, it is enough for me to believe *q* rationally and to believe rationally that if *q* is true, then so is *p*. I needn't also rationally believe that I believe *q*, although often enough I will rationally believe this.

By contrast, your belief *p* makes it rational for me to believe *p* only to the degree that it is rational for me believe that this is what you believe. Egoists and non-egoists, as I have said, can agree on this. They disagree over what else, if anything, is needed. Egoists insist that something else always is needed. I must have positive reasons for thinking that you are reliable. Non-egoists deny this.

Who is right, the egoists or the non-egoists? The non-egoists, I think; but I also think that much of the spirit of egoism can be accommodated within the non-egoist's stance. More on this later. I want first to explain why it is incoherent for us not to grant fundamental authority to others if we are not skeptical about our own intellectual abilities. Part of the explanation is that our belief systems are saturated with the opinions of others. In our childhood, we acquire beliefs from parents, siblings, and teachers without much thought. These constitute the backdrop upon which we form yet other beliefs, and often enough these later beliefs are also the products of other people's beliefs. We accept the testimony of those we meet; we listen to each other on television and radio; and we read each other's books and articles. We are not intellectual atoms, uninfluenced by one another. Our views are hugely shaped by the people around us. This suggests, even if it doesn't quite imply, that if we trust ourselves, we must in consistency also trust others. For insofar as the opinions of others have shaped our opinions, we wouldn't be reliable unless they were.

Of course, not everyone influences the beliefs of everyone else. I live in one place, and you in another, and we haven't had any contact. So, you haven't influenced me. Still, unless one of us has had an extraordinary upbringing, your beliefs have been shaped by an intellectual environment that is broadly similar to the one that has shaped my beliefs. Moreover, your cognitive equipment is broadly similar to mine. And so, once again, if I trust myself, I am pressured on the threat of inconsistency also to trust you.

This is not to deny the obvious. There are intellectual differences among us, and some of these differences are greater than others. The difference between my intellectual upbringing and environment and that of my brother is much less than the difference between my intellectual upbringing and environment and that of the Mandinka. Likewise, there are differences of intellectual ability, even among normal adults. Still, these differences are insignificant when compared to the differences between us and, say, turtles. It is easy enough to overlook how similar we are in intellectual capacity and background, since we tend to take our similarities for granted. It is our differences that fascinate us. A sign of this is that we make far finer distinctions about one another than we do about anything else, and among the characteristics that we most finely distinguish are ones concerning our intellectual capacities and backgrounds. The availability of so many distinctions can tempt us to think that we are radically different from one another, but any careful look will reveal that the intellectual capacities and the intellectual environments of all people about whom we know anything are largely similar to our own. As a consequence, others believe largely what we believe. Even those who are distant from us in time and place believe pretty much what we believe. They believe, as we do, that there are other human beings, that there are living things other than human beings, that some things are larger than others, that some things are heavier than other things, that some events happened before other events, and so on.

When I say that others believe largely what we believe, I am taking a position between two extreme positions, each of which, oddly enough, is motivated in large part by a radically holistic conception of concepts and beliefs. On the one side are those who argue that, given holism, no sense can be made of the idea that the beliefs of others are radically different from ours (Davidson 1986). On the other side are those who assume that people in other cultures have beliefs different from ours and who then go on to argue that, given holism, these differences are so great that we cannot even understand what it is that they believe; the concepts they employ are incommensurable with ours, and hence their beliefs are radically different from ours. I am rejecting both of these positions. My claim is that although it may be possible for the beliefs of others to be radically different from our beliefs, we know of no culture where this is in fact the case. What at first glance might appear to be radical differences among the belief systems of various cultures look more like surface differences when the huge backdrop of shared beliefs is adequately emphasized. The ancient Greeks, the ancient Incas, and the Indians of the Brazilian rain forest all believe pretty much what we believe (Hutchins 1980).

If the intellectual equipment and intellectual environment of others is broadly similar to our equipment and environment, then we must generally trust them insofar as we generally trust ourselves. We must regard them as generally reliable, and we must give their opinions at least some weight. It is incoherent for us not to do so, given that we trust ourselves.

Our reasons for trusting others, on threat of incoherence, may decrease as their distance from us in abilities and circumstances increases. The trust owed others can be a matter of degree. Still, insofar as the abilities and circumstances of even the most unfamiliar people are broadly similar to our own, we have at least some reason to trust the beliefs of anyone. We have these reasons even if we know little about their individual talents or training and nothing about their past reliability.

So, insofar as it is rational for me to believe that you believe *p*, I automatically have at least a weak reason to believe *p* myself. I don't need to know anything special about you. In particular, I don't need special reasons to trust your opinion, as the egoist suggests. I don't need these special reasons because, all else being equal, it is incoherent for me not to trust you, given that I trust myself.

The heart of this argument is a consistency claim. If I grant fundamental authority to myself, I must in consistency grant it to others. I must do so because it is reasonable for me to think that my intellectual faculties and my intellectual environment are broadly similar to theirs.

So, the distinction between derivative and fundamental authority is not that the former is motivated by reasons whereas the latter is not. Fundamental authority can be motivated by reasons; it's just that the reasons are negative ones. If my reasons for trusting others are based on positive evidence of their reliability—either evidence specific to their talents, information, and situation or evidence about the track record of people in general in giving testimony—then their authority is derivative. On the other hand, what I have been arguing is that even if I lack positive evidence of their reliability, I can still have reasons to trust them—the reasons being that it would be irrational for me not to do so, given that I have fundamental trust in myself and given that I think that my intellectual faculties and my intellectual environment are broadly similar to theirs. But if these are my reasons for trusting them, then as I am employing the distinction, their authority over me is fundamental, not derivative.

Of course, no argument of the above sort can be airtight. There are various ways of blocking its force. It's just that none is especially plausible. For example, one strategy is for me to assert that my intellectual faculties are fundamentally different from those of others. Another is to assert that the intellectual environment that helped shape my beliefs is fundamentally different from the environment that has shaped the beliefs of others. Still another is to assert that although my environment is broadly similar to that of others, it hasn't affected me in the way that the environments of others has affected them. I have somehow managed to rise above my environment.

Most of us at one time or another have been tempted to think of ourselves as distinctive in thought as well as manner. We want to believe that what we think and perhaps even how we think is out of the ordinary. Even so, in its most radical form, this is a view that not many of us would be willing to endorse. In our thoughtful moments, we don't think of ourselves as fundamentally different from others.

There is nothing inherently incoherent in my thinking that I was born with radically different abilities from others or that I was raised in a radically different way from others or that, unlike almost everyone else, I have managed to rise above the influences of my intellectual environment. Thus, there isn't anything inherently incoherent in my refusing to grant authority to others. Still, the vast majority of us would be willing to admit, at least on reflection, that our intellectual faculties are similar to others and that a large portion of our opinions have been influenced by the same kinds of factors that have influenced others and that we haven't cast off these influences. But then, insofar as we have intellectual trust in ourselves—i.e., insofar as we're not skeptics—it is prima facie reasonable for us to trust the opinions of others as well.

More could be said about the details of this argument, but there is a more pressing issue to pursue. Namely, even if this argument is correct, as I'm inclined to think it is at least in rough outline, it doesn't answer the question of how to treat the opinions of others when they conflict with mine. Is the prima facie credibility of their opinions defeated when I have conflicting opinions? I think that it is.

The presumption of trust in the opinions of others is generated, I have suggested, out of self-trust. For most of us, it is incoherent to trust by and large our own faculties and opinions and not to trust by and large those of others. But by the same token, the prima facie credibility of other people's opinions is defeated when I, who trust myself, have a conflicting opinion. It is defeated because they have made what is by my lights an inaccurate judgment.

This doesn't mean that it might not still be rational for me to defer to them, but it does mean that I need a special reason to do so. Often enough, I will have this special reason, but there's no guarantee that I will; and if I do not, I need not alter my opinion when faced with opinions that conflict with mine.

More completely stated, the thesis is this: if your opinion is to give me a reason to alter my opinion, it must be rational for me to believe that you have this opinion; if this is rational for me, then I have a prima facie reason to trust that opinion; but this prima facie reason is defeated if I have an opinion that conflicts with yours; if this prima facie reason is defeated, then your opinion gives me a reason to alter my opinion only if I have special reasons to defer to you about the matter at hand; these special reasons can come in the form of considerations that indicate that you are in an especially good position to ascertain the truth of the issue in dispute, or they can come in the form of considerations that indicate I am not in a good position to ascertain its truth.

For example, suppose it is rational for me to believe that I lack the training, skill, or information needed to make an accurate judgment. Then even if I have a different opinion from you about the matter in dispute, it can be reasonable for me to defer to you. Alternatively, suppose it is rational for me to believe that although I have relatively reliable information and abilities, you have skills or information that put you in an especially good position to evaluate the issue. Then once again, it can be reasonable for me to defer to you. It can be reasonable for me to defer despite the fact that my conflicting opinion defeats the prima facie authority of your opinion. Your fundamental authority for me has been defeated, but you do nonetheless have derivative authority for me.

Suppose you are no more and no less skilled than I, and we have the same information, but our opinions conflict. Even so, if you have devoted more time to thinking about this information than I have, I may still have reasons to defer to you. Your having spent more time on the issue may give me a reason to believe that I would have reached the same conclusion had I taken more time to think about the information at hand.

On the other hand, if we are equally skilled and equally well informed and we have devoted an equal amount of time and effort to thinking about the issue but we still disagree, there is room only for

Socratic influence. You need to convince me, to show me where I have gone wrong. I have no reason to defer to you.

Of course, often it won't be clear how strong a reason your opinion gives me to change my opinion. I may be less than fully sure how your skills contrast with mine or less than fully sure how much time and effort you have devoted to the issue in question. I may even be less than fully sure what it is that you believe. As a result, it won't be clear how, if at all, I should alter my opinion. But for the discussion here, it is best merely to note these complications and then ignore them, so that the main point is not lost. And the main point is that differences of opinion between myself and you tend to give me a reason for thinking that you are not to be trusted on the issue in question.

It's worth emphasizing again that this is not to say that it is permissible for me simply to ignore the opinions of others when they disagree with me. It is only to say that the prima facie trust that it's reasonable for me to grant to others is defeated when I have an opinion that conflicts with their opinion. So, if I don't have a special reason to defer to them, I don't have a reason to alter my opinion.

Notice also that even if I don't currently have a reason to alter my opinion, the conflict may very well give me a reason to investigate further the issue at hand. Intellectual conflicts inevitably raise the question of how good a position I am in, compared to others. A conflict of opinion thus puts me on guard; and if the issue is sufficiently important, the conflict will give me a reason to recheck my own reasoning or gather additional information or consult with others whom I might have stronger reasons to trust. On the other hand, if the issue is not an especially important one, it can be rational for me to retain my current opinion without further investigating it. Further investigations may not be worth the effort.

So, to repeat, when I have reasons to believe you have opinion *p*, this gives me at least a weak reason to have opinion *p* myself. I need not know anything special about you or your expertise. But this prima facie reason is defeated if I myself have a conflicting opinion. Even so, it may still be rational for me to defer to you if I have reasons to think you are in a better position to evaluate *p* than I am.

This account does justice to the insights of both epistemic egoists and non-egoists. Non-egoists are right in insisting that an attitude of credulity is ordinarily reasonable. If it is rational for me to believe that you believe *p*, I have a prima facie reason to believe *p*. On the other hand, in the most interesting cases, the cases where there is conflict of opinion, this prima facie reason in favor of *p* is defeated. So, with respect to these cases, the egoist is right in spirit if not in letter. If it is to be rational for me to alter my opinion, I need special reasons to trust you.

By "conflict of opinion," I mean an explicit conflict. If you believe a claim and I have no opinion at all about this claim, then—as I am using the phrase—there is not a conflict of opinion between us. Correspondingly, the prima facie reason in favor of the claim that your belief generates for me is not defeated.

This is an important point, since there are lots of issues about which I have no opinion, often because I'm not in a position to have one. Suppose I have only passing familiarity with an issue. Then I may have no opinion at all. I could take a guess—but even if I did, I wouldn't be willing to stand behind it, and hence it would be something more akin to a doxastic whim than a genuine opinion. But then, there is nothing to conflict with the opinions of others on this issue. Thus, all else being equal, I have a reason to defer to their opinions.

I can also fail to have opinions about topics with which I am familiar. Indeed, I can fail to have opinions about propositions that I have explicitly entertained. It is important to resist the idea that we always have some belief or another in propositions that we understand, if only a belief about their probabilities. Often enough, I will have no idea of how to assign even a probability to a proposition.

Consider the proposition that there is a man somewhere in Manhattan now standing on his head on a sidewalk. I wouldn't voluntarily make any assessment of the probabilities of this proposition. If asked how probable it is, I would respond that I have no idea. If forced, I might be willing to venture a guess; but the guess shouldn't be taken to represent my current opinion, and certainly not one that I would be willing to stand behind. If my view is to be represented by probabilities at all, it is some very large segment of the interval 0 to 1 that best represents it. But insofar as this interval represents anything, it represents a refusal to take a position. By contrast, when I think that the probability of a fair coin coming up heads is about 0.5, I am taking a position—a definite, albeit probabilistic, position about the chances of the coin coming up heads.

None of this is to say that when I have no opinion, I'm rationally required to take the word of others at face value. It's merely to say that one kind of defeater of the prima facie trust that it's reasonable for me to have in the opinions of others is not available. Their authority isn't defeated by the fact that I have a conflicting opinion, but there can be other defeaters. I can have special reasons to distrust their opinions—perhaps their track record on such issues isn't very good or perhaps they lack the relevant training. If so, it isn't reasonable for me to defer to them.

Still, in general it will be the case that the fewer opinions I have about a set of issues, the more likely it is that I have reasons to defer to the opinions of others. For example, if I am new to a field, I'm unlikely to have very many opinions about the field and hence there won't be many opportunities for conflicts between my opinions and those of others. Thus, there is plenty of room for deference.

Correspondingly, the more opinions I have about a set of issues, the less likely it is that it will be reasonable for me to defer. If I am an expert in a field, I'm likely to have an opinion about most of the issues in the field, and hence there are more opportunities for conflicts between my opinions and those of others. Thus, there is less room for deference.

Once again, I'm gliding over various complications for the sake of simplicity. For example, I have been talking in an all-or-nothing fashion about a number of issues that are more accurately regarded as matters of degree. Thus, I have been treating my willingness to stand behind an opinion (so that it isn't merely a doxastic whim) as an all-or-nothing matter, whereas in fact this is a matter of degree. As a result, the defeating function also comes in degrees. The more I'm willing to stand behind my current opinion, the more it tends to defeats for me the credibility of your opinion if it conflicts with mine. The less I'm willing to stand behind my opinion, the less it defeats the credibility of yours.

A truly adequate account of intellectual authority would do justice to these and other complexities, but I am not even attempting to do justice to them. My aim is the more modest one of sketching a general approach to issues of authority.

With this general approach in hand, let's reconsider the diary example. The supposition, remember, is that I have discovered a diary that lists the opinions of the diarist but I have no special information about the diarist. Even so, I have a prima facie reason to believe the propositions listed in the diary. I know the diarist believes them, and this gives me a reason to believe them as well. On the other hand, if a proposition listed in the diary is one that I disbelieve, then this prima facie reason is defeated. Moreover, since I have no other information about the diarist, I have no reason to alter my opinion in light of this conflict with the diarist. I have no reason, in other words, to grant the diarist derivative authority.

Let's now vary the basic scenario. Suppose I have reasons to think that the diarist has information or skills that I lack. Then even if I have a conflicting opinion, I have reasons to move my opinion in the direction of the diarist's opinion. A fortiori, if I have no opinion at all, I have reasons to adopt the opinion of the diarist.

Consider another variation. Suppose I have information that the writer of the diary was a contemporary of Chaucer. How should this information change my reaction to the opinions listed in the diary? It depends. If the listed opinion is one about everyday life in the fourteenth century, then presumably it is reasonable for me to defer. The fact that the diarist believes this proposition gives me a prima facie reason to believe it as well. Moreover, I'm unlikely to have a conflicting opinion since I don't know much about daily life in the fourteenth century. In addition, there's no reason for me to think that the diarist wasn't in a good position to have reliable beliefs about these kinds of matters.

On the other hand, suppose the diary also lists opinions about the motions of the planets, the causes of pneumonia, and the nature of fire. It won't be reasonable for me to defer to the diarist on these matters, even if I have no firm opinion about some or all of them. The prima facie credibility of the diarist's opinion is defeated, since given the general state of knowledge in the Middle Ages, there are reasons for me to think that the diarist wasn't in a good position to have reliable beliefs about these matters.

Now change the scenario so that I know that the diarist is my contemporary, and suppose that at least some of the listed opinions concern technical matters about which I have no expertise. Despite the fact that the issues are ones requiring expertise and despite the fact that I have no assurances that the diarist is an expert, I might not have any reason to discount the diarist's opinion. It is reasonable for me to grant prima facie credibility to the opinions of others. What this means, among other things, is that it is reasonable for me to assume that others have been intellectually responsible in forming their opinions. So, if the diary lists an opinion on a technical matter, it is reasonable for me to assume, all else being equal, that the diarist either is an expert or has relied on the experts. The difference between the opinion of this diarist and the opinion of the medieval diarist on, say, the nature of fire is that I have reasons to believe that even a responsibly functioning intellect in the Middle Ages was unlikely to get things right about such matters.

Let's now vary the information about me, rather than the diarist. Suppose I'm an expert about a matter listed in the diary. Then ordinarily it won't be rational for me to defer, although I should still be open to Socratic influence. If I'm an endocrinologist, for example, I should be open to influence on matters of endocrinology, and the diary might contain enough information to persuade me to change my mind on some issue. But it's unlikely to be rational for me to defer to the diarist on these matters. Indeed, part of my function as an expert is not to defer. It is to make up my own mind on these questions. If I don't, I am not doing my job (Schmitt 1985).

This is the second of two considerations that make it reasonable for experts to be less open to authority than non-experts. The first, as I mentioned earlier, is that experts tend to have extensive opinions about their areas of expertise. So, when they come across the opinions of others on an issue in their specialty, it is likely that they themselves will already have an opinion. If the opinion is a conflicting one, it will defeat the prima facie reason they have to trust the other person. By contrast, non-experts will tend to have fewer opinions about the subject, and hence there will be more room for authority. The second consideration is that when there is a conflict of opinion involving an expert, it's unlikely to be rational for the expert to think that the other person is in a better epistemic position. Hence, there is unlikely to be any special reason to defer. Moreover, this is so even if the other person is also an expert. With non-experts, the reverse is true. There are likely to be special reasons to defer. So, once again, there is more room for authority.[4]

Indeed, if I'm not an expert, I ordinarily will have reasons to defer to the experts even when all of their deliberations and data are available to me. This is so because ordinarily I will have reasons for viewing myself as less than fully competent to evaluate their deliberations and data. The more reasons I have to be unsure of my own abilities, the more likely it is that I have reasons to defer. On the other hand, if I myself am an expert and if all the deliberations and data of the other experts are available to me and I have taken the time to study their deliberations and data, it's unlikely to be reasonable for me to defer. I am in a position to make up my own mind rather than rely on them.[5]

To be sure, there are occasions on which it is reasonable for experts to defer to other experts. In part, this is the result of increasing specialization. As expertise is defined more and more narrowly, there are increased opportunities for experts in the same broad field to defer to one another. One's expertise is not so much in physics per se as in theoretical physics and not so much in theoretical physics per se as in string theory, and so on. So, it can be reasonable for string theorists to defer to other physicists about their narrow specialties, and vice versa.

Still, this increasing specialization doesn't affect the general point, which is that insofar as one succeeds in becoming an expert in a field, there is less room for intellectual deference. This helps explain why intellectual egoism looks more plausible when we are thinking about experts working on issues within their own expertise.

Change the scenario of the diary once again. Suppose I have assurances that the diary represents the opinion of most of my contemporaries. Does this give me a stronger reason to change my opinion than if the diary represents the opinion of an individual? It depends upon the issue. For some issues, it is significant that there is commonly held opinion about it; for others, this isn't especially significant.

Suppose the opinion held in common is that the hit-and-run driver in a recent accident had blond hair. Then I'm likely to have reasons to defer to this shared opinion. In part, this is so because with eyewitness reports there isn't much room for expertise. To be sure, some of us have better eyesight than others, some are more observant than others, and some even have special training to be observant in cases of accidents. Still, for the most part, those who are in roughly comparable positions to observe an event will have roughly comparable authority when it comes to making eyewitness reports about it. So, if their reports are independent and in agreement, it won't be easy for me to dismiss them on the ground that I have special expertise or on the ground that they lack it.

Moreover, I'm likely to have a reason to defer to the common opinion even if I too have witnessed the accident and have a conflicting opinion. Suppose that I, unlike almost everyone else who was there, remember the driver as having dark hair. Then the prima facie credibility of the other eyewitnesses is defeated by my conflicting opinion, but I still do need to explain why they all disagree with me—and it may not be easy for me to come up with this explanation. After all, in general I don't have reasons for thinking I'm especially privileged with respect to making observations, and likewise there need not be any obvious non-evidential consideration that's shaping the beliefs of the other witnesses.

On the other hand, suppose I think there is indecisive evidence for a commonly held opinion, e.g., that there is intelligent life elsewhere in the universe. Then there won't be much of a reason for me to defer. Given the lack of decisive evidence, it is reasonable for me to assume that something other than the evidence is guiding people's opinions. Perhaps they want it to be true that there is intelligent life elsewhere; perhaps this is a comforting thought for them. But whatever the explanation, it wouldn't be especially surprising if most people turned out to be wrong on this issue.

These variations of the basic diary scenario illustrate again how the characteristic dangers of both egoism and non-egoism are avoided by the position on intellectual authority I have been advocating. The skeptical dangers of egoism are avoided because we do not need special information about the reliability of other people's beliefs in order to trust them. It can be reasonable for us to grant fundamental authority to those about whom we know little or nothing. On the other hand, the conservative dangers of non-egoist positions are avoided because when our opinions conflict with the opinions of others, the prima facie reason we have to believe what they believe is defeated. On the issues in conflict, their fundamental authority for us is defeated, and this in turn leaves plenty of room for rational dissent from popularly held opinions.

This position gives due recognition to the fact that as intellectual beings, we are both social and autonomous. Despite the influence of others—indeed, because of it—we become intellectually independent, at least if all goes well. Our intellectual training develops and hones abilities that allow us to make autonomous judgments. To be sure, we cannot entirely shake off the influence of others, but no plausible notion of autonomy requires us to do this. What autonomy does require is that we be capable of evaluating, and sometimes even radically criticizing, the views, procedures, and standards of those around us (Foley 1993, pp. 85-88 and 117-131).

Notes

1. "The fourth and last *wrong Measure of Probability* I shall take notice of, and which keeps in Ignorance, or Errour, more People than all the other together, is that which I have mentioned in the foregoing Chapter, I mean, the *giving up our Assent to the Common received opinions*, either of our Friends, or Party; Neighborhood, or Country" (Locke 1959, IV. xx. 17).

2. "For, I think, we may as rationally hope to see with other Mens Eyes, as to know by other Mens Understandings. So much as we our selves consider and comprehend of Truth and Reason, so much we possess of real and true Knowledge. The floating of other Mens Opinions in our brains makes us not one jot the more knowing, though they happen to be true. What in them was science, is in us but Opiniatretry, whilst we give up our Assent only to reverend names, and do not, as they did, employ our own Reason to *understand* those *Truths*, which gave them reputation. . . . In the Sciences, every one has so much, as he really knows and comprehends: What he believes only, and takes upon trust, are but shreds; which however well in the whole piece, make no

considerable addition to his stock, who gathers them. Such borrowed Wealth, like Fairy-money, though it were Gold in the hand from he received it, will be but Leaves and Dust when it comes to use" (Locke 1959, I.iii.23).

3. From his discussion of miracles: "there is no species of reasoning more common, more useful, and even necessary to human life, than that which is derived from the testimony of men and the reports of eye-witnesses and spectators. . . . It will be sufficient to observe that our assurance in any argument of this kind is derived from no other principle than our observation of the veracity of human testimony, and of the usual conformity of facts to the reports of witnesses" (Hume 1975, X, 111).

4. Contrast with Gibbard who thinks there's always something suspicious about authority: "A conviction based on authority alone . . . is unsatisfactory. It is disquieting, especially if one suspects it goes against the way one would think matters through oneself with enough information" (Gibbard 1990, p. 231). Belief based on authority is not always as disquieting as Gibbard suggests. I'm often willing to defer to the experts even if I think I would come to a quite different conclusion were I try to think the issue through for myself. But this needn't be disquieting, if I have reasons to think that they have training and expertise that I lack.

5. For a different opinion, see Lehrer and Wagner (1981).

4

Speaking of Ghosts

C. A. J. Coady

Respect for fashion may be fine in the rag trade, but it should have no place in the avenues of the intellect. Hence I shall begin with an unfashionable thinker writing on an unfashionable topic: F. H. Bradley on spiritualism. Both may seem remote from the themes of this collection, but I aim to establish some links—although my efforts will not involve any attempt at the rehabilitation of Bradley's metaphysics or any endorsement of spiritualism.

In his vigorous essay, "The Evidences of Spiritualism" (1935), Bradley seeks to debunk the claims that spiritualist "phenomena" show something religiously important—in particular, the existence of a moderately enjoyable after-life into which we shall be inducted in disembodied form on the occasion of death. At the time he wrote, there was considerable enthusiasm for spiritualism. A great debate had raged throughout the late eighteenth and early nineteenth centuries about the phenomenon of "mesmerism"; many of the opponents of "animal magnetism" in its various forms treated it all as fraudulent and spoke of magic or spirit-mongering, whilst some of its supporters saw it as a spiritual phenomenon beyond scientific explanation. The fact that hypnotism, at least, became established as in part a genuine though still a puzzling and somewhat ambiguous reality encouraged some to think of a similar respectability descending on seances, poltergeists, or psycho-kinesis, and led others to think that this respectability might give some credence to claims relating to the immortality of the soul, or at least its survival of death.[1]

At the time Bradley was writing (in 1885), the Society for Psychical Research had recently been founded (in 1882) with one of Bradley's philosophical rivals, Henry Sidgwick, as its first president. Sidgwick was cautious, even sceptical, about the likelihood of the society's investigations unearthing genuine spiritual realities, and became even more so as time passed and the amount of fraud and confusion in the area became apparent; but with characteristic open-mindedness and curiosity, he was prepared to see such matters investigated. He had had a long-standing interest in apparitions, ghosts, etc., and seemed to think that a proper sifting of the evidences might at least offer some empirical support for certain religious claims.[2] It is this prospect that Bradley hopes to eliminate.

Bradley mounts a barrage of criticisms against the spiritualists. He argues that, even granting the reality of the reported phenomena, the argument that the causes of it are disembodied souls is weaker than a number of other hypotheses that might be offered in explanation (in particular, that they are embodied in a different type of matter); there is no reason to believe such souls immortal; there are problems about identifying such spirits with the human beings they claim to have been; and their communications and effects reveal a lower level of existence than ours, not a higher. But I do not want to pursue any of this, for I am interested in a certain epistemological assessment that Bradley makes of the supposed communications from what he calls "spirit-land." This assessment might seem to create certain difficulties for something that I want to argue for (and have argued for) about communications in *this* world, so discussing it should throw further light upon the entirely mundane, though in some respects mysterious, predicament in which we find ourselves as epistemic agents in our earthly social world. Consequently, in what follows, I will not only set aside Bradley's other arguments against the supposed status, or even the very idea, of spirits, but I will also ignore certain other objections to the acceptance of their testimony that turn on the impossibility or the very great improbability of there being any such entities. That is, it might be argued that disembodied spirits are a conceptual impossibility, or that they are a conceptual impossibility as continuants of deceased human beings, or that the prior improbability of such beings outweighs any credence we might otherwise be tempted to give to their supposed reports. Plausible arguments along these lines may certainly be mounted, but I am disregarding them for two reasons. The first is that I do not find them entirely persuasive, in either the impossibility or improbability versions, partly because of certain misgivings I have about the philosophical arguments for the impossibilities, and partly because our taking the reports of others seriously frequently conditions how we think of possibility and probability. The second, and perhaps more important, reason for neglecting such matters is that by so doing I can (like Bradley) concentrate upon a number of interesting and challenging questions that arise if we are not initially dismissive in this way.

THE EPISTEMOLOGICAL BACKGROUND

In my book, *Testimony: A Philosophical Study* (1992, also see 1973, 1975, 1981), I argued emphatically against a certain picture of our reliance upon the word of others. The picture is probably best articulated by Hume, but it is present in much post-Renaissance thought and indeed in the ancient and medieval worlds. The dominant figure in the picture is that of "the autonomous knower" who does indeed rely, and rely quite extensively, on the testimony of others, but who does so because he has independently checked on their reliability in a testimony-free way. The picture turns out to be ambiguous in certain respects: does the autonomous knower accept testimony because he has independently ascertained the reliability of this particular witness, or the reliability of some class of cognitive agents to which the witness belongs (and, if so, which class), or is it merely that he knows he can do one or the other of these checks if need be? I argue in my book that the answers are also multiply ambiguous and that once clarity is achieved it turns out that the autonomous knower is a chimera.

Part of the case for this involves showing that the plausibility of supposing that such testimony-free verifications of reliability are possible depends covertly upon accepting testimony-laden checks, observations, and falsifications. I am, for instance, confident that the claims of used car dealers (about the merits of the cars they offer) must be treated with considerable caution, though my only personal experience of a transaction with one of them happens to have been perfectly happy. Other than this, I have never done any sort of personal checking on their accuracy or veracity. Others have done it for me, and, without checking individualistically on them, I rely upon the inter-social network of informal checking that they have established. (Indeed, they rely in part upon it themselves.) Such often-ignored facts account for the way Hume and others persistently and unconsciously conflate individual and social readings of the term "observation," a conflation that gives so much impact to Hume's reductionist account of our ordinary dependence on testimony.

Such confusions are symptomatic of the fact that the reductionist picture in which the mythical autonomous knower figures so centrally is flawed at heart because, so I argue in *Testimony*, the existence of a common language in which reports are made and accepted or rejected already carries with it a commitment to some degree of unmediated acceptance of testimony on the ground floor of our cognitive endeavours. This reference to "ground floor" is not intended to invoke or comprehensively endorse those foundationist theories of knowledge that have recently been subjected to so much scorn and criticism. My view of that debate is that some parts of the foundationist enterprise are more worthy of support than others, and the same is true of its rival coherentist project. One thing that does seem to be right about the foundationist emphasis is the idea that individual perception, memory, and inference deserve a particular respect as sources of information in a way that speculation, guessing, and suggestion (whatever their other cognitive value) do not.[3] My claim about testimony is that it deserves the same respect as perception, memory, and inference. Indeed, the respect we owe to them requires us to accord it similar honour. This is because testimony puts us in touch with the perceptions, memories, and inferences of others, and a certain coherence between individual and communal resources underpins the individual's reliance on his or her own epistemic skills and achievements. This fact underpins an absurdity in the reductionist enterprise in that it is committed to the possibility of understanding fully what other speakers of the language tell us about the common world we inhabit, but of nonetheless also finding all of their reports mistaken or deceitful. The argument for this I have presented elsewhere and will not repeat here.

BRADLEY'S CRITIQUE

Let us turn then to Bradley. Bradley begins his critique of the spirit testimony with some general observations about testimony that put him squarely in the reductionist camp. Testimony, he insists, "can never be an independent source of information, side by side and on a level with personal observation. For it must by its nature involve an inference, and that inference must be founded on our direct knowledge. It *is* an extension of our personal experience, but an extension that proceeds from and rests on that basis." He then proceeds to admit our instinctive trust in what we are told, but rejects this as mere natural tendency and hence beside the point. It is, I think, correct that we must do more than note the natural tendency, but it is a complex question what that "more" must be. Bradley seems to think that, since we cannot accept "anything and everything just because it is offered to us by another intelligence," then we must use some criterion drawn from individual experience (and/or inferences from personal experience) to sift all the testimonies we receive. That we *sometimes* use individual experience to determine whether a witness is lying or mistaken can hardly be denied, but, of course, it doesn't follow from the fact that testimonial error can be sometimes so detected that it is always so detected, nor indeed that testimonial reliability is or must be established in that way. To think in that fashion would be like thinking that because we sometimes detect visual errors by tactile investigation then we must always do so and that we are right to trust our vision generally only because we have extensively verified its findings by tactile investigation. (In his early writings on the theory of vision Berkeley seems to have thought that something like this conclusion was true of the visual determination of depth, though the argument cited here played at most a subsidiary part in his advancing that conclusion.) It is also to the point that we sometimes detect visual errors, even occasionally about directly visual properties like depth or distance, by auditory means, but a parallel generalization about the dependency of sight upon hearing would be even more bizarre.

Although Bradley sails close to these absurdities about testimony, he attempts to avoid the most extreme of them. He says that he is "far from meaning" that individuals should believe only what they have themselves experienced or what does not run counter to their own experience. "It is not that we are confined to private experience," he proclaims, "but that this experience itself must warrant our leaving it, by giving us a reason for going beyond." This reason, in the case of testimony, is "an inference on our part to a mind in the witness which, first, is capable of having learnt the fact attested and, next, is able and willing to communicate the truth. We in short infer that the mind of the other may in these respects be treated as our mind; and in consequence we have merely to test its statements in the way in which we test our personal observations." Bradley's use of plural pronouns is clearly rhetorical, or at any rate distributive; he is talking of individual inferences and observations. Bradley thinks further that an individual's confidence that witnesses are broadly able to testify accurately (what I have called their competence) must be established by positive individual observation, whereas confidence in their sincerity ("absence of motive for untruth and deceit") must *in addition* be supported by the individual's *negative* experience. By this, he means that I may rightly take into account the fact that I have no experience of this witness that makes it plausible to suppose that he or she has a motive to deceive me. In short, I must positively establish (from solely individual resources) that the witness is competent to testify, and do what I can to establish in the same fashion that he or she is sincere, with the proviso that in establishing the second I can rely on an assumption that if the witness were insincere I would have found it out.

From this we can see that Bradley is proposing both an account of the epistemic status of testimony in our cognitive landscape and certain tests for determining the acceptability of particular depositions. He thinks that the latter follow from the former; but we should be alive to the possibility that there may be some useful insights in what he says about the tests, even if we reject his reductionist stance on the epistemic status of testimony. We do not and could not proceed as he claims we must, since the checkings and inferrings will turn out to be testimony contaminated in a variety of ways. But it is true that our confidence in the depositions of others relies upon their being competent and sincere, just as our confidence in our individual memories and visual perceptions relies upon the normal working order of the memory and perceptual mechanisms. What is debatable is the idea that because certain competence and sincerity conditions must obtain if testimony is to be reliable (both at large and in particular cases) then we must be able to satisfy ourselves that these conditions obtain, independently of any recourse to testimony, before we can rely upon it. There is, of course, an analogy here with a general puzzle in the theory of knowledge that goes by the name of the closure problem. Since there is an indefinite number of propositions that must be true if some particular proposition *p* is to be known, then it is tempting to conclude that we must (per impossibile) know independently that all of these propositions are true before we are entitled to be described as knowing *p*. So if we actually know that *p*—i.e., on the basis of perceiving *p*—then it must be true that we are not hallucinating, that we are not being deceived by a malignant demon, that we are not a brain in a vat, etc., and it is tempting to conclude that we cannot know that *p* unless we first know all these other things. If we take this route, then a deep and pretty general scepticism seems unavoidable; so this should give us pause about taking the route in the case of testimony. We could, of course, elect for widespread scepticism, but then this does not tell us anything interesting about the specific epistemological status of testimony, which is Bradley's (and our) target.

So we might agree that testimonies are unreliable if the witness is incompetent and/or intent on deceiving, but decline to be drawn by Bradley into placing the onus of demonstration where he does. The more plausible picture is that for all sorts of ordinary testifying we can (and must) presume competence and sincerity, though we quickly learn (at least as much from others as from our own individually ascertained mistakes) that there are contexts and circumstances in which an attitude of trust is inappropriate.[4] Even for expert testimony, though we will usually be more interested in positively establishing witness credentials, the route to doing so will seldom involve testimony-independent verification of such credentials. Indeed, in the case of expert testimony we are usually entirely at a loss to determine the existence and quality of such competence from our own resources. With expert witnesses we may (contrary to Bradley's suggestion about testimony in general) actually be slightly better placed by our own unaided efforts to determine insincerity rather than incompetence; and the test of "negative experience" might work slightly better on competence than on sincerity, in that if the witness were incompetent I might have heard of it.

What then of the spirits? Let us waive for the moment the foundational question about testimony (though, as we shall see, it will return) and ask instead how we should react to the spirit communications? Bradley is ready with a set of answers. We cannot be sure that the spirits have the competence to testify nor can we ascertain whether they are sincere. Indeed, the body of "evidence" that we have of supposed spirit communications suggests that the level of intelligence of the spirits is pretty low, so, if anything, we might conjecture that their observational and other skills are sub-optimal. As to their sincerity, the case is even more disturbing since we cannot apply "our criterion" any longer, for this reason:

> We have no knowledge of our own by which to check their statements, and, what is worse, we know nothing about their characters. We do not know their moral natures; and whether they have or have not a motive to deceive us, we are utterly ignorant. It is not too much to say that if they were spirits of evil, whose happiness was staked upon fooling us men, we might (so far as we know) have no means for discovering it. (Bradley 1935, pp. 604-605)

So Bradley concludes that we should place no trust at all in spirit testimony.

In fact, he proceeds to consider a further argument on behalf of the spirits, and we shall turn to that in due course; but let us pause to assess the state of play. In particular, does Bradley's mistaken outlook on the epistemological status of testimony undermine his conclusions about the spirits? Or is it, perhaps, rather that his correct views about the spirits help to undermine my claims about his mistaken outlook? I want to argue that, in spite of his mistakes about the status of testimony, Bradley is raising legitimate problems for the witness of spirits, and that, properly understood, these problems—rather than contradicting my account—throw further light upon its value.

EXPLORING SPIRIT-LAND

The basic difficulty about the spirits is that their world ("spirit-land") is cut off from ours entirely except for the testimony they give. So far as we know, we have no further interaction with them and the things that surround them other than their words. Bradley even raises the question whether these are words, i.e., whether the noises emanating from spirit-land are parts of language at all; and this is an issue to which we shall return. For now, let us assume that there is nothing problematic about the linguistic reality of their supposed utterances, and that we have eliminated the entirely plausible (and commonly verified) hypothesis of fraud. What we have are vocalised sentences in an earthly language (for simplification, let's assume English in what follows) apparently informing us of happenings and circumstances in another world inaccessible to our senses. As Bradley insists, we worldlings are in no position to make independent observations of spirit-land or of the behaviour and nature of its inhabitants, and this does seem to create a genuine worry about their reports. Note, however, that it is not only I as an individual who cannot check independently on the spirit testimonies, for I cannot get other worldling testimony that checks have been made. We worldlings as a community are cut off from spirit-land, except for the spirit communications. But why should this matter? Isn't the situation rather like that in which we laypeople confront the deliverances of experts?

This analogy is worth a little exploration. In the modern world, we are certainly deeply dependent on the word of those whose expertise is beyond our testing, and sometimes beyond our barest comprehension. It is tempting to think of the expert computer engineer or software whiz, or the expert mathematician or geneticist, as inhabiting a different world (or worlds) from the lay world. Simplifying greatly, let us think of these as two worlds: lay world and expert world. Why do so many of us trust the expert reports so readily and mistrust the spirit reports so emphatically? It cannot be because we can independently check the experts' reports and cannot independently check the spirits' reports, because we have conceded that we lay and world-bound cannot do either. Yet we do stand in a different relation to the experts than to the spirits. Enough of us do interact with the experts epistemologically (and, of course, in other ways) to tell certain things about their capacities and their likely sincerity. They are strange enough, no doubt; but their strangeness merges with their ordinariness and we can know about their characters and about the place their expertise occupies in a common world. Much of this is known to any one of us from the word of others, some lay and some expert, in ways that I have discussed in my book; but although the pattern is complex, it is also comprehensible. It provides the facts that lie behind our sense that the construction of lay world and expert world is highly artificial whereas our present world and the spirit world are really separate. Any one of us laity could set ourselves to become an expert, given certain favourable conditions; but we can only set ourselves to become a spirit by dying, i.e., departing from this world.

Is this a sufficient response? Well, it depends. This is the point at which to add to the spirit story an element that Bradley himself sees to be of importance. It is the fact that the spirits tell us not only about their world, but also comment on ours. We may not have access to their world, but they seem to have some access to ours, and we can judge the accuracy of what they say about mundane matters. As Bradley says, "The spirits tell us things that we ourselves verify. They are found intelligent and faithful in some things, and that gives us a reason to trust them beyond" (1935, p. 605). He then goes on to characterize this attempted support for spirit testimony as "irrational" on the grounds that the spirit "might yet be a witness not competent to speak of the things of spirit-land." Bradley's thought is that a particular spirit's veracity about mundane matters should be treated as the exhibition of a sort of exceptional capacity, rendering it insignificant from the point of view of testing the spirit's capacity to observe and willingness to transmit genuine information from spirit-land: "His capacity is not established by the strange and unusual. It is when he proves himself our equal in the highest that we have, that we should think him on our level" (pp. 605-606). And as to truthfulness, "By what logic does it follow that, if they speak truth in one thing, they will do it in another? That is the argument by which dupes are plundered perpetually" (p. 606).

Bradley's response seems at first blush too strong. Surely the fact that the spirits make claims about our world that we can and do verify must make some change to the evidentiary status of their testimony at large. Yet Bradley denies this. Since a good deal can turn on detail here, let us construct an example to make our discussion more concrete. Imagine a medium (and let us call her Madam Dunbar) going into a trance during which the suggestion is that she is the vehicle of a messages from "beyond." Her voice alters dramatically; the new voice tells the assembled audience that it is Henry Sidgwick, and then proceeds to give us detailed information from spirit-land—as, for example, that it is a very beautiful land, with charming houses and flowers that give off wonderfully fragrant scents. In addition, the voice tells us that he (Sidgwick) departed this life in 1900 and gives many details of Sidgwick's life that are beyond what one might expect the ill-educated Madam Dunbar to know, but which those philosophically and historically learned members of the audience know to be true. Moreover, the voice claims to be anxious to convey to us some interesting information about his former life, and, indeed, tells us that he wrote an article on the topic of egoism that eluded the grasp of his literary editors and has never been published. The voice tells us where this may be found and how it escaped the attentions of the executors, and later on we find an article as described, in a characteristic Sidgwickian mode with some novel thoughts on a familiar Sidgwickian theme. Furthermore, the voice tells us that the daughter of a Mr. Ducasse, a member of the audience, was taken ill half an hour before and is now in hospital nearby. This also proves to be true and very unlikely to be known to the medium. At subsequent performances, the voice (or what seems to be the same voice) produces equally useful information. And the question is this: do such verifications make the testimony about goings-on in spirit-land more credible?[5]

We should note, to begin with, that such verifications are usually taken not as evidence that the other testimonies of the spirits about spirit-land should be believed, but that the communicator really is who he or she claims to be. In the imagined example above, the evidences are supposed to support the claim that it is indeed Henry Sidgwick who has, from his superior viewpoint, communicated a piece of true information about this world. And indeed, if such a report were genuine, it would surely tend to support that hypothesis, though being also consistent with several other remarkable hypotheses—as that another spirit in the confidence of the Henry Sidgwick spirit had been passing this information as if the other spirit were the sometime Knightsbridge Professor at the University of Cambridge. But our question concerns the degree to which this accurate attestation about our world gives support to the spirits' claims about theirs. Here Bradley seems to be on surer ground. Our example provides reason to believe that the Sidgwick spirit has the capacity to observe and/or remember accurately events in our world, and an interest in conveying the truth about at least some such events. But how do we know that this capacity and interest carries over to events and objects of spirit-land?

This question needs to be treated with care. Bradley sometimes writes as though the mere logical possibility that the spirits may be malevolent or incompetent is enough to discount their standing as witnesses, but the logical impossibility of deceit or mistake would be far too strong a standard of admissibility. What is really at issue, as the earlier analogy with expert testimony suggests, is whether and how we can extend our normal easy trust in the word of others to the testimony of such unusual beings speaking on such unusual matters. And, as Bradley also points out, the issue is affected by the fact that the testimony is to matters of some weight—the existence and nature of an after-life. In the parallel case of expert testimony, it is akin to the acceptability of evidence on a matter of guilt or innocence, life or death. For these reasons, the evidential onus must shift somewhat from the normal conversational context. I want to explore this further by moving at this point away from spiritualism to another example that shares many of its features.

TALKING TO ALIENS

Quite a lot of people are confident that the material universe contains rational inhabitants other than human beings (and animals, if any of them be rational); others are not so confident but think it a serious possibility that extra-terrestrials exist. Amongst such people, the question has been raised of how we would detect and deal with communications from such beings, and various practical measures have even been implemented for monitoring radio signals from remote galaxies. Let us suppose that messages start arriving that purport to be from such beings. The messages are actually in what seems to be English. This is surprising, but explicable perhaps given the supposition that the aliens are so intelligent that they have worked out how we communicate by monitoring various signals emanating from our world. Their replies to our questions reveal a knowledge of our world, and even some knowledge of things in our world that we do not at the time know ourselves but that we come to confirm. They then tell us many things about their very remote world which are quite unlike most things in our experience. What credence should their reports be given? In particular, what weight should we place upon their communicative competence and honesty about our world in assessing the Bradleian supposition that they may be either incompetent or deceitful about theirs?

As to competence, I think the case is fairly clear, though it depends somewhat upon the nature and extent of the alien successes in our world. If their communicated information about our realities is impressive enough in variety and range, we are surely reasonable in assuming that they have the competence to comprehend their own world and the authority to speak of it. There may be interesting problems awaiting us about sensory properties they detect in their world that would not be accessible to us, or (for that matter) that they detect in ours that are currently inaccessible to us. On the other hand, the supposition that they are competent to cope with our world and to work out how to communicate with us, but yet incompetent to handle the environment in which they evolved, is too improbable—and possibly even incoherent—to delay us.

The Bradley challenge on malice is not so readily dealt with. How do we discount the hypothesis that their veracity about our world is a ploy for deceiving us about theirs? This is, indeed, one standard device of the conman: gain the victim's confidence by a limited display of honesty and then exploit it for dishonest purposes. Of course, the conman's strategy works by playing upon that fundamental trust in the word of others that underpins linguistic communication, and without which (so I argue in *Testimony*) a general system of actual linguistic communication would be impossible. Indeed, a shared language in which there were nothing but false reports would be an impossibility, and there is good reason to believe that any shared language will embody a norm of truthful communication that serves to vindicate that trust. But if so, shouldn't we trust the aliens, and their narrative surrogates, the spirits?

Not necessarily. The trusting conclusion doesn't follow from the premises, and it is important to see why not. For the aliens to speak English is for them to employ these signs, inter alia, for a great deal of truthful reporting, just as it is for us. But the hypothesis of a separate world is precisely an hypothesis that raises the possibility that such truthful reporting is segregated from an area of predominantly deceitful testimony, namely, the testimony they give *to us* about their world. Spies in a foreign land during wartime will need, for both semantic and prudential reasons, to speak many truths about the world they share with the foreigners, but this leaves them free to lie dramatically about their homeland. If we imagine our initial contact with the aliens proceeding in a different and more plausible way, we may see this more clearly. We receive signals that we cannot understand but that seem to be intentionally produced, and so we assume that the alien intelligences know something about earth and are trying to communicate with us. We try to contrive situations in which we and they are both able to confront common realities and describe them, and out of such teaching situations we strive to induct them into English. (We might indeed go the other way; but for my purposes it is simpler, as in reality it would be more feasible, to teach them our language rather than to learn theirs. Needless to say, there are numerous difficulties in the way of the "contrivance" I am suggesting, whichever path we take, and I am simply assuming, for the sake of the discussion, that these can be successfully negotiated.) That the aliens come to speak English with us, rather than merely mouth English sounds, is attested by the degree of agreement in judgement and accurate reporting that emerges in the world we share; and once this is established, we are eager to hear what they say about their otherwise-inaccessible world. But should we believe it?

Against trust, we have not only the real possibility embodied in our experience of the conman, but also the aliens' physical and cultural isolation from us. It is not just that we have so little to go on about their individual characters, but also that we have no chance to observe their ways of life and their biologies. They can tell us about such things, but the telling is isolated from the normal meshing with our own (communal) observations, inferences, and memories that is characteristic of terrestrial testimony. Encountering the members of an isolated tribe or community here on earth, an explorer or anthropologist may be able to understand from their economic situation, their type of isolation, their religious practices, that there exist areas of their life about which they are likely to lie to a foreigner. He or she can understand this partly because of what can be assumed to be shared, and found not to be shared, on the basis of encountering the tribespeople engaged in living their normal (though strange enough) lives. It is quite otherwise with the aliens. We may be encouraged that they share enough with us to communicate, but this degree of community is relatively thin, especially when it comes to assessing what may well be claims of great moment about their world, claims upon which our lives might depend, or the future of our political arrangements.

Yet the aliens' world is not totally divorced from ours, and it may be that they tell us things about their world that do provide a meshing of sorts with our experience via our otherwise well supported theories about the universe. I mean here more than consistency with our cosmological theories. Suppose they tell us things that are partly thus consistent, but partly require adjustment to our theories in ways that have testable consequences for us and also provide a new and intellectually attractive synthesis and simplification of our existing theories. The consequences are confirmed and the new theory is elegant and powerfully explanatory. In such circumstances, though we may not be able to rule out various versions of the conman hypothesis, we will have yet more reason to admit their competence, and have striking confirmation of their veracity about certain aspects of their world that are beyond our observational reach.

So we may be reassured about their capabilities for testimony, but what of their general sincerity? I think we now know enough about the aliens for it to be not irrational to trust them, though it would be going too far to say that we *know* that they are trustworthy. It seems that what we have is a sort of intellectual deadlock in which the responses of believing other things that they say about alien-land, or disbelieving, or suspending belief, will be essentially contestable. We may be forced out of the attitude of suspended belief by the necessity to act, if, for instance, they tell us something about their world that, if true, requires us to act dramatically here and now in ways that involve considerable loss, or, rejecting the message, to continue as we are with the prospect of considerable loss if their communication be true. For such cases, we cannot adjudicate what it is rational to do in the abstract; we need to know more about the details of the message, its context, and the stakes. We move here into the area of decision theory and the various principles for choice there much debated. Where the details are filled out in a certain way, we may also find ourselves in the terrain sketched by William James in "The Will to Believe" (1898) so that we may face something like a leap of faith or a leap of mistrust.

BACK TO THE SPIRITS

What then of the spirits? There are two striking points of dissimilarity between their circumstances and those of the aliens. The first is that they are even *more* removed from us than the aliens because they do not now inhabit our world in the way that the aliens do. After all, the aliens (by hypothesis) live in the same spatio-temporal world governed by the same physical laws as we do. Their experiences (relayed to us by testimony) may lead us to adjust our present understanding of those laws; but in the case of the spirits, what they communicate about spirit-land is irrelevant to our understanding of the laws of physics.[6] In considering the aliens we were tempted to hold that their "other-worldliness" was almost enough to remove their testimonies from the sort of mesh with the rest of our terrestrial lives that allows testimony the fundamental and significant epistemic role it has for us. This temptation, I argued, is somewhat resistible just because of the ways in which the alien world is not totally alien. But can we mount any resistance in the case of the "other-worldliness" of the spirits? The second point of dissimilarity suggests that we may be able to do something here; it reminds us that the spirits are, in a way, *less* removed from us than the aliens, since the supposition is that they (or some of them) have been ordinary members of our world and that we may become denizens of theirs. We are certainly right to heed Wittgensteinian and pragmatist warnings about the natural homes of our concepts and the dangers that inhere in too adventurist a departure from them, but we should also be wary of a certain intellectual timidity or parochialism that sometimes accompanies the warnings; we often cannot tell that our cognitive resources have been stretched too far until we try stretching them.

The two points of difference, therefore, pull in opposite directions. The fact that the spirits are more distant than the aliens (though not strictly "distant" at all) suggests that we have even less grip on their competence and sincerity with respect to spirit-land than we do with the aliens. The fact that the spirits (or some of them) are the spirits of our dead no doubt needs to be made intelligible and, if intelligible, then needs, in addition, to be made believable. But supposing this can be done, then the holding of such identifications is bound to make some difference in the credibility we can accord to reports about spirit-land. To return to my example of the ghost of Henry Sidgwick: given what we know about Sidgwick's honesty in his earthly life and given the details of the story told above, we surely have some reason to trust his word (if indeed it is his). At least we know a lot about what his character and capacities *were* by contrast with our knowledge of the aliens, and this should count for something, even if there are still such possibilities as that his character in the after-life has been transformed for the worse.

There is a further point that Bradley makes, and that we mentioned earlier, about the language in which spirit reports are made. Bradley alludes only in passing to this problem and clearly does not regard it as decisive, but it does raise an interesting issue (though I am not altogether clear that it is the same issue that Bradley himself has in mind). What Bradley says is this: "When we communicate amongst ourselves we are sure that our system of signs is trustworthy. If it were not so the practical results must show it; and this is in the end the sole test that we have. But when we converse with spirits have we got that assurance; and if not, do we possess any other?" (1935, p. 604). I interpret Bradley here not as casting doubt upon whether the spirits are really speaking English—though this is a doubt that one might initially raise and that he may indeed have been raising—but as asking a question about the adequacy of English (or any other earthly language) to the realities of spirit-land.

The doubt about whether they are really speaking English is like the doubt about whether something that looks remarkably like a human face on a huge rock was carved by a sculptor or made by the beating of the sea. This doubt is settled by our having no evidence of a sculptor who could do *that* but plenty of evidence of what the sea can do, and by certain facts about the vagaries of interpretation. Similarly for the story Russell tells about the supposed Scottish ghost who used to wail repeatedly, "Once I was hap-hap-happy, but noo I am meeserable," but whose utterances turned out to be the effects of a rusty gate spit and a strong wind (1948, p. 192). The spirit communications, as I am supposing them here, however, are palpably in English inasmuch as they not only resemble English sounds but betoken intentions to communicate via those sounds (susceptible of a familiar Gricean analysis of some kind) that mesh with the observable world in a number of standard ways, including the style of verification imagined in the ghostly Sidgwick story, but also less amazing ones like statements about the room in which the seance took place. If a deflationary explanation is available here, it will not invoke the effects of wind or sea but the fraudulent intentions of the medium or her allies.

A more interesting worry, which Bradley may have been getting at, is whether the resources of English are adequate to the realities of spirit-land. This is a point at which spiritualism necessarily connects with traditional religion and theology since not only are many religions concerned to stress some form of after-life for human beings, but they usually connect it with such transcendent realities as God and disembodied intelligences. Nor is this connection merely one of accidentally overlapping subject matter, since the modern spiritualist movement is in part an outgrowth of—or, as many would insist, a deviation from—Christianity, and inherits something of its metaphysical substructure. A common theological problematic within that tradition (and within others) concerns how our natural languages can be used to characterise transcendent realities—most notably, of course, divine realities, but also less exalted ones. Theories of analogical predication, *via negativa*, and so on have been responses to the problem. Without going deeply into any of this interesting material, we may nonetheless take the lesson that the business of reporting on spirit-land is no simple linguistic exercise like reporting on a visit to New Jersey (much as a visit to certain parts of New Jersey might seem like an after-death experience). When the spirits offer what seem to be plain descriptions, they may well be using English expressions in an extended sense that would make their reports no straightforward matter to interpret. It is a familiar, though somewhat mysterious, fact that sounds can be described with a colour vocabulary (recall Locke's reference to the blind man's description of the sound of a trumpet as scarlet), though this possibility does not involve a very secure grasp upon what is thereby conveyed, nor upon much in the way of practical response. If there were people who only described sounds in this way and we overheard their conversations, we might be seriously misled about their environment. Perhaps something similar is true about the spirit communications.

This seems to me to constitute a good reason for some caution about the understanding of the precise content of spirit communications. Our earlier conclusions suggest that Bradley's critique (bolstered as it is to some extent by his mistaken reductionist approach) is far too strong a rejection of spirit testimony. For certain suppositions about spirit reports, his main arguments fail to show that it is irrational to believe them, though they may well show that it is not irrational to disbelieve them. Our development of his hint about language, however, raises the spectre (appropriately enough!) that trusting their reports may have us believing propositions whose sense is much more elusive than it seems at first blush. Here, there is some analogy with our relation to the reports of experts where our beliefs in what they tell us (about black holes, anti-gravity, the latest bizarre particles, or even mere super-conductors) are often justified even though the content of these beliefs is not fully, and is sometimes only dimly, within our lay grasp. We are indeed justifiably confident that some of these contents are fully understood by somebody within our community, and it is precisely here that the analogy with the spirits becomes more tenuous. To the degree that it continues to hold, we may be entitled to believe what the spirits tell us ("not irrational to believe") whilst admitting that we have at most a very partial grasp upon the precise import of their descriptions. But there is a standoff, because those who refuse to give any credence to the spirit reports of spirit-land (even whilst admitting, as our hypothesis supposes, the reality of the spirits) cannot be accused of irrationality.

Notes

1. For an excellent history of the fortunes of "mesmerism" or hypnotism, and associated phenomena, since the time of the founding father, Franz Anton Mesmer, see Gauld (1992).

2. Sidgwick's work in this area, and his motivations, are thoroughly discussed in Broad (1953a).

3. Popper explicitly denies this, but for reasons that seem to me unpersuasive. Interestingly, one of his reasons for rejecting the idea that perception, memory, etc. are sources of knowledge is that, if we are looking for sources, then most of what we know comes from testimony. See Popper (1968). But instead of treating this as a refutation of the idea that there are sources of knowledge, it seems more sensible to add testimony to the list.

4. Thomas Reid (1975) makes this point about the way children begin with an attitude of total trust and modify it in the light of experience.

5. This mildly facetious story is based loosely upon some characteristic reports of medium messages from beyond. Of particular interest is one of the "verifications" apparently provided by the Swedish mystic Emmanuel Swedenborg. Swedenborg's assistance was sought by a Countess de Marteville in 1761 because she was being pressed for payment of a very large sum of money by a goldsmith who claimed to be owed it for a silver service provided to her husband before his death as a gift for the Countess. The Countess was convinced that her late husband had paid the account, but could find no receipt or relevant correspondence to prove as much. Three days later, Swedenborg reported to the Countess that he had managed to contact her dead husband who revealed that the money had been paid to the goldsmith seven months before the Count's death, and that the receipt was in the Count's bureau. The Countess insisted that she had searched the bureau to no avail, but Swedenborg explained that his information was that there was a secret compartment behind the left-hand drawer in which the receipt would be found. It was. Or so the account has it. See Wilson (1987, p. 56).

6. With regard to spiritualism and "science," we should be alive to the possibility that some of the phenomena grouped together under the heading of "the paranormal" may be ill assorted. Telepathy, for instance, may turn out to be a phenomenon of this world, explicable by some enlarged version of current science, or even perhaps showing limits to any comprehensive science that would still deserve the name "physics." But it is doubtful that spirit communications could be so understood.

5

A Conservative Approach to Social Epistemology

Hilary Kornblith

It is undeniable that social factors play an important role in human cognition. Epistemologists have often ignored this fact, and epistemology has suffered for it. I thus wish to join the chorus of those who urge epistemologists to pay serious attention to the sociology of knowledge. On my way of viewing things, this is a straightforward extension of the naturalistic approach to epistemology. Just as naturalists have made much of the importance of seeing knowledge in its proper psychological setting, we should also recognize the importance of the social setting in which knowledge is naturally and inevitably found.

My enthusiasm for much of what is now called "social epistemology," however, remains limited. Some have made quite remarkable claims about what follows from the social character of knowledge and justification. The locus of epistemic evaluation, some tell us, is first and foremost the group, and only secondarily, if at all, the individual.[1] When we focus our epistemological theories on the group, rather than the individual, some tell us that we come to see the intimate relationship between knowledge and power, with such old-fashioned ideas as truth dropping out of the picture altogether.[2] The world itself, on some views, is said to be a social construction, and thus epistemology must come to terms not only with the social production of belief, but also with the social production of the objects of belief.[3] These are radical claims, and I reject them all.

What I wish to do here is present an account of the importance of social factors in epistemology which flows directly from a naturalistic epistemology: an account which will leave important room for input from the study of group processes and institutions, but will leave the overall structure of our epistemological theories substantially unchanged. I know this approach is far more conservative than many would like to see, but I think that it is at least worthwhile seeing to what extent such a conservative extension of naturalistic epistemology can take account of social factors in cognition—factors which I agree are important and which I agree have been unduly neglected.[4]

In the first section, I explain what naturalistic epistemology is and what the motivation is for this approach. In the second section, I explain how this motivation suggests a program of research in epistemology which would draw on work in sociology in a way comparable to what one sees in the very rich body of literature in epistemology now drawing on work in experimental psychology. In the third section, I ask whether work in individual psychology becomes irrelevant once one recognizes the importance of the social dimension in knowledge; I argue that it does not. In the next section, I suggest that there is a special set of questions and concerns which must occupy epistemologically relevant social studies of science—questions and concerns which are only a small part of the work being done by sociologists of science. Finally, I attempt to explain why it is that the very narrow scope I propose for a social epistemology of science is so badly out of fashion.

NATURALISTIC EPISTEMOLOGY AND ITS MOTIVATION

Knowledge is a natural phenomenon.[5] It involves an interaction between human beings and the world around us. If we are to understand knowledge properly, we must examine it from two different perspectives. We should ask two different questions about the relationship between us and the world we inhabit. First, what is the world that we may know it? And second, what are we that we may know the world?

An important part of an answer to the first question is that the world is divided by nature into kinds. Natural kinds are homeostatic clusters of properties, i.e., clusters of properties which are bound together by nature in stable relationships (Boyd 1988, 1991). It is in virtue of the existence of natural kinds that inductive inference is possible, for when nature binds properties together in such homeostatic clusters, the presence of some of these properties is a reliable indication of the presence of others. Were it not for the existence of natural kinds, if just any set of properties might be found naturally occurring together, then inductive knowledge would be impossible, for one could never reliably infer the presence of any properties from the presence of others. The existence of real kinds in nature thus constitutes the natural ground of inductive understanding of the world.

Although inductive knowledge is thus made possible by the existence of real kinds in nature, it is only in virtue of the sophistication of our innate endowment that we may exploit such natural regularities and turn them to our cognitive advantage. There are two features of our innate endowment which allow us to tap into these regularities. The first has to do with the structure of our concepts. We are innately endowed with a rich conceptual structure which presupposes the existence of natural kinds. Our concepts have what Douglas Medin and Andrew Ortony (1989) call "an essence placeholder." That is, it is a presupposition of the very form of our conceptual structure that the natural world is divided into kinds having unobservable essences. These essences are sets of properties which are responsible for the observable characteristics of kinds, and which determine the conditions of kind membership. Although we typically do not know what the essential properties of a kind are, we nevertheless presuppose that kinds have such essential properties. The fact that we have concepts which are antecedently structured in this way allows us efficiently to pick up on the presence of natural kinds in our environment.

The second feature of our innate endowment which explains our inductive understanding of the world is the set of inferential tendencies which are native to us. We have a tendency to project features of kinds which we take to be essential to them, so that exposure to a single member of a natural kind is often sufficient to prompt rich and reliable inductive inferences about the kind in general. Our inferential tendencies work together with our conceptual structure to help project the features of natural kinds which tend to be bound together in nature. Such inferences are not, of course, infallible, but they are remarkably reliable. The reliability of such inferences is assured by the way in which our psychological structure dovetails with the real causal structure of the world.

There are a number of features of this account which are deserving of special emphasis. The possibility of knowledge depends on a firm fit between our native psychological endowment and the causal structure of the world. Were the world wholly unstructured, it could not be known by creatures of any sort. A rich causal structure is thus required if knowledge is to be so much as possible. By the same token, human psychology must be richly structured as well, and structured in a way which dovetails with the structure of the world. We are thus doubly fortunate: to live in a world which is knowable at all, and to be endowed with a psychology which makes it knowable by us. That these two preconditions of knowledge are satisfied cannot be determined a priori, but only through extensive empirical investigation. It is precisely this empirical investigation which is the task of a naturalized epistemology.

The result of this inquiry is a rich account of how knowledge is possible. This possibility requires explanation because human knowledge is such a remarkable achievement. Our sciences may not only provide us with a detailed account of the world around us and a detailed account of ourselves; they may also provide an account of how we could have been in a position to provide those very accounts.

At the same time, the result of a naturalized epistemology is not just an explanation of the possibility of knowledge, interesting and important as I believe that to be. Epistemology has traditionally been viewed as an enterprise which may contribute to the advancement of knowledge itself by correcting and refining the ways in which we arrive at our beliefs. This is one tradition in epistemology which I believe should not be abandoned. Indeed, the improvement of our epistemic situation can best be effected through the kind of empirical investigation I have just proposed.

When we properly understand how it is that human psychology fits in to the causal structure of the world, we simultaneously come to an understanding of our epistemic strengths and weaknesses. Much of our psychology is so constructed that we may quickly arrive at an accurate understanding of the world. But this feature of many of our psychological processes also gives rise to a characteristic pattern of errors when those processes go to work in nonstandard environments. By better understanding the environments in which our psychological equipment works well, and also understanding the environments in which we are most liable to err, we put ourselves in the best possible position to give constructive advice on the improvement of our epistemic situation. Here, a naturalized epistemology offers rules for the direction of the mind which fulfill the critical role to which traditional epistemologies have long aspired and yet have served so badly.[6]

The constructive and critical role of a naturalized epistemology is not, however, limited to proposing small refinements of processes and procedures of which we already make use, or strictures on the environments in which we may apply valuable techniques already in place. The empirical investigation of our belief-forming processes and procedures may at times uncover massive error, not as a by-product of otherwise epistemically constructive forces, but processes and procedures which, from an epistemological standpoint, are wholly pernicious. Here too, a naturalized epistemology will serve as a source of epistemic advice, as a guide for the proper conduct of inquiry. Here too, it is through careful empirical investigation of the reliability of our belief-forming processes that epistemology may play its critical and constructive role.

In the account I have presented thus far, I have ignored the many social factors which play a role in the acquisition of knowledge. I now turn to examine how such factors may be integrated into this account.

THE IMPORTANCE OF SOCIAL FACTORS IN A NATURALISTIC EPISTEMOLOGY

Knowledge is a socially mediated phenomenon. That social factors play a role in the production of belief is sometimes transparent, as in cases of deference to expert opinion. But the influence of social factors extends far beyond such cases, and pervades our entire corpus of beliefs. The influence of social factors begins at birth, for language is not reinvented by each individual in social isolation, nor could it be. Because language acquisition is socially mediated, the concepts we acquire are themselves socially mediated from the very beginning. Social factors shape the way in which we view the world in subtle and pervasive ways.

A naturalized epistemology investigates the mechanisms of belief production and retention. Thus far, this has resulted primarily in an examination of perceptual and inferential mechanisms—ones which are located entirely within individuals, and ones which are typically investigated in ways which abstract away from their social setting. But the mechanisms of belief production and retention extend far beyond the perceptual and inferential equipment located in individual heads, and include social structures and institutions which are equally appropriate objects of investigation. Just as we wish to know whether our natural inferential tendencies are likely to give us an accurate or a distorted picture of the world, we also need to know whether our social institutions and practices are helping to inform us or to misinform us. And just as we need to examine our perceptual and inferential equipment against the background of the natural environment in which they operate, we also need to investigate these mechanisms against the background of the social environment in which they operate. Such investigations are straightforward extensions of the naturalistic project in epistemology.

Now the fact that our beliefs are socially mediated does not *by itself* assure that social factors are worthy objects of epistemological investigation. After all, when I come to form a belief on the basis of someone's testimony, the fact that air is the medium through which that person's utterance is conveyed does not suggest that naturalistic epistemologists ought to be especially interested in investigating *its* properties. Air is certainly a pervasive medium in the transmission of belief, but it is of no special interest to epistemologists.

Why then should social factors be of special interest? Consider the phenomenon of deference to societally recognized experts. This phenomenon is present not only in our culture, but in other cultures as well. Is it a reliable method of forming beliefs or not? Obviously, a lot will depend on the way in which the society goes about recognizing experts. In some societies, those people who are thought of as experts about a certain subject matter are, in fact, not at all well informed. In such circumstances, deference to societally recognized experts is a bad practice from an epistemological point of view. In cases where the experts are well informed, deference to experts may be a fine thing. But we may only address the question of the reliability of deference to experts by examining the institutions through which a society confers the title of expert. We need to see whether these institutions are structured in such a way as to confer the title of expert on people whose opinions are likely to be accurate. The fact that one and the same phenomenon—deference to experts—may be reliable in one social setting and yet unreliable in another, assures that social settings are an appropriate object of epistemological investigation. Changes in air pressure, temperature, and the like do not have similar effects on the reliability of belief-producing processes, in spite of the fact that air is a pervasive medium for the transmission of belief.

Note too that the way in which social factors play a role in determining our concepts is just as clearly relevant to epistemological inquiry. We acquire our conceptual repertoire largely unself-consciously and uncritically in the course of language acquisition. The transmission of our conceptual repertoire is a social phenomenon, and qua social phenomenon, it looks very much the same across cultures. Whether the acquisition of a culturally transmitted conceptual repertoire aids in the acquisition of true belief or inhibits it, however, will vary dramatically from culture to culture. In prescientific cultures, for example, much of the culturally inculcated conceptual structure serves as a vehicle for misguided belief and unreliable inductive inference. If we are properly to understand and evaluate the ways in which conceptual structure thus affects belief acquisition, we will need to look at the social mechanisms which serve to create, maintain, and develop a culture's conceptual repertoire, and we will need to determine the extent to which these cultural forces are truth linked. Such an investigation is of a piece with the examination of individual mechanisms of inference to determine their reliability, and, as such, should play an important role in a naturalized epistemology.

Now, in spite of all of this, there is still one way in which these social factors could drop out entirely and play no independent role in epistemology. I will discuss the phenomenon of deference to experts, but what I say here will apply equally to other social factors.

Suppose that the phenomenon of deference to experts looks like this. Individuals frequently arrive at their beliefs in areas about which they have little or no first-hand knowledge by deferring to people they judge to be experts. When they do this, at least in the typical case, they have very good reason to believe that the societally recognized experts do have true beliefs. Moreover, the reasons people typically have for judging the experts to be experts do not themselves, at bottom, involve still further deference to experts. The appeal to societally recognized experts is thus entirely parasitic upon the exercise of individual reason.

If this picture were correct, then the social phenomenon of deference to experts would be of no independent epistemological interest. We could investigate cases of belief formed by way of deference to experts in the very same way in which we investigate other cases of belief formation. In particular, no examination of social structure would be required; we would need to examine the reasons which individuals have for their beliefs, and nothing external to them. Moreover, as I've said, what is true of the phenomenon of deference to experts is true of other social phenomena as well: they would simply drop out of the epistemological picture as unworthy objects of independent epistemological investigation.

Now I think that this line of reasoning is extremely attractive to many people and it has a good deal to do with the fact that social influences on belief formation have been so little investigated by epistemologists. Some fine work has been done to show that this picture of deference to experts is not correct,[7] and I will not rehearse the arguments here. What I do want to point out, however, is why those who have already endorsed a naturalistic approach to epistemology should never have found the above picture of deference to experts attractive.

The account of deference to experts sketched above is motivated by an internalist account of justification. It suggests that any legitimate case of deference to experts must be grounded in information accessible to the agent whose belief is so justified. If this kind of argument were sound, it would also show that the reliability of belief-forming processes is irrelevant to the justificatory status of an agent's beliefs; what is relevant, instead, is what the agent may conclude about the reliability of his or her belief-forming processes on the basis of information which is internally accessible.[8] Now I will not present an argument against this kind of internalist account of justification here,[9] but it should be clear enough that anyone who accepts a naturalistic epistemology must reject this picture. The burden of naturalism has been to argue precisely that this internalist picture is misguided, and that features of an agent which are not internally accessible are nevertheless determinative of the justificatory status of an agent's beliefs. Once one allows, however, that justification need not be internally accessible, the picture of deference to experts as grounded in individual reason loses its appeal.

Indeed, one can say something far stronger than this. There is a striking parallel between the ways in which features of our psychological mechanisms affect our beliefs and the ways in which features of our social situation affect our beliefs. Features of our psychological mechanisms affect the content of our beliefs from birth, and thus long before we are in any position to make judgments about the reliability of those mechanisms. When we do begin to investigate the reliability of our belief-producing processes, those processes have already had a pronounced effect on us, an effect which influences the character of that investigation. This influence is one which it is simply impossible to bypass. One cannot somehow step outside one's beliefs and one's belief-producing processes and then conduct inquiry without them. But the same is true of the social influences on one's beliefs. These too operate from birth. Their influence on our concepts and belief contents begins long before we are in any position to investigate them, and thus, once such investigation begins, it is inevitably mediated by the very factors which we wish to investigate. Here too, the hope of somehow putting one's investigation beyond the influence of the factors one wishes to investigate cannot be fulfilled. But this just puts the inquiry into the effects of social factors in the same boat as the inquiry into the effects of psychological factors. And the case for the importance of the latter investigation has, I believe, been amply made out. The fact that we must make use of our processes of belief acquisition in order to investigate them does not rob the inquiry of its point, nor does it preclude the discovery that there are important defects in the processes we are born with. The same may be said of the analogous investigation of social factors in belief formation. There is no guarantee, of course, that this investigation will inevitably uncover the truth, but it is a lesson of modern epistemology that we will have to make do without guarantees.

We may thus conclude that the investigation of social factors in cognition is an essential part of a naturalistic approach to epistemology.

IS THERE STILL ROOM FOR THE INVESTIGATION OF NONSOCIAL FACTORS IN COGNITION?

The very considerations which motivated an investigation of psychological factors in cognition thus also license an investigation of social factors. We may now wonder, however, whether this latter investigation does not threaten to take over the entire field. Once we allow that social factors play a pervasive role in cognition, is there any room left for nonsocial factors to operate? Is cognition simply social all the way down? What I would like to do is sketch what the various options here look like, and I will argue that both of the extreme positions are entirely untenable. Precisely where the chips will fall in the remaining continuum, however, is not yet clear.

The position that cognition is just social all the way down occupies one extreme. On this view, the explanation of why an individual came to hold one belief rather than another is ultimately, and in every case, social. Although human beings are endowed with certain native psychological equipment which is not itself socially determined, and although cognitive phenomena are a product of the interaction of social and psychological factors, the influence of social phenomena is so great that the cognitive phenomena which are a product of this interaction may be directly read off the social factors which play a role in producing them. On this view then, there are, of course, nonsocial factors which play a causal role in the production of individual belief, but differences in individual belief will always be explained, at bottom, by an appeal to social phenomena.

Notice that even if this extreme view were true, it would not make the study of individual psychology, and other nonsocial factors in cognition, irrelevant to epistemology. First of all, a complete causal account of the production and retention of belief would require a discussion of nonsocial factors even on this view. Second, this causal account of the role of nonsocial factors would be absolutely essential to the epistemic evaluation of our beliefs. For example, if it were discovered that absolutely everyone reasons by way of a certain inferential process *p*, and that differences in individual belief were due to different social inputs to that process, we would still need to know whether p is a process which is reliable in the environments in which it operates, and this would inevitably require identifying p and understanding how it interacts with the various possible social inputs. The epistemic evaluation of the beliefs which result from p would thus require an examination of nonsocial phenomena. Even on the view which assigns the largest possible role to social phenomena, then, the study of individual psychology and other nonsocial factors in cognition is not made irrelevant to epistemic evaluation.

Nevertheless, this extreme view is one which we may decisively reject. Not all individual differences in belief are socially determined. If Danforth and Hillary have different views about the moral permissibility of abortion, this may, of course, be explained by differences in socialization. But if Hillary believes that there is a table in front of her when Danforth denies that there is a table in front of him, this will, in some cases, be explained by the fact that there is a table in front of Hillary but no table in front of Danforth. In a very wide range of cases, differences in perceptual belief are not explained by social factors at all.[10] The view which gives social factors full responsibility for explaining differences in belief may thus be rejected.

It is equally clear that we must reject the view which occupies the other extreme: the view that all individual differences in belief are to be explained by nonsocial factors. It is important to note that even if such a view were true, it would not undermine the relevance of social factors in cognitive and epistemological investigations. Because social factors clearly play a causal role in belief acquisition, their relevance to epistemological investigations is assured even if they were to play no role in explaining individual differences in belief. But, of course, they do sometimes play a role in explaining individual differences. When Jack and Jill each defer to the experts, they may arrive at radically different beliefs if their societies recognize different experts. The view which gives social factors no role to play in explaining differences in belief is a nonstarter.

On any account, then, belief acquisition and retention must be seen as a product of both social and nonsocial factors, and both kinds of factors will come in for investigation in the course of epistemic evaluation. Moreover, on any reasonable account, both kinds of factors will play a role in explaining individual differences in belief. There is still room for a great deal of disagreement about the relative weight of these two kinds of factors. Some will attempt to explain most of the variation in belief as due to variation in social environment, while others will see it as due primarily to variation in individual psychology or nonsocial environment. On any account at all, however, there is a great deal of work to be done on both the social and nonsocial sides of epistemology.

SOCIAL EXPLANATION OF BELIEF AND ITS CONNECTION TO TRUTH

When social factors are identified in the etiology of belief, there are two kinds of question one can ask about the connection between these factors and truth. First, one may ask whether the role which the identified social factor plays is conducive to the production of true belief. Second, assuming that the first question has been answered in the affirmative, one may ask whether the presence of the social factor itself has any special connection with the production of true belief. These are important questions for epistemologists to be asking, and they point in the direction of an important class of social explanations.

Let us consider, again, the phenomenon of deference to experts. I was recently interested in answering a certain question about dinosaurs and, in order to answer it, I called on a faculty member at my university who is said to know about such things. I deferred to someone my social group judges to be an expert, and I believed what he told me. Now let us suppose that this person is generally right about such things. In this case, then, my method of deferring to his judgment was a reliable one. More generally, if the people my social group judges to be expert on, say, scientific questions are genuinely well informed on such matters, the method of deferring to socially recognized experts is, in my social group, a reliable one.

We may now ask a question, however, about the process by which a society comes to confer the title of expert on certain individuals. Even if those which my group takes to be experts are, as a matter of fact, well informed in the appropriate areas, we will want to know the extent to which this is a matter of good fortune, and the extent to which it is a matter built into the structure of the social institutions upon which I rely.

Consider the way in which someone comes to be recognized as an expert on dinosaurs. There is a certain pedigree which is required here. As in other areas of study, one needs to train with someone who is recognized as an expert. There are certain journals which are recognized in the field as prestigious, and publication in such journals is required in order to attain a high degree of recognition. There are certain kinds of institutions, such as universities and natural history museums, affiliation with which brings a certain degree of credibility. Now if we merely describe this as a social phenomenon in which people in a position of power or authority are, in virtue of that position, able to confer certain privileges on others, then this particular institution may look no different from one in which members are chosen for a country club. Such a description is not inaccurate, but it is extremely misleading. If we thus abstract away from the purposes the institution is designed to serve, and from the purposes it succeeds in serving, we will surely fail to understand a good deal about the institution. If we go no further than to point out that the title of expert is conferred on individuals in a way which parallels membership in a country club, we will have lost sight of the features which make each of these institutions the kind of institution it is.

One central purpose of scientific institutions—although not their only purpose—is to discover truths about the natural world. There are features of the social organization of science which are designed precisely to further that purpose, and some of these features, moreover, succeed in furthering that purpose. It would be simply absurd to deny this. Now if this were all there is to be said about the sociology of knowledge, it would be a very boring field indeed. So let me say something about what I think is interesting about the field.

The attainment of true belief is not the only purpose of scientific institutions, nor are the features of our institutions which are designed to serve this purpose always successful. Scientific institutions have quite practical aims as well, some of which are laudable, such as the betterment of the human condition, and others not. Even in the case of laudable aims, there are interesting questions about the extent to which these aims are contributory to the more theoretical aim of understanding the natural world, neutral with respect to that aim, or, rather, in conflict with it. And of course there are the ways in which scientific institutions may be abused for political purposes—cases in which the epistemic authority of the institution may be highjacked or perverted. Finally, there are features of the institution which may come about quite by chance, especially in small fields, where the influence of a single individual may play a role in shaping the path of future work in ways which are radically disproportionate to that person's actual understanding of relevant matters. Examples of each of these phenomena are so easy to provide, and so familiar, as to make it unnecessary to provide them here.

In investigating the social structure of the institution of science, sociologists may play a role in keeping the institution honest and keeping it well aimed on the path to truth. This is of a piece with the normative role of epistemologists generally: to evaluate and recommend correctives in our procedures for acquiring and retaining beliefs. Sociologists may only play this role, however, if they examine the social structure of our institutions with an eye toward their effectiveness in getting at the truth. Descriptions of social structure which abstract away from their connection to truth are worse than useless in this epistemological endeavor, for they group together institutions and practices which, from an epistemological point of view, may be radically different.

We need to have a better understanding of the relationship between the goal of attaining truth and the other goals which shape our scientific and cultural institutions, and we need a better understanding of the internal mechanisms of these institutions which are designed to monitor their effectiveness in achieving these goals. There is every reason to think that such an investigation will itself provide a check on our institutions, and help to push and prod them in the right direction. Social investigation of our institutions has always served as a source of informed criticism. It is no less appropriate, and need be no less effective, in the cognitive realm.

There is a certain ideal which we wish to see instantiated in the social structure of our epistemic institutions. We want them to serve in the production, retention, and dissemination of true belief. But more than that, we want them to be guided toward the truth in ways which include the requisite self-monitoring mechanisms. We have institutions which include mechanisms designed for this purpose; there is peer review, and there are ethics panels, and so on. The ideal which we wish to see instantiated, however, is an institution which does not merely achieve these results as a by-product of other more integral features; rather, the very essence of the institution should be its connection with true belief. It is for precisely this reason that sociological studies which abstract away from questions about truth cannot serve epistemological purposes.

I do not mean to suggest that sociological studies of scientific institutions which abstract away from questions about truth are of no value. There are certainly legitimate questions about power structure, for example, which will lead to a system of classification grouping scientific institutions and country clubs together. But while such social studies of science will help answer interesting questions about power, they divide the social world in ways which are irrelevant to epistemology. Not all legitimate systems of sociological classification are relevant to epistemology, even when they apply to institutions which are epistemologically interesting. When we epistemologists look to the sociology of science as a source of deeper understanding, then, we need to make sure that the categories and questions which inform those studies are ones which will also inform our epistemology. This can only occur when the connection with truth is at the focal point of investigation.[11]

TRUTH-LINKED EXPLANATION: UNDERMINED OR REINFORCED?

The picture I have presented is not at all new; indeed, it is quite old-fashioned. Accounts of the sociology of science which allow truth to play a role are not as central to the field today as they once were. I want to say something about why this might be so. On my account, much of contemporary work in the sociology of science is badly misguided. How, if I am right, could so many people have gotten things so badly wrong?

I believe the answer to this question lies in a view about the relationship between explanations of belief acquisition which allow truth to play a central role and those which allow social factors to play a central role. What I want to suggest here is that truth-linked explanations have gotten a bad name in the sociological literature because it is widely assumed that such explanations are automatically undermined by successful social explanations. The view that social explanations and truth-linked explanations are, of necessity, competitors, however, is false.[12]

Let us consider an example. Suppose that John believes that pteranodons fly, and he arrived at this belief by consulting a well-known authority on dinosaurs. One might think that the proper explanation of John's belief will make reference to its truth. Just as a proper explanation of my coming to believe that there is a table in front of me (when there is a table in front of me) will appeal to the external cause of my belief—namely, the table—so explaining John's belief about pteranodons will also involve an appeal, in the end, to the fact that pteranodons do, after all, fly. In both cases, it seems, a truth-linked explanation is called for.

Nevertheless, the truth-linked explanation of John's belief may well be undermined if it should turn out that a social explanation of his belief should be correct. Suppose the dinosaur authority with which John consulted had a large, impressive office; he spoke in a self-assured, indeed, condescending manner. The office and the unpleasant manner were really what influenced John; he would have believed almost anything uttered by someone who was housed in such an office and who spoke in such a manner.[13] If we fill out our example in this way, it seems, our initial attempt to explain John's belief by appealing to its truth has been undermined. Truth-linked explanations are often defeated when social explanations of this sort are found to be true. It is the supposition that social explanations, if true, will automatically defeat truth-linked explanations which fuels the current dissatisfaction with a social epistemology such as my own. Once I make room for social explanations of belief acquisition, it will be thought, I thereby undermine my concern with the truth. The only alternative, some may argue, is to deny that there are accurate social explanations of belief acquisition; and that, I agree, would be a mistake.[14]

Is it correct, however, to assume that successful social explanations of belief acquisition automatically defeat truth-linked explanations? It is not. The reason our truth-linked explanation of John's belief is defeated is not simply that there is a proper social explanation of his belief. Rather, the proper social explanation of his belief shows that John's method of belief acquisition is not sensitive to the truth. The features which influence John are not ones which are reliably connected with the truth, for rude people in big offices frequently make pronouncements on all manner of things of which they know nothing. It is not that just any social explanation of John's belief would defeat the truth-linked explanation. Instead, it is certain features of this particular explanation which make for defeat.

Consider, instead, a different social explanation of John's belief. Imagine this time that John is not so easily impressed by big offices and bad manners. John has consulted with someone who has written many books about dinosaurs with reputable publishers; this authority has a special chair of dinosaur studies at a distinguished university, and is a noted authority on the very kind of dinosaur about which John has inquired. Let us further suppose that the following story about publishers, universities, and the social structure of John's society is also true: these institutions reward people who are recognized as knowledgeable by those who are already in positions of authority within the institutions, and, most importantly, those who are in positions of authority within the institutions are themselves properly connected with the truth. There is no reason why such a thing couldn't happen; and clearly enough, if it did, the truth-linked explanation of John's belief would be reinforced, rather than undermined, by the social explanation.

The proper question for social epistemology is thus, as I have been urging, a question about the relationship between our social institutions and the truth: .To what extent do our social institutions allow for, and reinforce, socially coordinated belief acquisition which is truth-linked? Under what conditions do they instead interfere with the acquisition, retention and dissemination of true belief? These are the questions upon which attention must be focused, and they are questions, I fear, which have received far too little attention.

CONCLUSION

I have argued that social studies of science have an important role to play in a naturalized epistemology, but not all social studies of science are equal from an epistemological point of view. As epistemologists, we need to look to well-informed work in sociology if we are to fill out the program which naturalistic epistemologists have set for us. The work in sociology which will be relevant, however, must have epistemological concerns at heart.[15]

Notes

1. E.g., Sarkar: "*the primary subject of rationality in science ought to be the basic structure or form or organization of the scientific community whose members are engaged in the pursuit of shared goals*" (1983, p. 80).

2. See, e.g., Rouse: "Knowledge is power, and power knowledge. . . . Theories are to be understood in their uses, not in their correspondence (or noncorrespondence) with the world" (1987, p. 24).

3. Thus, e.g., Woolgar: "The argument is not just that social networks mediate between the object and observational work done by the participants. Rather, the social network constitutes the object (or lack of it)" (1988, p. 65).

4. I am not alone in favoring this conservative approach. Alvin Goldman (1992) and Philip Kitcher (1990, 1991, 1992) have also defended and practiced the kind of conservative social epistemology I favor. See also Schmaus et al. (1992).

5. Here I summarize an approach to understanding human knowledge which I have defended in detail in Kornblith (1993).

6. I have discussed this feature of traditional epistemologies in Kornblith (1989).

7. I am thinking especially of Schmitt (1987a,b) and Coady (1992). See also Hardwig (1985, 1991).

8. For just such an argument, see BonJour (1985).

9. But see Goldman (1980) and Kornblith (1988, 1989).

10. This is not to deny that social factors play a role in explaining the acquisition of these beliefs. After all, it would be impossible to have these beliefs without having the requisite concepts, and these concepts are socially acquired. This is analogous to the point that individual psychological factors would still need to be acknowledged as playing a role in belief acquisition and retention even if all individual differences were to be explained by social factors.

11. Unfortunately, much work in the sociology of knowledge does not meet this requirement. Indeed, in many cases, the entire enterprise gets off on the wrong foot. Thus, Barry Barnes, in explaining what knowledge is for the sociologist, comments,

> An immediate difficulty which faces any discussion of the present kind is that there are so many different conceptions of knowledge. Some of these can be set aside, for sociological purposes, by taking knowledge to consist in accepted belief, and publicly available, shared representations. The sociologist is concerned with the naturalistic understanding of what people take to be knowledge, and not with the evaluative assessment of what deserves to be so taken. (Barnes 1977, p. 1)

David Bloor also sees some connection between naturalism and this approach to knowledge:

> The sociologist is concerned with knowledge, including scientific knowledge, purely as a natural phenomenon. The appropriate definition of knowledge will therefore be rather different from that of the layman or the philosopher. Instead of defining it as true belief—or perhaps, justified true belief—knowledge for the sociologist is whatever people take to be knowledge. (Bloor 1976 [1991 edn, p. 5])

The idea that knowledge is a natural phenomenon, however, should in no way suggest that the connection between knowledge and truth needs to be ignored.

12. A similar issue is raised by Nicholas Sturgeon (1992) in his discussion of the relationship between moral and nonmoral explanations.

13. There is a good deal of work in the sociology of science which seems to assume that scientists are no more attuned to the truth than John is. Instead of the naivete of the subject I describe, however, scientists are portrayed as hungering after power and entirely uninterested in the truth. Thus, Shapin and Schaffer write, "The contest among alternative forms of life and their characteristic forms of intellectual product depends upon the political success of the various candidates in insinuating themselves into the activities of other institutions and other interest groups. He who has the most, and the most powerful, allies wins" (1985, p. 342).

14. The assumption that social explanations automatically compete with truth-linked explanation is found explicitly in such sociologists of knowledge as Mannheim (1936, 1952). Where some have seen this as a reason for limiting the scope of sociological investigation (because the proper explanation of so much of science is so obviously truth-linked), more recent sociologists have, to a large extent, seen this as a reason for abandoning truth linked explanation (because it is so obvious that there is room for a sociological investigation of belief acquisition of all sorts). The common premise that social explanation competes with truth-linked explanation is thus used, by different authors, to reach radically different conclusions. My own view is that the mistake lies in this common premise.

15. I am grateful to David Christensen and Fred Schmitt for helpful comments on a draft of this chapter.

6

Contrasting Conceptions of Social Epistemology

Philip Kitcher

I

The history of epistemology has been dominated by an individualistic perspective on human knowledge, most dramatically displayed in Descartes's scenario for the aspiring knower who was resolutely contemplating the dubitability of beliefs in the privacy of a stove-heated room.[1] Like other epistemologists before and after him, Descartes did not overlook the obvious fact that all of us learn from others. Individualists have believed, however, that this epistemic dependence could be transcended, holding that we have available to us individualistic grounds for accepting some propositions and that this set of propositions can be used to assess information we receive from others. Proceeding in this fashion, we can ultimately calibrate informants, much as we calibrate instruments, so that all that we claim to know comes to be based upon the exercise of our individual judgment.[2]

Neglect of social epistemology thus results, I believe, from (typically tacit) acceptance of a reductionist program. It is assumed that there is a set of propositions—the individualistic basis—that we can know without reliance on others. Given this individualistic basis, we are supposed to be able to assess the reliability of potential sources by checking their deliverances against propositions in the basis. Once a source's reliability has been evaluated in this way, simple inductive inferences can lead us to employ that source in instances in which individualistic checking is impossible. So it is assumed that all that we take ourselves to know can be obtained by relying only on sources whose credentials have been individualistically checked.

To the best of my knowledge, nobody has ever carried out this reductionist program in any detail. There are plainly two sources of problems: one arising from the possibility that we employ sources for whom comparisons with the individualistic basis are far too slender to support the extensive use we make of them (think, for example, of the paucity of ways in which we can check directly the deliverances of national news media); the other stemming from the worry that there may be no propositions that we can know without being epistemically dependent on others. These points are analogous in obvious ways to objections encountered by logical empiricist programs for the reduction of "theoretical" knowledge; and just as the issue of the theory-ladenness of perception was crucial to that debate, so too, it seems to me, the second concern, which stresses the social dependence of all our knowledge, is fundamental to the prospects of individualistic reduction.[3]

Both in our abstract thinking and in our perceptual experience, the conclusions we draw depend on the conceptual repertoire that we deploy and on the habits for reaching or inhibiting belief in which we have been trained. Early absorption of the lore of our societies affects us even at those points at which we appear most able to take our epistemic lives into our own hands. These points can probably best be appreciated by considering the differences between our formation of belief, both in perception and in reasoning, and the analogous processes that occur in others whose initial socialization is different.[4] Unless we hold, as Descartes did, that there is some presuppositionless point from which we can begin inquiry, we must abandon the individualistic reduction as a failure. But, since my primary purpose in what follows is to contrast different styles of social epistemology, I shall not try to present the argument in detail, leaving would-be individualists the challenge of showing that prospects for reduction are brighter than I have taken them to be.

Social epistemology begins at the point of rejecting the individualistic reduction. One may go on in a number of different ways. I shall start with an approach that remains relatively close to the individualistic tradition.

II

According to a venerable conception of knowledge, the primary subjects of knowledge are individual human beings. To talk about the knowledge current in a community is to say something, possibly quite complex, about what the members of that community know. Ascription of knowledge to individuals turns on recognizing that they have beliefs with special properties: beliefs that are true and that are "properly grounded," "justified," or "warranted." So one comes to the traditional formula, "*X* knows that *p* just in case *p* and *X* believes that *p* and *X* is justified in believing that *p*" or its more sophisticated modern equivalents (for example, "*X* knows that *p* just in case *p* and *X* believes that *p* and *X*'s belief that *p* was formed by a process that is reliable (in the appropriate sense)").[5] Theories of knowledge that begin from this familiar type of account may venture into social epistemology solely because they are persuaded of the breakdown of the individualistic reduction canvassed above. In consequence, the exact point at which epistemology becomes social is in the appreciation of the possibility that whether or not a subject is justified (or whether or not a belief-forming process counts as reliable in the pertinent sense) turns on the properties of other people or of the group to which the subject belongs.

For purposes of convenience in what follows, I shall assume a (bland and undeveloped) version of a reliabilist account of knowledge—although I believe that the distinctions I shall draw and the questions I shall raise would emerge in strictly parallel fashion, given any of the main alternatives to reliabilism. We can thus present the elements of a *minimal social epistemology* as follows:

(1) Individuals are the primary subjects of knowledge. To ascribe knowledge to a community is to make an assertion about the epistemic states of members of the community.
(2) *X* knows that *p* if and only if (a) *X* believes that *p* and (b) *p* and (c) *X*'s belief that *p* was formed by a reliable process.
(3) The reliability of the process that produces *X*'s belief that *p* depends on the properties and actions of agents other than *X*.

My designation of this position as *minimal* is intended to prepare the way for recognition of far more radical versions of social epistemology. As we shall see, these may reject the individualistic assumption (1), modify conditions (2b) and/or (2c), and make corresponding alterations—in (3).

However, before considering these possibilities, I want to explore the epistemological agenda for a position based on (1)-(3).

One primary task for a theory of knowledge of this form consists in understanding the reliability of various types of belief-generating processes. Part of this task consists in recognizing the standards of reliability that should be invoked in particular contexts—the law courts, the laboratory, the everyday transmission of information, for examples—and aspects of identification of such standards surely involve questions of social epistemology.[6] However, the main social epistemological project consists in the investigation of the reliability of various types of social processes. Once we have recognized that individuals form beliefs by relying on information supplied by others, there are serious issues about the conditions that should be met if the community is to form a consensus on a particular issue—questions about the division of opinion and of cognitive effort within the community, and issues about the proper attribution of authority. I shall refer to the field of problems just outlined as *the study of the organization of cognitive labor.*[7]

Just as individualistic epistemology concerns itself with those processes that promote an individual's attainment of true belief, so too social epistemology should be concerned with the organization of communities of knowers and with the processes that occur among knowers within such communities that promote both the collective and the individual acquisition of true belief. Consider, for instance, the problem of consensus formation. Communities that set lenient standards for the adoption of a proposal made by some subset of their members as part of community lore are evidently more likely to pass on false beliefs than those that are more exacting. By the same token, communities that demand exacting independent checks of such proposals will be inclined to waste valuable cognitive efforts. How should the balance be struck?

We have here a well-defined optimization problem that can be treated precisely by making assumptions about the cognitive capacities of individuals and about the positions that they hold within the society. To the extent that we can make realistic presuppositions about human cognitive capacities and about the social relations found in actual communities of inquirers, we can explain, appraise, and *in principle* improve our collective epistemic performance. In similar fashion, the standard institutions of inquiry can submit to precise critical analyses.

The considerations of the last paragraph suggest a way of thinking about the requirements on knowledge that enables us to defuse an important objection.[8] Reliabilist analyses of knowledge and justification (as well as other approaches to the problem of analysing "*X* knows that *p*") often seem to take as their target the precise reconstruction of our everyday intuitions about what would count as instances of human knowledge. But why should these ordinary intuitions be privileged? Why should we want to exhibit the structure of the concept of knowledge we currently possess? The obvious answer is that an explicit account of the everyday concept might enable us to improve it or to replace it with a more adequate concept. However, skeptics may legitimately demand to know what criterion of adequacy is alluded to here. What turns on whether we define "knowledge" in one way rather than another, or on whether we set this or that standard of reliability?

Recognizing the role that classifying propositions as items of knowledge plays in the achievement of consensus, and thus in both the transmission of belief and the shaping of further inquiry, enables us to reply to this skeptical query. Assume that the ultimate standard for appraising the processes that guide our investigations is their propensity to lead to the community-wide acceptance of truth (or, better, of significant truth).[9] Proposals for classifying beliefs as justified or as known under conditions that vary with respect to the type of reliability that is understood can be evaluated according to the social roles that such classifications would play in the genesis of community-wide true belief. Some standards for justification, for example, might be too liberal in that they would allow too easily for the introduction and dissemination of error. Hence the problem of deciding how consensus should properly be formed is deeply relevant to the issue of the standards that analyses of knowledge and justification should satisfy. Analytic epistemology thus presupposes answers to questions in social epistemology.

III

The enterprise of the preceding section is attractive: it offers a plethora of precise, challenging problems, all connected with the central issues of the theory of knowledge, and all virtually unexplored. Nonetheless, for all its charms, this project is not what most of those who take the social turn in epistemology find exciting and liberating.[10] In the rest of this essay, I want to explore various ways in which one can try to reject some of the traditional epistemological assumptions that are taken over in (1)-(3), and thus make a more radical break with the epistemological past. My own bias in favor of the more limited conception of social epistemology outlined in section II will be evident in what follows. Nonetheless, because the issues are complex, I cannot hope to offer detailed, knockdown arguments in favor of that conception. Instead, I intend to identify the major issues that divide various conceptions and to see what notions must be clarified if the debate among them is to be more fruitfully pursued.

A relatively minor deviation from the project of section II consists in retaining the overall conception offered in (1)-(3) but retracting a part of the individualism maintained in (1) by allowing that there may be properties relevant to collective inquiry that cannot be reduced to properties of and relations among individual inquirers. The optimality analyses envisaged in section II—and those articulated in preliminary attempts to work out the enterprise envisaged there—adopt as their preferred framework the language of rational decision theory, microeconomics, and other parts of social science that are resolutely committed to methodological individualism. In principle, one might want to allow for an expansion of this framework to incorporate references to irreducible collectivities (or collective properties). While I hold no brief for reductionism in general (recognizing the limitations of particular types of reductionist programs in biology and psychology),[11] there seems to be no reason to be committed to an expansion of this framework in advance of detailed arguments that show why specific social facets of inquiry are affected by irreducible social factors. Casual gestures in the direction of Durkheim are not sufficient. For it is not only a matter of controversy whether Durkheim's alleged social facts are needed to explain the phenomena that concerned him,[12] but also quite possible that there should be irreducible social causes in some areas of human life (for example, suicide, forms of religious life) and not in others (for example, the growth of human knowledge).

As I have already remarked, this is a minor deviation, and one that could quite easily be accommodated. A more consistent methodological holist would, I suspect, be far more inclined to question the principles (1) and (2) than to try to tack some social causes onto a fundamentally individualist project. One important criticism of the version of social epistemology developed in section II is that it slights the social by making the most individualistic parts of social science—psychology, microeconomics—central to the development of social epistemology. If we were to start, instead, with sociology, political theory, or cultural anthropology as our paradigms of social science, we might develop a far more *social* social epistemology.

Consider many of the slogans that are currently fashionable in discussions of social epistemology: "knowledge is power"; "knowledge circulates in communities"; "knowledge is institutionalized belief."[13]

These slogans invite us to invert the traditional picture of knowledge as produced by individuals, who may be dependent upon the epistemic efforts of *other* individuals, and as becoming community-wide knowledge through recognition of the characteristics of what has been individually produced. Instead, we should regard the community-wide knowledge as primary, identifying individual knowledge with belief that accords (in some sense to be explained) with the knowledge current in the community. As it stands, this thesis is vague.[14] I suggest the following more precise version of it: starting with an account of community knowledge, the social epistemologist proposes that items of individual belief count as knowledge just in case, first, the propositions believed are members of the set known in the community and, second, the processes that underlie the formation of the beliefs are of types approved as knowledge-generating within the community. Social epistemologies of this form thus reject (1), and they may also diverge from (2b) and (2c).

One source of the repudiation of (1) lies in appreciation of the multiplicity of ways in which contemporary scientific knowledge is embodied—in printed texts, in pictures, in instruments, in experimental systems, in artifacts, in social institutions.[15] Faced with this diversity of forms of knowledge, philosophical focus on the beliefs of an individual may seem a peculiar obsession. Moreover, when we examine the different embodiments of knowledge, it may appear that what they have in common is not any propositional content with a distinctive status, but rather an ability to be employed in various ways, to direct the activities of people and other things. The experimental apparatus enables us to control certain phenomena. The diagram serves to display what we ought to perceive. These, like other embodiments of knowledge, are devices for intervening in nature and for regulating our social conduct. To count something as knowledge is to recognize it as having a certain power.

Despite the suggestiveness of these ideas, the account of knowledge they "embody" seems to me intolerably vague. What sorts of entities can count as items of knowledge? What differentiates those entities of these types which are pieces of knowledge from those which are not? *One* route that social epistemology can take at this juncture is to adopt a full-blooded relativism, averring that the types of entities that can count as items of knowledge are as diverse as the "forms of life" in which they are embedded, and that the standards of knowledge are simply those of social acceptance. It is enough that an instrument, diagram, or text is "reproduced and circulated," or that it forms "part of an enduring network" within a society—under such conditions it counts as an item of knowledge *within that society*. There are apparent losses in settling for relativism—most obviously, the possibility of drawing a distinction between what is current in a society and what is genuine knowledge—and I shall explore these later. For the moment, I want to step back and ask if the phenomena that inspire the "multiple embodiments" approach to knowledge really demand a break with the traditional conception of knowledge as something that is located in (or possessed by) an individual subject.

In recent years, philosophers (as well as historians and sociologists of science) have become, quite rightly, impressed with the "craft knowledge" of scientists (and others).[16] Part of the story is no news: epistemology has always recognized that subjects have both skill knowledge (knowing how) and propositional knowledge (knowing that).[17] Many interesting debates have raged around the possibility of showing that an apparently irreducible piece of skill knowledge is really underlain by propositional knowledge.[18] Whether or not the champions of deep propositional representations are right about our ability to learn a language or to perceive three-dimensional objects, it seems initially that our most striking abilities to control natural phenomena are dependent on instances of human propositional knowledge. We would not be able to synthesize compounds or to design organisms with specifiable properties unless some person(s) had come to know propositions about molecules in the one instance or about genes in the other.

Detailed studies of the replication of apparatus and of experiments have made it plain that scientists sometimes have skills that cannot be articulated as propositional recipes: field geologists know what unconformities look like, molecular biologists know how to run gels, and so forth.[19] I shall suppose that there is no reduction of these skills to items of tacit propositional knowledge that the adept fail to articulate. Nevertheless, these pieces of knowledge are still localized in individuals: particular subjects have (or lack) the skills. Moreover, a plausible individualistic analysis of skill knowledge suggests itself. Associated with each skill is a set of manifestation conditions, under which the subject should display a particular type of performance. X knows how to Z if and only if, when conditions $M(Z)$ are realized, X Zs (where $M(Z)$ are, of course, the manifestation conditions associated with *Z*ing). Let us now ask if the point about the diverse embodiments of knowledge can be accommodated by showing how the various entities acclaimed as pieces of knowledge obtain that status as the result of the skill knowledge and propositional knowledge of individuals.

Consider the double helical model of the structure of DNA, copies of which can be found in innumerable laboratories around the world. Why does this count as an item (or embodiment) of knowledge? We have already looked briefly at the suggestion that this status accrues because of the ways in which the copies are treated and the ways in which they function in social interaction. An alternative (traditional) proposal is that the DNA model is an embodiment of knowledge because there are people who know that DNA molecules correspond to the arrangement of wires, plastic, and metal in certain specifiable respects. In saying that the model is an item (embodiment) of *community* knowledge, we recognize that, first, there is a class of people within the community who know the propositions that record the correspondence and, second, (almost) everyone else in the community believes that this class includes all the people who are reliable with respect to matters of that kind.[20] In similar fashion, a picture of the stages of meiotic division counts as an item (embodiment) of knowledge because there are people who know that the processes of cell division correspond to the picture in certain specifiable respects. (And again, we can account for the community knowledge in terms of the recognition that the people in question are those who are reliable about such matters.) The air pump counts as an embodiment of knowledge because the pump can be used to achieve certain interventions in nature; that is, the pump serves as a prop in manifestations of certain types of skill knowledge. (It is also true that people know that when the air pump is employed under specifiable conditions certain effects will be produced, but the skill knowledge outruns the propositional knowledge.)

I claim that the prospects for giving an individualist account of the phenomena of craft and community knowledge are quite bright. We thus encounter an obvious asymmetry. While the sociologizing program based on the rejection of (1) seems headed either for relativism or for vagueness, the approach sketched in section II seems to have resources for coping with the phenomena that its rival takes as principal sources of motivation. Let us now turn to consider the possibility that relativism may have independent attractions.

IV

Much of the point of classical epistemology and philosophy of science arises from distinguishing between what people think (even when they are in entire agreement) and what is correct. Truth, and its relatives, enter discussions of knowledge in two places: first, and most obviously, in the claim that what is known must be true (2b);[21] and second, in the understanding of reliability as grounded in the propensity for generating true belief. Traditionalists presuppose that the notion of truth is epistemically independent, that we are not to reduce the notion of truth in terms of what people know, or believe, or what the members of a society accept. Precisely this epistemic independence of the concept of truth inspires the radical versions of social epistemology to break with tradition.

On what grounds? What is wrong with the traditional invocation of an epistemically independent notion of truth? Three main arguments figure in the recent literature.[22] The first campaigns for relativism by appealing to the fundamental tenets of the Strong Programme in the sociology of knowledge (most notably, the Symmetry Principle). The second invokes a venerable anti-realist attack on the correspondence theory of truth. The third rests on a thesis about the underdetermination of our claims about reality by our encounters with reality. I shall consider these arguments in turn.

The Strong Programme in the sociology of knowledge is based upon the attractive idea that *all* beliefs should submit to causal explanation, and that this causal explanation will involve social causes.[23] In effect, the arguments of sections I and II have already acknowledged this basic point, although they have resisted the idea that the social causes to which we must appeal violate the principle of methodological individualism. (The minor deviation envisaged in section III would introduce Durkheimian entities into the explanatory apparatus.) Thus, in a certain sense, all the conceptions of social epistemology so far envisaged—even the most traditional—honor the Symmetry Principle. All suppose that "the same types of causes" must be invoked to explain both true and false beliefs. For, if we are out to explain *X*'s belief that *p*, we shall surely do so by identifying *X*'s cognitive capacities, *X*'s interactions with reality, and *X*'s social background. Even in cases of perception, *X*'s socialization will be relevant, if only to help us understand why *X* forms a belief under the conditions that obtain and why *X*'s belief employs the categories that it does. Hence, *at a very general level*, the same types of causes will be invoked to understand any belief, irrespective of its truth value.

To make the Symmetry Principle imply more exciting, relativistic, conclusions, it is necessary to interpret it in a much stronger—and quite controversial—way. "Type" is, of course, highly ambiguous, and the ecumenical conclusions of the last paragraph depended on individuating types very broadly. If, however, we individuate types narrowly then, *so long as we make traditional assumptions about truth*, the Symmetry Principle yields highly counterintuitive consequences. To see this, suppose that we think of processes like the following: (a) perceiving macroscopic objects in good light; (b) forming conclusions about probabilities through the use of careful sampling and the use of Bayes's Theorem; (c) forming beliefs by listing the first thirty-eight propositions that come into one's head, assigning them numbers 00, 0, 1-36, spinning a roulette wheel, and believing the propositions that correspond to the first six numbers that come up; (d) ingesting large quantities of alcohol, going outside in the twilight, and forming beliefs about the numbers of objects of various kinds that are present; and (e) forming beliefs about probabilities by using small, biased samples or using the gambler's fallacy. The processes that I have described are far more narrowly individuated than my earlier references to causal factors involving social background, cognitive capacities, and interactions between the subject and nature. If we suppose that the Symmetry Principle applies to the more specific processes (a)-(e), then it will follow that each of these processes should be invoked to explain the presence of both true and false beliefs *and indeed that each should be invoked equally often in this enterprise.* For otherwise there would be an asymmetry: as we listed the true beliefs and false beliefs that were explained, we should find that some processes turn up more frequently in the explanation of true beliefs while others occur more frequently in the explanation of false beliefs.[24]

Now the symmetry required here is intuitively absurd, and one's first thought is that only a fetishistic devotion to symmetry at all costs could inspire one to think that processes of types (c)-(e) are equally likely to generate true beliefs as processes (a) and (b). This thought is perfectly correct so long as we are taking for granted a nonepistemic notion of truth, and assuming that some of the most stable claims that are widely shared across different cultures are true. However, if one has *already* adopted the view that the only notions of truth that are coherent are those that identify truth with some type of institutional or community-wide belief, then the impression of absurdity can be dispelled. For in that case it is possible to hold that different types of processes can equally be made part of a community's standards for truth, so that, while the symmetry may be broken *locally*, the breach of symmetry can and must be explained in terms of the particular choices that the community has made. While we live in a culture that has institutionalized processes like (a) as truth promoting, others might just as well (and perhaps even do) take processes like (d) as truth promoting.

If the line of argument that I have constructed is correct, then appeal to the Symmetry Principle alone should not force us to adopt a version of social epistemology more radical than that discussed in section II (possibly with the deviation alluded to in section III). For there is no compelling motivation for adopting the Symmetry Principle in the strong sense in which types of processes are individuated narrowly.[25] Defenders of nonepistemic approaches to truth will view such adoption as leading quickly to absurdity. However, for those who already believe that traditional, nonepistemic, notions of truth must be abandoned, the absurd consequences are artifacts of a misbegotten approach to truth, and the Symmetry Principle can be given a far stronger interpretation. The popular belief that acceptance of the Symmetry Principle thus leads to relativism seems to me to be quite mistaken. Only in the context of independent arguments against nonepistemic notions of truth does the principle obtain that kind of force. At best, the first line of argument can only reinforce conclusions that have already been reached on different grounds.

On, then, to the second line of argument. This begins with the suggestion that traditionalists are committed to a particular type of nonepistemic notion of truth, to wit, the correspondence theory. It then suggests that the notion of correspondence is incoherent (some versions) or idle (others), so that the only useable notion of truth is one that identifies truth with some type of acceptance.[26] Both parts of the argument can be (and have been) questioned. A currently fashionable approach to the treatment of truth proposes that no elaborate theory of truth is required. We can avoid identifying truth with any type of acceptance without embracing the correspondence theory of truth, simply by adopting a minimal (or deflationary) conception of truth.[27] I shall not examine the credentials of this inviting line of escape, since I believe that it ultimately fails.[28] Instead, I shall try to meet the challenge to correspondence truth head-on.

Correspondence theorists claim that there are linguistic/conceptual items that correspond (or fail to correspond) to parts of nature. Their opponents typically inquire how this correspondence is *set up* or how it is *checked*.[29] Allegedly, to establish or to scrutinize the correspondence between thought/language and reality would require the attainment of some perspective from which both sides of the dichotomy could be viewed and the connections between them identified. Since there is no such out-of-theory position, no sense can be given to correspondence or failure to correspond, and the notion of correspondence is senseless/incoherent/useless.

I shall call this argument the "Inaccessibility of Reality Argument"—or the IRA, for short. The IRA is a terrorist weapon which anti-realists employ with enormous confidence. I believe that the confidence is misplaced.

As I have already noted, many of our interventions in reality are guided by our representations of objects that we manipulate. Some of these representations are public (for example, maps, diagrams, descriptions), some are internal states. Realists believe that there are referential relations between elements of representations and entities that are typically independent of the subject who has/uses the representation. These referential relations, together with the state of reality, jointly determine the truth values of statements and the accuracy values of other forms of representations (such as maps, diagrams). Such, at least in roughest outline, is the correspondence theory of truth—or, more generally, of accuracy—to which real realists are committed.

Now why should anyone accept this idea of correspondence, and how can the correspondence ever be checked? To answer such questions, we do best to start from a situation in which ordinary people occupy a position analogous to that transcendent perspective denied by the IRA. Imagine that you are observing the behavior of another person and that you know not only what that person desires and intends but also how she represents the objects with which she interacts. Your explanation of the success of that person's behavior will appeal to the accuracy of her representations: she gets what she wants, to the extent that she does, because she represents the objects whose properties she controls, modifies, or compensates for in her own actions in ways that correspond to their actual dispositions. Reflection on such cases should bring home to us the importance of explaining the behavior of *others* by recognizing their representations, the correspondence of elements of those representations to objects that are independent of the individuals under study, and the connection between accurate (true) representations and success in dealing with those objects.[30]

None of this presupposes any problematic perspective because we, the observers, are part of the story. If you like, the entities that are independent of the subjects whose behavior is explained are "internal" to the worldview of the observer(s). But real realists think that this point about the presence of an analyst is trivial. Why should the relations between the subject, the subject's representations, and the independent objects depend on the presence of another to note them?[31] Why should the presence of an observer affect the connection between accurate representation and success? Why should the case of any of us—or of all of us—be any different?

Real realism is the position that makes an analogical move from the everyday situation in which we observe and explain the behavior and the behavioral success of another to the predicament of all of us. Just as I recognize objects that are independent of those I observe, referential relations between elements of others' representations and those objects, and a connection between accurate representation and successful behavior, so too I suppose that there are objects independent of me (and indeed of all of us) that there are referential relations between elements of my representations and those objects, and that the success of my interventions in nature correlates with, and so signals, the accuracy of my representations. Not to take this view of myself would be to grant myself a peculiar status, perhaps privileged, perhaps underprivileged—and would indeed involve an *unmotivated* asymmetry.

The line of thought that I have sketched represents what I take to be the central tendency of realism (hence my label "real realism"). There are many complications that need to be addressed if it is to be made completely clear and persuasive;[32] but, since the forms of the IRA that emerge in discussions of social epistemology are typically *very* quick and straightforward, I shall not take up the subtleties here. Suffice it to note that, given the approach I have adopted, there is no reason to claim that acceptance of the correspondence theory of truth requires some transcendent perspective, or that it presupposes some privileged position for the epistemic subject in which reality directly manifests itself.[33] The story I have told frankly admits that all of our representations are partially produced by causal processes that extend back into our societies and their historical progenitors.

Some approaches in contemporary epistemology proceed far too swiftly from appreciation of the socio-historical situatedness of the knower to dismissal of the independence of what is known. Feminist epistemology offers important insights in its recognition that each of us occupies a standpoint, and that standpoints make epistemic differences. But, in light of my response to the IRA, I propose that the way to extend this insight is not to dismiss the ideal of objectivity, nor to reject the correspondence theory of truth, which supplies its most obvious underpinnings, but rather to probe systematically the ways in which different standpoints make available more or less epistemically apt dispositions, more or less reliable ways of generating true beliefs. There are differences between subjects, or between temporal stages of the same subject, according to their dispositions to acquire true beliefs or to be moved by reliable belief-forming processes. Some of these differences are surely traceable to the distortions introduced by social biases or personal prejudices. We can recognize the differences without supposing that there is some perfect state in which the world is inevitably made manifest to us.

Reliabilists should thus insist that some standpoints are better or worse than others with respect to particular types of propositions: given that the issue is to determine whether *p*, the chances of doing so may be greater if one's circumstances are one way rather than another. I doubt that issues about the character of the ultimate constituents of matter will be resolved on the top of a kitchen table (even in Utah) or that those who know nothing of population genetics will be able to settle controversies about sexual selection. More interesting instances of the foibles and virtues of particular standpoints are familiar from the history of science. Membership of a particular ethnic group within a particular society may interfere with one's ability to acquire true beliefs about the distribution of characteristics that are believed to be important to human worth (witness the history of nineteenth-century craniometry).[34] By the same token, gender-associated biases can render invisible some of the most important features of the phenomena under study—a point dramatically demonstrated by the changes that have been wrought in primatology since the entry of many women into primatology in the 1970s.[35]

The claim that a particular standpoint is preferable to others can thus be recast in terms of the relative reliability of the processes that standpoints make available. We should assess any such claim by drawing on what we think we know about the deliverances of the contending standpoints. Yet it seems initially unlikely that any single standpoint will be preferable across the board. There will surely be occasions on which the critique of the outsider is needed to stimulate a community that has fallen into complacency, and other circumstances in which the comments of the marginalized are useless because they are ignorant.

At this point, we can fruitfully return to the project of social epistemology envisaged in section II. Instead of thinking of the merits of rival standpoints that individuals might adopt, each of which might influence their chances of obtaining true beliefs, we should consider what *distribution* of standpoints might serve the community best, facilitating the goal of reaching consensus on the truth.[36]

I conclude that the IRA does not force us to relativism or any other position that abandons the correspondence theory of truth. Nor does the rebuttal of the IRA presuppose that there is some privileged epistemic position in which access to REALITY is achieved, or even that there is a unique best epistemic standpoint. So far we seem to have combined realism with social epistemology in a way that avoids those deficiencies that motivate more radical departures.

V

However, another argument remains to be confronted, and the picture here is far more blurred. As noted in my outline reply to the IRA, an important part of the story is the connection between success (construed as getting what one wants) and accuracy of representation. Any such connection can be undermined if one can argue that there are rival schemes of representation that are equally successful. Appropriate instances of such schemes of representation can be sought either in cross-cultural variation or in history. I shall not try to discriminate the two forms of argument.[37]

Much work in the sociology of scientific knowledge, and, derivatively, in social epistemology, starts with the topic of variation in belief.[38] Different groups of people—culturally distinct contemporaries as well as temporally separated societies—may hold radically different views about all sorts of things. There is no challenge to the traditionalist's invocation of truth and the demand that propositions known be true so long as these differences can be explained in terms of differences in success: for in such instances we can appeal to the correlation between success and accuracy to distinguish genuine knowledge. Trouble arises, however, if the practices of both groups are successful, that is, if neither has problems in coping with reality. Under those circumstances, the idea of explaining success by appeal to accuracy of representation founders—since not both of the representations can be accurate—and it is tempting to claim that we can simply make do by noting the success of the practice itself. "It works because it's true" can no longer be sustained as more informative than the bare recognition that "it works."[39] Invocation of nonepistemic truth becomes idle.

There are popular, rather casual, ways of making the general argument. One is to appeal to the "Duhem-Quine thesis." Now there should be no doubt that the writings of Duhem, Quine, and others contain important, challenging arguments about the underdetermination of something by something else. But it is important to be quite exact about the somethings. In the most obvious versions, Duhem and Quine are concerned with the possibility that incompatible sets of statements might prove observationally equivalent, either in the sense of yielding the same set of observational consequences or in the sense of accommodating the same set of stimulations of nerve endings. (There are intricate problems in explicating "observational consequence" and "accommodating" that need not concern us here.)[40] It is important to separate versions of the thesis and to assess their plausibility and equally important to connect those versions with the prima facie quite different situations envisaged in the rebuttal of the IRA, which involve recognition of *local* successes. The argument from the Duhem-Quine thesis needs considerable development if it is to show that there are alternatives to commonsense ideas about the nutritive value of different substances *that would abandon or reverse our most basic ideas on this subject*, and that would be equally successful in keeping us alive.

When we consider commonly cited examples of cultural variation, it is quite clear that the situations studied by Duhem and Quine are very different from those relevant to the assessment of the connection between practical success and representational accuracy. Consider the differences between the claims of Western biology about plants and animals, and those advanced in non-Western cultures and eagerly pounced on by aspiring relativists. The non-Westerners, we are told, are equally successful, even though their practice employs different representations. But there is no sense of empirical equivalence, or even of "accommodation of the same sensory stimulations," behind this notion of "equal success." The successes are of quite different types, since the biologists want to engage in activities with respect to plants and animals that diverge from those favored by the non-Westerners. If there is an issue raised by the citation of this kind of example, it is the question, "Are there different types of success that should be accommodated by different sets of representations?"—not, "Are there different sets of representations that will generate exactly the same practical successes?"

Now the issue of the potential relativity of success, to which we have been led, may itself look threatening. To understand the extent of possible trouble, let us consider the example of those non-Western societies that hold what we regard as radically false beliefs about the properties of certain taboo animals. It is quite possible that we should find, after detailed analysis, that these false beliefs play an important part in the way in which members of the society cope with reality. Suppose, specifically, that the false beliefs are invoked to defuse various types of social friction, and that, in consequence, these beliefs are partially responsible for the social order that members of the culture value. Thus we have an example of two societies in which incompatible claims are made about certain kinds of animals, both of which facilitate successful practices.

I believe that we should question the terms in which I have described the example, specifically by breaking up the blockish notion of "successful practice." My hypothetical non-Western culture is successful in certain types of social intervention; and if we pursued the example in more realistic detail, we would find that this success can be traced to tacit understanding of how to manage certain types of interchange among people who are potentially in conflict. Perhaps the same type of understanding is also found in Western societies, and is hidden only because those societies do not regularly confront the kinds of situations in which it would be applicable. But the important point is that what we view as the faulty beliefs about animals are not implicated in any way in the generation of successful interventions (whether predictive or manipulative) with respect to those animals. Hence it would appear possible to achieve a broader set of representations that would incorporate the Western biological views and the non-Western social understanding in a system that would preserve both sets of successes. Because there would be no internal inconsistency, there would be no challenge to the link between success and accuracy.

The discussion of the preceding paragraph indicates the lines along which we should seek resolution of cases in which incompatible beliefs apparently figure in distinct successes. A full resolution of the issues concerning underdetermination must await the outcome of attempts to show that the recipe will work for the examples which have been most frequently cited in the cause of relativism. But our preliminary verdict should be that the case against realism is so far not proven.

VI

I save until the end what has increasingly come, it seems to me, to be a major source of motivation—if not of argument—for a radical version of social epistemology founded in relativism. For those whose voices have traditionally been silenced, or ignored, an epistemology that seeks objective standards may appear inevitably oppressive, so that resistance to it is based more on concern than on the construction of detailed arguments. Thus some contemporary scholars might view the dialectic that I have sketched in earlier sections as itself something that needs to be transcended.[41] For those sections envisage truth as emerging from the clash of ideas and knowledge as obtainable by finding and occupying better (though imperfect) epistemological positions. Mindful of the harm that has been done by treating some standards as objective, some conclusions as established, and some positions as superior, radical critics of traditional epistemology propose that we rethink our reigning metaphors. They envisage different ends for inquiry—not the control of nature grounded in the apprehension of truth, but the enhancement of human life through the sympathetic exploration of rival viewpoints and the development of attitudes of care and concern.[42]

While I believe that these considerations are powerful and significant, and that they call for detailed exploration of the ways in which the growth of human knowledge has affected human well-being,[43] the fault may lie not with the epistemological notions of objectivity, truth, and epistemically superior position but with the ways in which those notions have been too hastily applied to support the prejudices and further the interests of a dominant group. Fallibilism is a commonplace of twentieth-century epistemology, but it by no means follows that our sense of our own fallibility is represented in our epistemic practice. Concern for objectivity seems to me potentially liberating and, by the same token, ignorance is confining; but the history of inquiry (most vividly, the history of studies of human behavior) shows clearly how ignoring our own fallibility may have profoundly damaging consequences. The challenge for the more conservative versions of social epistemology is to respond to genuine concerns about the oppressive force of standards without abandoning the benefits that the search for such standards makes possible.

Two different errors thus seem to me to hinder fruitful cooperation in social epistemology. One is the frequent tendency of radical social epistemologists to assume that certain kinds of conclusions have been definitively established and that they can dismiss any enterprise that retains connections with the objectivist notions of traditional epistemology. I do not pretend that the arguments of the preceding two sections have been worked out in detail: as my notes below indicate, there are numerous thorny issues that need to be explored. But those arguments do reveal that the passage from traditional epistemology to the "social construction of reality" or to the "study of knowledge as a form of power" is far more bumpy than is usually appreciated.

The countervailing error results from appreciation of the fact that many radical proposals are based on swallowing lines of arguments that appear dubious. Hence epistemologists feel entitled to neglect the considerations from history, sociology, and anthropology that motivate those radical departures. If the disease of radical social epistemology is premature theorizing (specifically, the jump to quick dismissal of important epistemological concepts), its counterpart in more traditional programs is neglect of the phenomena and insensitivity to the human consequences of epistemological overconfidence. I hope that even an outline account of some rival possibilities may point the way towards a more constructive dialogue.

Notes

1. This paper grew out of my commentary on the presentations given by Helen Longino and Joseph Rouse at an American Philosophical Association symposium on social epistemology in December 1991. I have tried to place the contrast between their approaches and my own in a more general setting, concentrating less on the details of their proposals than on the kinds of positions advanced not only in their work but in the writings of David Bloor, Harry Collins, Steve Fuller, Donna Haraway, Sandra Harding, Bruno Latour, Steven Shapin, and others. In the text I am primarily concerned to identify the logical relations among various controversial theses. Attributions of these theses to individual authors and texts are confined to footnotes. I am grateful to Longino and Rouse for the stimulus provided by their papers and discussions. I would also like to thank Fred Schmitt for his penetrating and constructive comments on an earlier draft.

2. For this conception of calibrating potential informants, see Kitcher (1992, 1993, ch. 8).

3. Classic attempts to formulate the reductionist project are Carnap (1967) and Goodman (1955). For a more liberal version, see Carnap (1958). Concise presentation of the position and its foibles are given by Quine (1969a). The *locus classicus* for the attack on the reductionist position is Sellars (1963a).

4. For a somewhat more extensive formulation of this argument, see Kitcher (forthcoming a).

5. See the extensive literature that followed Gettier (1963). The developments are reviewed in Shope (1983). For reliabilism, the classic source is Goldman (1986).

6. See Goldman (1991a).

7. For formulation of this project, see Goldman (1987b), Hull (1988), Kitcher (1993, especially ch. 8). Implementation is begun in Goldman and Shaked (1991) and in Kitcher (1990, 1991, 1993, ch. 8).

8. Launched forcefully by Stich (1990, pp. 89-98) against the project of the first part of Goldman (1986).

9. For this conception of the goals of inquiry, see Kitcher (1993, ch. 4).

10. I suspect that the project I have sketched seems almost indistinguishable from classical epistemology ("positivism") to those like Bruno Latour, Donna Haraway, Andrew Pickering, Sharon Traweek, and the many others in sociology, anthropology, and history of science who want to develop a more radical critique. I hope that the first sections of this chapter reveal that there are significant differences among philosophical proposals that are often lumped together under what is taken to be an insulting label. (There is some irony in the fact that while outsiders view the charge of positivism as especially damning, philosophical research on the work of the Vienna Circle and its affiliates is revealing how subtle and insightful were the ideas of the logical positivists.) The goal of the remaining sections is to show how large is the gulf that more radical thinkers urge us to cross—and how some of the motivating forces they take for granted are, in fact, far from compelling.

11. Fodor (1974); Kitcher (1984).

12. See, for example, Papineau (1979, ch. 1).

13. See Rouse (1987), Latour (1987), and Bloor (1976 [2nd edn, 1991]).

14. For discussions of this thesis, I am indebted to Fred Schmitt.

15. These points are forcefully made by Rouse (1987), and Latour (1987), Latour and Woolgar (1979). For cogent arguments against the bias of thinking solely about scientific knowledge in propositional terms, see Hacking (1983).

16. See Polanyi (1958), Hacking (1983), and Collins (1985).

17. For an admirably clear presentation of these points, see Ryle (1948).

18. See, for example, Marr (1982) and Chomsky (1980).

19. The *locus classicus* is Collins (1985).

20. Equally, some embodied knowledge might be founded in individual *skills*, rather than in individual propositional knowledge. As Fred Schmitt pointed out to me, there is no reason to suppose that all embodied knowledge reduces to individual *propositional* knowledge. The embodiment of knowledge is, I suggest, best understood as grounded in individual items of knowledge, together with the public recognition of the achievements of the knowers.

21. This is a standard way of formulating (2b), but friends of deflationary approaches to truth are likely to protest that invocation of truth is quite unnecessary here.

22. Main sources of the arguments I discuss are the writings of defenders of the Strong Programme in the sociology of knowledge (see, particularly, Bloor 1976 [2nd edn, 1991]; Barnes 1974; Shapin 1982; Shapin and Schaffer 1985), defenders of empirical relativism in the study of scientific knowledge (Collins 1985), and a variety of other approaches to the history, sociology, and anthropology of science (Pickering 1984; Latour 1987; Haraway 1990; Keller 1985; Traweek 1988). The arguments are often presented in very abbreviated form in these sources. More extensive, and subtle, versions can be found within recent philosophy. See, for example, Putnam (1981), Rorty (1980), and Fine (1986). I outline responses to some of the more subtle lines of argument in Kitcher (1993, forthcoming a, and especially forthcoming b).

23. See Bloor (1991).

24. Moreover, as Fred Schmitt pointed out to me, since the Symmetry Principle is an *empirical* principle, similar belief-forming processes should be found in the genesis of roughly equal numbers of *actual* true beliefs and *actual* false beliefs. In approaching situations of scientific decision-making symmetrically, sociologists of science do not of course make a priori assumptions about the correctness of various scientific claims. But it seems to me that they often presuppose that particular, quite specific, types of processes will yield true and false beliefs with roughly equal frequency. One should ask whether this is a different a priori assumption, and, if not, what its empirical basis is.

25. A fortiori there is no motivation for the slavish devotion to symmetry confessed in Latour (1991).

26. Sophisticated approaches along these lines can be found in Rorty (1980) and Putnam (1981). Much simpler versions appear in the writings of Bloor, Barnes, and many other writers cited in note 20 above. Helen Longino (1990) attempts to show how objectivity is possible within a framework that identifies truth with consensus belief in societies that follow certain types of procedures, but I do not see how her approach avoids collapse into relativism.

27. See Horwich (1990). Both Fine (1986) and Rouse (1987) develop their accounts of scientific knowledge on the basis of this type of account of truth.

28. This is argued in outline fashion in Kitcher (forthcoming a), and at greater length in Kitcher (forthcoming b).

29. The argument thus comes in two slightly different forms: one that inquires into how the correspondence between word and world is set up; and the other that asks how it is checked. Sophisticated versions of the former line of argument culminate in Putnam's intricate considerations about reference (e.g.,

Putnam 1981). The latter form of argument leads to debates about the connections between truth and the explanation of success.

30. The issues here are extremely complex, as Putnam (1978, 1981, 1983), Horwich (1990), and Field (1986) make clear.

31. As Rorty (1980, p. xxvi) insightfully notes, part of the motivation for strong versions of realism stems from the recognition that "our beliefs have very limited causal efficacy." As the text indicates, I draw far more from this point than Rorty would expect.

32. Most importantly, there is a compelling need to respond to the arguments of the first two chapters of Putnam's (1981). I try to discharge this duty in Kitcher (forthcoming b).

33. See Longino (1991) and Harding (1993).

34. See Gould (1981).

35. See Haraway (1990) for thorough documentation of the point. While the more radical claims made in some parts of this book (and, even more, in Haraway's subsequent writings) strike me as based upon fallacious arguments, her indictment of the male-dominated practice of mid-twentieth-century primatology is both powerful and moving. For further brief discussion of a range of issues raised by Haraway and others (which may correspond more closely to their aims), see section VI.

36. See Kitcher (1990).

37. For separate treatment, see Kitcher (forthcoming a).

38. See the early pages of Bloor (1976 [2nd edn, 1991]).

39. This is a central theme of the introduction to Rorty (1980).

40. For an extremely insightful discussion of some of these issues, see Laudan and Leplin (1991).

41. I suspect that this would be the attitude of Donna Haraway, Sharon Traweek, and Evelyn Fox Keller.

42. Although these themes are touched on in various philosophical, anthropological, and sociological works, I find them most lucidly expressed in Belensky, Clinchy, Goldberger, and Tarule (1986).

43. See the closing paragraphs of Kitcher (1993). I should note that similar points were made long ago by Paul Feyerabend (1978).

7

The Fate of Knowledge in Social Theories of Science

Helen E. Longino

INTRODUCTION

My project has been to develop an analysis of scientific inquiry that both acknowledges the social dimensions of inquiry and keeps room for the normative and prescriptive concerns that have been the traditional preoccupation of philosophers.[1] Is such a project really feasible? Many sociologists and philosophers answer in the negative.

Philip Kitcher (1991 and this volume), for example, claims that in spite of my intention to provide a new account of objectivity and a way of thinking about inquiry that integrates its social and cognitive dimensions (see Longino 1990), the account I do provide cannot rise above a relativism that is incapable of distinguishing between evolutionary theory and creationism (or your disreputable program of choice). He does this by extracting from my account a definition of knowledge that exhibits this weakness. That definition will be the subject of my remarks later in the chapter.

Sociologists and anthropologists of science, on the other hand, have taken themselves to offer a significant challenge to the philosopher. Through a number of different case studies, they have argued that scientific knowledge is not developed by the application of procedures ratified by epistemological norms of the sort recognized by philosophers. Instead scientists negotiate, borrow, barter, and steal—use any means necessary—to get their interpretations accepted, their aim being to survive or win in the game of science. Science is socially constructed. This motto has become both a rallying cry and a banal comment. It turns out, however, that it does not mean the same thing to all. And the difference makes a difference.

Philosophers have engaged most with the "strong program" in the sociology of science associated with the University of Edinburgh and represented in the work of Barry Barnes and David Bloor (Barnes 1977; Bloor 1976 [2nd edn, 1991]; Barnes and Bloor 1982). This program has attracted the attention of a number of philosophers—for example, a sympathetic if critical reading by Mary Hesse (1980), and much less temperate responses from Larry Laudan (1984), among others. According to the strong program, both good and bad, successful and unsuccessful science must be explained in the same way. One can't explain good science by appealing to rationality and bad science by appealing to distorting social factors. In both kinds of case, what does the explanatory work is interests: ideological/political interests; professional interests; individual career interests. Science is socially constructed in the sense that the congruence of a hypothesis or theory with the social interests of the members of a scientific community determines its acceptance by that community (rather than a congruence of theory/hypothesis with the world).

The strong program theorists present two sorts of theoretical argument. Appeals to Wittgenstein's later philosophy or to Mary Hesse's Quinean account of concept formation undergird an argument to the social nature of classification systems. The relativism is supported by arguments challenging the notion of privileged descriptive categories or of a common basic level of sense experience, and by arguments concerning the impossibility of a noncircular justification of principles of inference. There is no general argument to the effect that all scientific judgments have a social content. Instead, the various case studies are intended to exhibit a congruence between the scientific positions and the social values of participants in scientific debates. The combination of theoretical arguments with the case studies then has this form: cognitive, or rational, factors cannot explain why *S* thought as she or he did (because they fail in any case), therefore the appeal of *T* for *S* was precisely the congruence of *T* with *S*'s social values. Beliefs and attitudes about society or one's proper place in it determine scientific content or what scientific content is accepted. But the fact that the boundaries of classificatory categories are conventional and determined by a linguistic community does not show that the boundaries are adopted because of their semantic relation with social values. And what the arguments against basic experiential categories or "rational" justifications of inductive reasoning really support are anti-foundationalism, not relativism. So while the case studies are intriguing, they do not demonstrate that in every instance of scientific judgment the protagonists had no reason but interests for the scientific choices they made.

In many ways more compelling are the empirical laboratory studies done by Karin Knorr-Cetina, Bruno Latour, and others. Although they have different social-theoretical frameworks within which they present their studies they show that science is social in a different sense than it is social for the strong program theorists: the procedures of science are social in the sense of involving social interactions. Moreover, the "slice of life" documentation of those interactions shows (in the laboratory cases studied) that the procedures by which scientists certify results and validate hypotheses involve a hodge-podge of "internal" and "external" considerations. These theorists then conclude from this that it is not possible to distinguish between the purely cognitive and the social—or interest-laden—bases of hypotheses. The normative concerns of philosophers are, hence, idle: the wheels of prescription may spin in philosophy, but they fail to engage the gears in actual epistemic communities.

Latour (1987), for example, enunciates as a rule of method that if we want to understand scientists and engineers we must follow them as they enroll allies and establish networks, and not appeal to anything like "mind" or cognition until all the routes of social explanation have been exhausted. He clearly thinks that, when all such explanations *have* been exhausted, there will be nothing left in need of explanation. The allies that can be enrolled include not just other members of the scientist's community, but the elements of nature whose behavior the scientist is trying to explain, predict, use, or reproduce in the laboratory. Latour's language rather playfully suggests that natural "actants" can find it in their interest or not in their interest to cooperate with the investigator. But it's not clear that an unpacking of "enrolling allies" would not reintroduce the cognitive elements Latour wishes to banish.[2]

Karin Knorr-Cetina, in an essay (1983) outlining the elements of her constructivist approach to science, claims that the features of scientific practice that it reveals "defeat the hope of the philosopher of science to find the set of criteria that govern scientific selections." In this essay she construes "the epistemological question" as the question, "How is that which we come to call knowledge constituted and accepted?"—a question to which she gives answers invoking the social processes and interactions in the laboratory and between the laboratory and its worldly environment. What I find striking about this "defeat" of the philosopher is that the game is won before it is even engaged, by the way the questions are cast. With respect to her epistemological question, one might respond that no, the epistemological question is not how that which we come to call knowledge is constituted and accepted, but what we think we're saying when we claim knowledge or make a knowledge attribution. What distinguishes knowledge from other doxastic states, such as opinion or belief? With respect to the defeat of the philosopher, we might respond that the hope of the philosopher of science is not to find the criteria that do govern scientific selections, but to find the criteria that ought to govern them.

This brief review suggests that both the sociologist and any philosopher at least as traditional as Kitcher agree that the fate of knowledge as it is treated in social theories of science is to collapse into what is believed or what is accepted. If philosophers are interested in analyzing the concept of knowledge and in figuring out what norms our use of such a concept commits us to, why should we remain interested in the sociological approach? There are at least two reasons. Firstly, whether or not we are naturalists, philosophers have rightly or wrongly taken the sciences to be the best model we have of knowledge production. Studies of how it actually works should surely be of interest to us even if they challenge our preconceptions. While Knorr-Cetina's investigations reveal social interaction at the heart of the scientific enterprise, her results do not defeat or displace the philosopher so much as raise new questions or change the field upon which philosophical concerns are engaged. Secondly, feminists have been interested in this work because it provides a model for thinking about how masculinist interests could get incorporated into so-called good science as well as in methodologically disreputable science. Feminists have offered analyses of the content of specific research programs in the sciences that demonstrate their congruence with (and, in cases, support of) masculinist ideology and their satisfaction of methodological norms. It is puzzling how this could happen on most philosophically orthodox accounts of scientific practice. Any general account that throws the standing of methodological norms into question has thus seemed a more attractive alternative. But what the empirical work demands is an account of knowledge that incorporates the social dimensions of science into the epistemology of inquiry, rather than one that shows that (much) practice departs from traditional epistemological conventions. The latter demonstration permits the riposte that good science does not express the biases decried by feminist critics, while the former enables demonstrations of masculinism in the most prized of research programs (cf. Longino 1992).

Both the feminists and the sociologists can be understood as rejecting what we might call an "unconditioned subject," that is, a knower guided only by content- and value-neutral methodological rules (cf. Longino 1993). Individual knowers are instead conditioned by various aspects of their social location—from their dependence on government agencies and industry for funding, to their location in an intellectual lineage, to their position in the race, gender, and class grid of their society. The problem with recognizing the social locatedness and, hence, conditioned character of individual epistemic subjects is that it seems to force us into choosing between relativism and demonstrating the epistemic superiority of one among the various social locations. I wish to reject this choice, which I see as arising from a continued commitment to individualism in epistemology. The question towards which the rest of this essay is addressed is whether any recognizable concept of knowledge can be recovered from a more thoroughly social account of inquiry.

WHEREIN IS KNOWLEDGE SOCIAL?

Elsewhere (Longino 1990), I argued that an individualist bias in philosophy stood in the way of solutions to problems—such as underdetermination—confronting the possibility of scientific knowledge. Some may see the solution afforded by a social account of knowledge as worse than the problem. I would argue, in contrast, that scientific knowledge is produced by cognitive processes that are fundamentally social and that an adequate normative theory of knowledge must be a normative theory of social knowledge—a theory whose norms apply to social practices and processes of cognition.

Although in that earlier work, I appealed to present features of scientific practice, the main argument was an epistemological one: only if we understand scientific inquiry as fundamentally social, and scientific knowledge as the outcome of discursive interactions, is it possible to claim that scientific inquiry is objective. Here I would like to concentrate on a different sort of argument, namely, conceptual arguments to the effect that observation and justificatory reasoning—central elements of scientific knowledge construction—are themselves social.

1. Observation. Ethnomethodologists and sociologists practicing discourse analysis have argued that establishing what the (observational) data are is a social matter. Ascertaining what the results of an experiment are, what is a real result and what an artifact of the experimental situation, what are new data (constituting a genuine anomaly) and what an experiment gone wrong, is accomplished by "negotiation," or critical discussions among group members.

Michael Lynch has used ethnomethodological analysis to uncover the conversational work that anchors the interpretation of data. In a piece on digital imaging in astronomy Lynch and Samuel Edgerton (1988) describe the intersubjective and socially interactive process of interpreting and clarifying the salient features of galactic images. Karin Knorr-Cetina has made similar sorts of observations, although without the trappings of ethnomethodology. In a paper with Klaus Amann (1990), she reports on a study of a molecular biology laboratory using gel electrophoresis techniques to identify the molecular constituents of a sample of DNA. The two sociologists identify various discursive interactions that propel a group of investigators to progressively more definite accounts of what is actually exhibited on a given film. The final representations, the ones used in publication, are constructed by synthesizing a number of films—introducing a second level of integrative sociality.

Of course, what happens in one or two laboratories is not evidence that scientific observation is intrinsically social, rather than contingently so on the occasions reported. But more conceptual considerations do support thinking of scientific observation as dialogical in nature. Observational data consist in observation reports that are ordered and organized. This ordering rests on a consensus as to the centrality of certain categories (the speed of a reaction vs. the color of its product), the boundaries of concepts and classes (just what counts as an acid), the ontological and organizational commitments of a model or theory, and so on. Observation is not simple sense perception (whatever that might be), but an organized sensory encounter that registers what is perceived. I leave open whether this registering is linguistic (see below); it does involve classification and categorization that notes similarity and dissimilarity with other items of interest.

Furthermore, not just any observation will do. To have value as data, observations must have a stability that allows their transfer from one laboratory to another. If we are going to treat observational data as data, we need assurances that an apparent or purported regularity really is one. The requirement of the repeatability of experiments is a requirement for the intersubjective accessibility of data serving as evidence because it is a requirement that anyone similarly placed with similar equipment would see (perceive) the same thing. Nature has been enrolled as an ally when the experimenter has found a way to stabilize her or his results across different perspectives.[3] Even when an experiment is not actually repeated (which is the case for the majority of experiments), the presupposition of its results being used as evidential data is that anyone similarly placed would observe the same thing.

Harry Collins (1983, 1991) has argued that only in cases of controversial science (e.g., cold fusion, parapsychology, molecular memory) does anyone go to the trouble of actually trying to produce the same results with the same methods. We might say that only in such cases does anyone attempt actually to determine the publicity or intersubjective accessibility of experimental results. Collins is trying to expose the repeatability requirement as window dressing not supported by actual practices. On the view urged here, the invocation of the repeatability criterion in controversial cases demonstrates that the presupposition in the "normal" case of the unchecked taking of a set of observations or measurements as data is that they are and will remain stably accessible across changes in context or point of view. In the case of doubt as to its satisfaction, the presupposition is tested by bringing different perceivers to the situation (identical or a replica) and ascertaining intersubjective invariance. From this point of view, then, the studies of Lynch and Knorr-Cetina are not at all surprising. If intersubjective invariance is an important feature of observational data, then of course experimenters will consult with one another to establish or impose definiteness on initially "flexible" data. Indeed, since one of the professional aims of researchers is to get their data and interpretations taken up by others, the very kind of sociality to which Knorr-Cetina and Latour draw our attention guarantees that researchers will aim for intersubjective invariance of observation. Otherwise, their work will perish.

The point here is not that an individual scientist could not engage in experimentation or make observations on her own. Indeed, the sensory capacities of individuals are crucial. The claim of sociality is the claim that the status of the scientist's activity as *observation* depends on her relations with others—in particular, her openness to their correction of her reports. This is what enables the transformation of "it seems to me that *p*" into "*p*." There is no way other than the interaction of multiple perspectives to ascertain the observational status of individual perceptions.[4]

2. Reasoning. The second main cognitive element in the production of scientific knowledge is reasoning, which traces lines of evidentiary support between data and theories and hypotheses. Individual brains or minds, of course engage in calculation. But reasoning (at least scientific reasoning) is not mere calculation; it is bringing the appropriate considerations to bear on judgments. Justificatory reasoning is part of a practice of challenge and response: challenge to a claim is met by the offering of reasons to believe it, which reasons can then be challenged on grounds both of truth and of relevance, provoking additional reasoning. Reasoning, thus, gets its point in a social context—a context of interaction among individuals, rather than of interaction between an individual and the object of her or his cogitations. What counts as an

appropriate consideration, as a reason, is determined and stabilized through discursive interactions.

In the empirical sciences, observational and experimental data function as the appropriate sorts of considerations. But even when described and categorized, their precise relevance to particular hypotheses and theories is not self-evident.[5] Both ascertaining the evidential relevance of data to a hypothesis and accepting a hypothesis on the basis of evidence require a reliance on substantive and methodological background assumptions. Just as not any old observations will do, so not just any old assumptions will do. In general, every assumption upon which it is permissible to rely is a function of consensus among the scientific community, is learned as part of one's apprenticeship as a scientist, and is largely invisible to practitioners within the community. Although invisible, or transparent, to members of the community, all such assumptions are articulable and hence, in principle, public. This in-principle publicity makes them available to critical examination as a consequence of which they may be abandoned, modified, or reinforced. Just as not all experiments are repeated, not all assumptions are in fact so scrutinized; but the presumption in inference is that they would survive, if scrutinized.

This critical examination is a social activity, requiring the participation of multiple points of view to ensure that the hypotheses accepted by a community do not represent someone's idiosyncratic interpretation of observational or experimental data. The inferences that build scientific knowledge, then, are not the inferences made by individual researchers, but inferences that proceed through discursive interactions. Of course, the invisibility—within a community—of many of its background assumptions as assumptions means that a closed community will not be able to exhibit those assumptions for critical scrutiny. These sorts of worries also affect the discussion of observation: the degree of intersubjective invariance of a set of observations will be limited by the degree of perspectival variation. These are the worries that generate the normative aspects of this view to be discussed in the following sections.

Knowing

The results of both reasoning and observation are socially processed before incorporation into the body of ideas ratified for circulation and use. What deserves the honorific "knowledge," on this view, is an outcome of the critical dialogue about observation, reasoning, and material practices among individuals and groups holding different points of view. It is constructed not by individuals, but by an interactive dialogic community. The conceivability of such a figure as Robinson Crusoe is frequently invoked as a counterexample to the above claims. Isn't it possible for some particular isolated individual to engage in inquiry that would qualify as scientific, to produce systematic knowledge of her surroundings that would count as science? Cannot she engage in that critical scrutiny on her own? Several points need to be made in rejoinder. First of all, in imagining Crusoe's critical scrutiny of her reasoning and observation, we simply import the community into Crusoe's head. Secondly, Crusoe's conversation with herself is parasitic on her past and potential interaction with others. She must rely on meanings and practices developed in the social setting from which she has been set adrift; and she must regard the results of her cognitive activity as tentative, awaiting ratification by the community of which she is still, in intention, a part. We can regard her activities as science only if they stand in this relation to the activities of others. Individuals are not replaced by a transcendent social entity, on the view being advocated. Rather, without individuals there would be no knowledge: it is through their sensory system that the natural world enters cognition; it is their proposals that are subject to critical scrutiny by other individuals, their imaginations which generate novelty. The activities of knowledge construction, however, are the activities of individuals in interaction, of individuals in certain relations (of criticism and response) with others.

A knowledge-constructive community extends beyond the laboratory in several important ways. As Knorr-Cetina (1981) reminds us, researchers are sensitive to the opportunities (for further support, interest) that can be engaged by taking certain research directions rather than others. And whether anyone pays attention will depend on how researchers can link their work up with that pursued elsewhere. The critical exchanges occur not only within the laboratory or research unit, but between it and other researchers as well as members of the larger community who have an interest in the outcomes. The dialogue will then involve aspects which are not classically cognitive—enrolling, in Latour's words, various sorts of allies who can provide an audience or increase the prospects of future development and/or funding. But it also involves elements that are epistemic in nature: is the pattern on film A sufficiently like the pattern on film B? Is this result an expression of the material under investigation or an artifact of the instrumental set-up? It is not purity, but responsiveness to epistemic considerations that is important. As David Hull (1988) says of the systematists he chronicled, knowledge may be a by-product of the activities that obtain the primary results (e.g. credit) desired by scientists; but, because of the rules by which the game is played, it is still a product. It is not purity, but responsiveness to epistemic considerations that is important in determining epistemological status.

While intersubjective interaction is a necessary feature of scientific cognition, not just any form of interaction will do. If the point of intersubjective interaction is to transform the subjective into the objective, then those interactions must not simply preserve and distribute one subjectivity over all others, but must constitute genuine and mutual checks.[6] This end can be served by specifying features of the design and constitution of a community that facilitate transformative criticism and enable a consensus to qualify as knowledge. Four such features or conditions can be identified.

1. There must be publicly recognized forums for the criticism of evidence, of methods, and of assumptions and reasoning.
2. There must be uptake of criticism. The community must not merely tolerate dissent; its beliefs and theories must change over time in response to the critical discourse taking place within it.
3. There must be publicly recognized standards by reference to which theories, hypotheses, and observational practices are evaluated and by appeal to which criticism is made relevant to the goals of the inquiring community. With the possible exception of empirical adequacy, there needn't be and probably isn't a set of standards common to all communities. The general family of standards from which those locally adopted are drawn includes such cognitive virtues as accuracy, coherence, and breadth of scope, and such social virtues as fulfilling technical or material needs or facilitating certain kinds of interactions between a society and its material environment or among the society's members. The point of requiring public standards is that, by explicitly or implicitly professing adherence to those standards, individuals and communities adopt criteria of adequacy by which they may be evaluated. The satisfaction of goals of inquiry is not ascertained privately, but by evaluation with respect to shared values and standards. This evaluation may be performed by anyone, not just by members of the community sharing all standards. Furthermore, standards are not a static set, but may themselves be criticized and transformed in reference to other standards, goals, or values held temporarily constant. Indeed, as in the case of observation and the assumptions underlying justificatory reasoning, the presupposition of reliance on such standards is that they have survived similar critical scrutiny.
4. Finally, communities must be characterized by equality of intellectual authority. What consensus exists must be the result not of the exercise of political or economic power, or of the exclusion of

> dissenting perspectives, but a result of critical dialogue in which all relevant perspectives are represented. This criterion is meant to impose duties of inclusion; it does not require that each individual, no matter what her or his past record or state of training, should be granted equal authority on every matter.

Education is required to prepare members of a society to make useful contributions, and researchers with a lot of experience or a record of "getting things right" may be more deserving of attention than others.[7] Exclusive attention to those who have earned the greatest cognitive authority, however, can lead to the neglect of new or "different" voices that ought to be heard. The more important function of measurements of degree of cognitive authority, then, is identifying—so as to be able to disregard—those who consistently get things wrong. The public standards mentioned in condition 3 have two objects. One is to impose obligations on acknowledged members of a knowledge-productive community to attend, restricting them to criticism that is relevant to their cognitive and practical aims. The other is to limit the sorts of criticisms to which a community must attend, restricting them to those which affect the satisfaction of its goals. The point of condition 4 is that such criticism may originate from an indeterminate number of points of view, none of which may be arbitrarily excluded from the community's interactions without cognitive impairment.

These features are features of an idealized epistemic community. In practice, then, they are criteria of knowledge-productive capacity that take the critical interactions of communities and their institutions as their domain of application. As such they constitute norms applying to the social practices and processes of cognition, norms whose satisfaction assures that theories and hypotheses accepted in the community will not incorporate the idiosyncratic biases (heuristic or social) of an individual or subgroup. We might call them "conditions of effective criticism." A community satisfying these conditions—that is, a community with means of disseminating and responding to criticism, whose members hold themselves answerable individually and collectively to a set of standards and reach consensus as a result of discursive interactions including all relevant perspectives and uninhibited by political or economic power—will qualify as a knowledge-productive community. Since the norms represent ideals that can be partially satisfied, this qualification is a matter of degree.

What's Known

Elsewhere (Longino 1993), I have proposed that this account of knowledge is most compatible with the treatment of scientific theories as models. There I appealed to the model treatment as an escape from what looks like a fatal dilemma. The account requires diversity in the community to generate critical discourse. But if diversity is seriously pursued, the consensus required for the application of theories to problems will be elusive; and if consensus is pursued, then critical oppositional positions will at some point have to be silenced, or at least ignored. Do we then aim for consensus or dissensus?

This dilemma seems forced upon us if we are still in the grip of an ideal of absolute and unitary truth—a final truth—whose attainment is the goal of scientific inquiry. Linked with this ideal is a residual individualism. The account of theories as models is intended to address the first source of the dilemma. Let me address the residual individualism first. "The community" is a misleading sobriquet. In a context of thinking about scientific knowledge we may be tempted to suppose that it refers to some entity—for example, the global scientific community, the scientific community whose aim is discovery of the truth about the world. Subcommunities may then be thought of as microcosmic replicas of the global community, each adding its mite to the stack. This is a bad picture. To think or see in these terms is still to see the knowledge-productive features of a knower as internal to the knower, or as a matter of the relation between knower and known, rather than a matter of the relatedness of the knower to other knowers. It is to fail to take into account the situated character of communities, their location in history and their constitution by their histories and their orientations to specific goals. It is to see pluralism as a means to its own overcoming in a final consensus.

The alternative is to see communities as themselves fluid entities overlapping both in values and standards and in membership. No community is ever complete in the sense of containing all possible perspectives within itself. Scientific knowledge is not a product of the final consensus, but consists in whatever theoretical apprehensions of the natural world are stable enough to permit elaboration and application for some period of time. Temporary and provisional unity around some goals and standards within a community permits the elaboration of ideas and hypotheses sufficiently for their application to problems. Whether their success can be called "knowledge" depends on the inclusion in their dialogue of all those perspectives having a bearing on the subject matter. It is on this matter of inclusiveness that attributions of knowledge are most clearly a matter of gradation. The notion of all relevant perspectives involves a diachronicity impossible to achieve, including as it must an as yet unrealized future. What perspectives must be included in community dialogue? Those that are live options for anyone both sharing some of the community's goals and with whom the community could reasonably be supposed to be in contact. This is of course dependent on the technologies of travel and communication available to a community.

If there is no "perfect" community but only successions of multiply related communities pursuing inquiry to satisfy local goals, then the ideal of an absolute and unitary truth—a final truth—is an empty notion. It decontextualizes what is meaningful only within the context of its constitution. The notion of models is introduced in part to provide an object or medium of knowledge suited to the provisionality, partiality, and pluralism inherent in this conception of epistemic communities. What counts as a model for this purpose is a pretty heterogeneous assemblage: sets of equations, specifications of structure, visual representations, mental maps, diagrams, three-dimensional objects like the wire and plastic models of the DNA molecule, or four-dimensional models that incorporate change or motion. The model approach to theories is intended as an alternative to the view that theories are sets of propositions. On this latter view, the adequacy of a theory is a matter of the truth by correspondence of the propositions constituting the theory. A model, by contrast, is neither true nor false; but its structure, or the structure of a subset of its elements, may be identical to a structure in the world. This isomorphism permits the mapping of the relations and structures and processes of the model onto some portion of the world. Elements of any portion of the world stand in many relations to many other elements. A model selects among those relations, presenting the results of that selection as a coherent, interrelated set. Many models can be isomorphic to some portion of the world as long as elements in the models stand in the same relations to each other as some set of elements in that portion of the world do to each other. The choice of a model, therefore, is not just a function of its isomorphism (or the isomorphism of a subset of its elements) with a portion of the world, but also a function of the relations it picks out being ones in which the users of the model are interested. It must represent the world in a way that facilitates the interactions its users seek to have with the modelled domain.

There is another reason to think of theories as models. Often research programs are guided not by an explicit theory, but by a sense of how things in the domain under study are related. This sense remains unarticulated in the generality in which it is held, and is expressed only in specific accounts of particular instances. I have called such a sense an explanatory model (Longino 1990), for it functions as a model of how explanations of particular phenomena in a domain are to be structured. In behavioral endocrinology, for example, behavioral patterns of various sorts are attributed to hormonal exposures at critical periods of organismic development. There is no explicit general theory, only a number of studies linking different behaviors to different hormone levels. Each of these, however, acquires significance on account of its similarity to the others. It is as though researchers are working with a general picture of a class of systems behaving in similar fashion, without ever articulating a general theory that then requires support. Such a theory, as a picture, is nevertheless a crucial element in the research, determining the way researchers look at and think about the systems under study, the questions they ask, and the experiments they design.

Models, whether tacit or elaborately articulated, guide our interactions with and interventions in the world. To see the products of scientific inquiry as models is to understand scientific knowledge not as reified in a set of propositions detachable from knowers, but as an ability to understand the structural features of a model and to understand and act in the world as it manifests that structure. Treating theories as models, then, also enables the expression of one of the ways in which scientific inquiry shapes and in a sense produces the world in which we live. Inquiry gives certain features, relationships, and processes significance by incorporating them into a coherent (if still partial) framework. A model works to the extent that it is possible to interact with the modelled domain as though it were constituted of just those elements. As Ian Hacking suggests in his discussions of laboratory sciences, one of the keys to the success of those sciences is the ability of researchers to create in the laboratory a world in which only those elements and processes postulated in a model are interacting (Hacking 1988). It is a small step to the supposition that what is recreated in the laboratory is what's real about the natural domain under study.

WHAT'S KNOWLEDGE

This is all very well, you might say, but what has happened to knowledge in the course of this analysis? Like the sociologist, haven't

I simply retained the term but jettisoned the concept? This is essentially the question asked by Philip Kitcher in the comments mentioned earlier. He does this by extracting an analysis along the lines of a traditional analysis of "*S* knows that *p*"—including an attitudinal clause, a success clause, and a procedural clause—from earlier versions of ideas of the sort developed in the preceding section. He uses his critique of this analysis to argue that the account from which it is drawn is incapable of expressing what we intend to convey by knowledge claims or attributions. I disagree with this verdict—in part because I think the analysis extracted doesn't quite capture the ideas, and in part because I disagree with Kitcher's assessment of what he does include. Let me first discuss Kitcher's extraction, and then present an alternative version.

Kitcher proposes the following as a reconstruction of the account of knowledge.

KNOWLEDGE I. *S* knows that *p* if and only if
(i) *S* believes that *p*;
(ii) *p* is effective in directing *S*'s actions towards the attainment of goals that are validated by the society to which *S* belongs; and
(iii) *S*'s belief is produced by a process that the society in question would validate (providing it meets criteria of proper cognitive design).

He worries that both the second and the third clause would permit us (counterintuitively) to say that creationists know that the world was created between four and seven thousand years ago. He presents the analysis as an analysis of propositional knowledge because he views proponents of models as committed to some propositions—for example, that a model is isomorphic with, or similar to, the modelled domain—and thus sees no reason to abandon the analysis of scientific knowledge as propositional knowledge or truth as the appropriate dimension of evaluation. I shall take up these issues in turn, drawing on the remarks of the previous sections.

Creationism. Kitcher's point in bringing up creationism is to demonstrate that, despite my aspirations to offer an analysis robust enough to support the normative judgments we make about knowledge (e.g., she knows, he doesn't), the analysis actually offered fails. So, for creationism substitute any egregiously wrong-headed set of claims about the natural world. Kitcher claims that both the second and third clauses of his extraction allow the creationist to know that the world was created between four and five thousand years ago. The second clause requires that *p* be effective in directing *S*'s actions towards the attainment of goals that are validated by the society to which *S* belongs. Something like this is consistent with the sociologists' accounts.

Now, for all my suspicion of truth, I think Kitcher is right to question its replacement by this pragmatic criterion. How does it allow egregiously wrong-headed beliefs to be knowledge? Kitcher does not elaborate, but it is worth doing so to see just why an exclusively pragmatic criterion of success will not do. Since it is not clear how a proposition by itself could be effective, let us suppose that what is meant is that acceptance of or belief that *p* is effective. What goals might be served by belief or acceptance that the world was created four to seven thousand years ago? Perhaps awe of the almighty, which is surely a goal validated by the creationist's society. But awe of the almighty is itself an intermediate goal, instrumental in achievement of the final goal, which is presumably salvation, or eternal life with god. How the second clause permits flawed beliefs depends on how it is read. If to be effective in directing someone's actions towards the attainment of a given goal requires that the goal be realizable, then the creationist knows only if eternal life with god is a genuine possibility (and god chooses to reward such belief with eternal life). If attainability is not required, then the creationist may know as long as acceptance of *p* effectively directs *S*'s actions towards that goal, even if it is not realizable. What's counter-intuitive about this clause is that, in general, beliefs which have no real-world correlates would be admitted as instances of knowledge (provided the other clauses were met). Even if god had created the world billions of years ago, she might reward the hapless creationist with salvation just for believing against so many odds, thus making *S*'s belief effective in the ways required. Part of what is counterintuitive is that it is the fact of *S*'s acceptance that is effective, rather than any relation between the content of what is accepted and elements, structures, and processes represented by that content. The earlier discussion of models invoked satisfaction of goals as an important element in assessing the adequacy of representations, but only as a supplement to model isomorphism. The kind of example just developed shows that efficacy in goal satisfaction is not a sufficient success condition in itself. Furthermore, in the case of a proposition, success need only consist in its content's being the case. Goal satisfaction is not required. Thus, I reject Kitcher's reconstruction of the success clause.

Kitcher also faults the third clause for permitting creationist knowledge. That is the clause requiring that *S*'s belief that *p* be produced by a process that the society in question would validate (subject, of course, to that society's meeting criteria of proper cognitive design).

How does this clause ratify wrong-headed beliefs? A society will validate processes of inquiry that result in its or its members' having beliefs which satisfy clause (ii). But the parenthetical addition of proper cognitive design is important here. Let us suppose that proper cognitive design means satisfying the four conditions of effective criticism discussed above. That means that there must be critical exchanges in which the full variety of perspectives are represented and that they are treated as equally capable of generating significant challenges to theories. For the creationist belief to be ratified by this clause, all participants to the dialogue would have to share an overriding commitment to the goal of salvation or to the intermediate goal of fostering awe of the almighty. But this is to limit the included perspectives by content, not by past performance.

Kitcher thinks the creationist claims cannot be criticized without the adoption of methodological norms that are not forced on individuals (or groups) simply by virtue of their commitment to a practice of open criticism and discussion. But this is not at all obvious. A practice of genuinely open criticism and discussion requires an openness to all perspectives: no claim or belief can be held immune to criticism. Creationism must withstand critical scrutiny and challenge to count as knowledge. Moreover, the supposition that additional methodological norms would be required presupposes an insulation of cognitive goals from practical and social goals—an insulation that we have no good reason to assume. A commitment to salvation that ratified procedures of inquiry warranting creationist beliefs about the origin of the universe would be in conflict with other goals of an inquiring community, and could be shown to be in such conflict if the community were indeed open. So, while I think Kitcher's version of the procedural clause is reasonably close to what I've been arguing for, his rejection of it is based on a lack of appreciation for its strength.

Propositions versus Models. If an account of propositional knowledge is to be given within the social approach, all that really requires modification is the third condition. The following is a better reconstruction than Kitcher's.

KNOWLEDGE II. If $S_1 \ldots S_n$ are members of an epistemic community C, then $S_1 \ldots S_n$ know that p if and only if

(i) $S_1 \ldots S_n$ believe that p;

(ii) p; and

(iii) $S_1 \ldots S_n$'s believing that p is the result of warranting practices adopted by C in circumstances characterized by

a. public forums for critical interaction,

b. uptake of criticism,
c. public standards, and
d. equality of intellectual authority among diverse perspectives.

Kitcher attributes an account of propositional knowledge to me for two reasons. Firstly, propositions are standard objects of knowledge in philosophical analysis, and their conditions of success and failure are clear: truth and falsity. Of this point, more in a moment. Secondly, he states that in spite of my talk of models, I'm still committed to a treatment of propositional knowledge. There are two ways to understand this latter claim. One is as the assertion that models are all well and good, but we still have propositional knowledge. To which I say, yes, I can know that the cat is on the roof, and I can know that the dial is at .5 on the meter, but a great deal of what we call "scientific knowledge" is just not like that kind of knowledge. That is, much of what we call "scientific knowledge" has as its object not singular propositions about mid-sized objects, but patterns and relationships among entities beyond our powers of sensory detection and between such entities and the objects and relationships we do detect. We have a choice, then, between limiting the possible objects of knowledge to those within our powers of detection and attempting to find an analysis that permits us to speak of knowledge in those cases in which direct determination of truth and falsity is not possible. Treating models as media of knowledge is one way of developing a more expansive conception of knowledge.[8]

A second interpretation of the claim that in spite of my talk of models I'm still committed to a treatment of knowledge as propositional knowledge is that, even in a model treatment of theories, whatever knowledge is involved is propositional knowledge, namely, knowledge that the model is similar to the real-world system of which it is a model. There are three problems with this view. Firstly, it unnecessarily restricts knowledge to the contemplative and fails to give expression to the ways in which scientific knowledge involves active engagement with its objects. Secondly, knowledge of similarity may not be what is asserted in claims to knowledge. We can know that a model is empirically adequate—that is, that a subset of its elements is isomorphic with a subset of the elements of the modelled domain—without knowing or needing to know the full extent or respect of similarity of the model to the modelled domain. Thirdly, given the elasticity of "similar," it is not clear what one knows when one knows that a model is similar to a real-world system. So it is not clear that propositional knowledge of this sort is any better or clearer than possible alternatives.

The more general point about propositions and models is that both are means of representation used in the sciences. Absent a principled argument to the effect that one rather than the other medium of representation can count as knowledge, any analysis of scientific knowledge in the sciences ought to be able to accommodate both forms. Talking about models as media of knowledge enables us to include as cases of knowledge those representations of portions of the natural world that are nonpropositional, that are nevertheless empirically adequate, and that provide us with a framework within which to carry out inquiry and successfully to pursue practical projects. The point of extending an analysis of knowledge to include such representations is to show how the distinction between knowledge and opinion can be preserved under such extension. What follows, then, is a proposal that draws on the earlier discussion. While it is modelled on the traditional form of analyses of knowledge, both the object of analysis and the analyzing conditions depart from it somewhat in content.

KNOWLEDGE III. If $S_1 \ldots S_n$ are members of an epistemic community, W is some real-world system or portion of real-world system, and M is a model (of that system), then $S_1 \ldots S_n$ know W as M if and only if

(i) $S_1 \ldots S_n$ represent W as M, and act with respect to W as if it were M;

(ii) a subset of elements of M is sufficiently isomorphic to a subset of elements of W to enable $S_1 \ldots S_n$ to satisfy their goals with respect to W; and

(iii) $S_1 \ldots S_n$'s representing W as M is the result of warranting practices adopted by C in circumstances characterized by

a. public forums for critical interaction,
b. uptake of criticism,
c. public standards, and
d. equality of intellectual authority among diverse perspectives.

The knowledge defined here is similar to knowledge by acquaintance. It differs from traditional accounts of acquaintance (e.g., Russell's) in that it is mediated rather than direct. This mediation makes possible both partiality and pluralism, since it leaves open that W may also be known as M', i.e. that M does not exhaust the features (processes/interactions/elements) of W. M and M' may equally be ways of knowing W. To illustrate with a mundane example: my students know me as a teacher; while my mother knows me as a daughter. Different features of my personality, capacities, and so on are highlighted in these representations of me which determine how these different knowers will act with regard to me. Their different representations also elicit different behaviors from me. Thus I confirm those representations in the contexts in which they are activated. Or think of a collection of objects of different materials and two models: one containing the two-place transitive relation {larger than} and names for the objects; the other containing the two-place transitive relation {heavier than} and names for the objects. These models will order the elements in the domain differently, but each can be an adequate representation of the domain for certain purposes.[9] The analyzing conditions are intended to preserve the pluralism and partiality inherent in this expression of the analysandum.

The attitudinal condition has two components: representation and action. Both are required as a replacement for belief. "Representation" conveys the intentionality of belief, while "action" conveys its commitment. The medium of representation, however, is not (or not necessarily) a proposition, but may be a set of equations, a diagram, a mental map, a structure made of linguistic or physical elements. The point of the representation is the kinds of actions it makes possible for $S_1 \ldots S_n$ in *W*, whether they be designing a new superconducting material, orienting the Hubble space telescope, or preparing a bacterial plasmid for production of some biological substance. This aspect of the condition expresses the active and productive character of scientific knowledge.

The success condition requires partial isomorphism of the model, rather than truth of constituent propositions. The requirement of isomorphism is a very weak requirement, especially when the isomorphism is only partial. It is satisfied as long as some elements of *M* stand to one another in relations structurally identical to those in which some elements of *W* stand to one another. It is not necessary that all the structural relations of a set of elements be represented in order that a given model or portion of a model be isomorphic with that set. Not every possible model will be (partially) isomorphic with its intended domain, but many models will be.[10] Given that isomorphism is so easily obtainable, it is not a sufficient condition of success. The success condition requires a degree of isomorphism sufficient to enable $S_1 \ldots S_n$ to act in *W* in such a way as to satisfy their goals. Clearly, isomorphism of the observational elements of *M* with the experienced elements of *W* is necessary to meet this condition, which leaves open whether any more isomorphism is required or even to be had.

This success condition also allows for changes in the sorts of experiences we may wish for or can have. Technological changes make possible finer experiential discriminations, and what counts as a satisfactory level of isomorphism at one time in the context of one set of needs and capacities may not count as such in the context of a different set. Hence, more extensive or different isomorphism may be required at a different time. While this condition has some of the flexibility of the more purely pragmatic version, its externalism enables escape from the problems attendant upon that version because it requires a relation with the modelled domain that holds independently of the fact that $S_1 \ldots S_n$ so represent it. Their goals are satisfied by acting in *W* in the ways made possible by representing *W* as *M*, not as a reward for faith.

The procedural condition is essentially the same in both proffered analyses and in this version is explicitly supplemented with the criteria of knowledge-productive capacity. When these are explicit, it's less plausible to think that the warranting procedures would permit egregiously wrong-headed views to count as knowledge. And if they did, I think we would be required to reconsider our judgment of egregious wrong-headedness. That is, if a community *C*'s representation of *W* as *M* continues to be warranted by the procedures of *C* that have been modified in response to free and open criticism referencing some goals of *C*, then it is not clear that there are any further grounds (beyond simple disagreement) for criticism. The worry so often expressed is Kitcher's worry: won't this analysis license creationism? The correct response to such a worry is two-fold. Firstly, if the creationists meet the conditions, they are not the creationists we love to hate. Secondly, it is satisfaction of condition 3 that gives even Western scientific communities whatever claim they have to our doxastic allegiance. For the only non-question-begging response to challenge must be this: "We are open to criticism; we do change in response to it; and while we may not have included all possible perspectives in the discursive interactions that underwrite our methodological procedures, we've included as many as we have encountered (or more than others have)." It doesn't follow, however, that the standards and warranting procedures could not change further in response to new sorts of criticisms. (Indeed, if feminist, environmentalist, and other critics of the sciences are successful, the standards and the knowledge they legitimate will change.) The point is that there is nothing further—that appeal to standards or methodological norms beyond those ratified by the discursive interactions of an inquiring community is an appeal to transcendent principles that inevitably turn out to be local.

CONCLUSION

In this essay, I've argued that the sociologists are wrong to dismiss the concerns of philosophers, but that philosophers are equally wrong to ignore the empirical studies of sociologists. Philosophical analysis converges with sociological observation in concluding that the processes of knowledge construction in the sciences are importantly social. This does not mean that norms are idle, but that they must be articulated for social rather than individual processes, and that the norms that bind individuals are those that come out of the public standards of a community. I've discussed a set of conditions for effective discursive interaction and shown that the distinction between knowledge and opinion that underlies our use of those terms, and hence the normative content of "knowledge," can be expressed within the terms of a social theory of scientific knowledge.

The view has elements of both construction and constraint. We select representations partly on the basis of their efficacy in satisfying our needs. But that very efficacy is a function of those representations' relations with their intended domains, and hence our selection is constrained by the need for some isomorphism with those domains. Furthermore, to count as knowledge, those representations must be the outcome of discursive interactions in circumstances that meet the identifiable conditions for effective community criticism. Not every representation counts as knowledge. The idea of social construction often evokes visions of science displaced by social interests and social content. But on the view of social knowledge developed here, such displacement would occur only in contexts of flawed discursive interaction. While the account of inquiry shows how social values can permeate scientific inquiry, the sociality that constrains is procedural. Norms of practice emerge as communities engage in specific practices with specific goals. Norms of inquiry are generated and validated by communities of inquirers with specific cognitive needs. Philosophers can reflect on the congruence (or incongruence) of practices, norms, and goals, and participate in the discursive interactions that constitute knowledge construction in our communities. We can reflect on the conditions for effective discursive interactions. All we are proscribed from doing is articulating context-independent rules (as distinct from conditions) of inquiry that must hold for all communities. The epistemology that results may lack the grandeur of traditional theories of knowledge that legislated for all, but what it lacks in grandeur it will gain in robustness.

Notes

1. I wish to thank Richard Grandy and Jeffry Ramsey for discussing earlier drafts of this essay with me, Fred Schmitt for his extensive and provocative comments, and all those who responded to spoken versions of this essay.

2. For an argument to this effect, see Brown (1989).

3. The condition of reproducibility, which involves stability across different apparatus as well as across different observers (see Cartwright 1991), signifies an even stronger alliance than repeatability.

4. This is the epistemological dimension of what Joseph Rouse (1987) and Jerome Ravetz (1970) discuss as standardization—a practical aim whose satisfaction enables the transfer of results from laboratory to laboratory and to the world outside the laboratory.

5. None of this is to deny that theoretical considerations play a role in the selection, reporting, and description of observational and experimental results. For a good account of the role of theory in observation, see Hesse (1980).

6. Goldman's (1987b) rejection of consensus reflects a similar concern. He's rightly worried that mere consensus doesn't rule out error, but his commitment to epistemological individualism prevents him from exploring conditions under which consensus might function as a criterion of justifiability.

7. This is the argument in Kitcher (1992).

8. Another way is to adopt a pluralistic definition of truth that allows more latitude in the sorts of propositions whose truth we deem ourselves able to ascertain. (See Hacking 1992).

9. Thanks to John Martin for this example.

10. Nor does invocation of isomorphism presuppose a preexistent determinate structure of the world that models must somehow match to be adequate. The isomorphism requirement is compatible with the view that determinacy is determinability in some system of representation.

8

Good Arguments

Richard Feldman

No doubt there are many virtues that an argument can have and thus many features that may lead us to describe an argument as a good one. However, I believe that there is a core notion of a good argument that we typically have in mind when we evaluate arguments and when we teach students to work with arguments. It is this notion that I will attempt to analyze in this chapter.

In the first part of the chapter I will discuss some accounts of what a good argument is, drawn from logic. In the second section I will examine some accounts of good arguments that emphasize the social role of arguments. In the final section I will describe and defend an epistemological account according to which good arguments are analogous to justified beliefs.

I

One place to find discussions of what good arguments are is in textbooks of symbolic logic. The standard logical views hold that a good argument is a valid argument, or perhaps a valid argument with true premises. We can formulate this "deductivist" view as follows:

> L1. An argument is a good argument if and only if (i) it is valid and (ii) it contains true premises.

The standard logical notion of validity makes it a formal or syntactic matter. Arguments are valid if they are of the proper form. Philosophers at times also appeal to a semantic notion of validity, according to which an argument is valid provided its conclusion must be true if its premises are true. The difference between using the syntactic and the semantic notions of validity in L1 becomes clear when we consider simple little arguments such as this:

Argument 1
(1) Jones is a brother.
(2) Jones is male.

According to the syntactic account, this argument is not valid. According to the semantic account, presumably, it is valid. Since the word "valid" as used in L1 is a technical term, there is no point in debating whether the syntactic or the semantic account of validity is "right." However, there may be some point in deciding which, if either, figures in the best account of good arguments.

I think that it is best to classify Argument 1 as an invalid argument. The reason for this is that it leads to the simplest and most readily applied system of argument evaluation. It is clear that Argument 1 depends in one way or another on the implicit premise:

(1.5) All brothers are male.

If you say that Argument 1 is valid, presumably this claim will rely upon the further claim that (1.5) is necessarily true. (You might just say that (1) "necessitates" (2), but presumably that would be the case only if (1.5) is necessarily true.) That judgment seems reasonable enough in this case, but other cases are more troublesome. Consider arguments relying upon implicit generalizations, such as these:

All causes precede their effects.

No airplane travels at the speed of light.

Any person whose head has been severed from his body for more than an hour is dead.

It's hard to say whether these are *necessarily* true. Consequently, it is hard to say whether the arguments upon which they depend are valid (in the semantic sense).

We can eliminate the need for judging the necessity of these statements by rejecting arguments such as Argument 1 as invalid. We can say instead that they are incomplete statements of larger arguments. In the case of Argument 1, the larger argument is as follows:

Argument 1a
(1) Jones is a brother.
(2) All brothers are male.
(3) Jones is male.

This argument is unquestionably valid. Assessment of it will eventually require an examination of the truth value of its second premise. However, we need not determine the modal status of the premise to complete this evaluation. Again, this may not seem to be a great advantage in this case; but for the other generalizations mentioned above, avoiding inquiry into their modal status is desirable.[1]

Thus, I think that arguments such as Argument 1 do not provide any good reason to adopt the semantic notion of validity. This is not to say that the syntactic standard of validity is without difficulties. It is most readily applied to formal languages, rather than to natural languages. Still, typically, the arguments we wish to assess can be cast in ways that make assessment of their validity straightforward.[2] By following the approach recommended here, such reconstructions of arguments will make explicit the assumptions upon which the arguments rely. It is difficult to see anything harmful about that. I will assume, therefore, that we can make sense of a syntactic notion of validity for natural language and that it is that notion that is being used in accounts of good arguments.

Deductivism is open to what I believe is a decisive objection. There are lots of good arguments that are not deductively valid (on any account of validity). Familiar enumerative inductive arguments are prime examples. For example, suppose that I am assigned the job of picking up the guest speaker for the sports banquet. All I know about the speaker is that he is a professional basketball player. I am trying to decide whether to drive my own small car or use my wife's larger car. I decide to use the larger car since the speaker is over six feet tall and therefore more comfortable in the larger car. Part of my reasoning here looks like this:

Argument 2
(1) Almost all professional basketball players are over six feet tall.
(2) The guest speaker is a professional basketball player.
(3) The guest speaker is over six feet tall.

This is, or at least could be, a good argument. Obviously, arguments following the pattern of Argument 2 are not valid. Thus, it appears that to demand deductive validity of good arguments is to demand too much.

There are a variety of ways in which one might defend the deductive requirement. I will mention two. Both hold that although Argument 2 is no good, it can be modified to be made good. Our intuition that Argument 2 is a good argument is supposed to be accommodated by the fact these replacement arguments are good. The first response calls for modifying the conclusion, replacing it with this:

Probably, the guest speaker is over six feet tall.

Perhaps one could then argue that the revised argument is valid. I will not undertake a detailed discussion of this approach here. In my view, there is no interpretation of "probably" that makes the revised argument suitable. On subjective and epistemic interpretations, the revised argument is not valid. On other interpretations, the conclusion of the revised argument is not suitably similar to the conclusion of the original argument. (See Feldman forthcoming, for discussion.)

The second response to the objection to deductivism begins with the observation that one can always add a conditional to an invalid argument to construct a valid argument. Thus, one can add a conditional to the premises of Argument 2, with this result:

Argument 2a
(1) Almost all professional basketball players are over six feet tall.
(2) The guest speaker is a professional basketball player.
(3) If almost all professional basketball players are over six feet tall and the guest speaker is a professional basketball player, then the guest speaker is over six feet tall.
(4) The guest speaker is over six feet tall.

Argument 2a, apparently, is valid.

A full discussion of this proposal requires a detailed examination of possible interpretations of conditionals such as (3). I will discuss the topic only briefly here. If (3) is a material conditional, then it is false if (1) and (2) are true and (4) is false. So, in that situation, Argument 2a has a false premise and therefore is not a good argument according to L1. However, I think that the original argument, Argument 2, could be a good argument in such a situation. One of the central features of inductive arguments is that good ones can lead to false conclusions. So, Argument 2a, with (3) taken to be a material conditional, is not a suitable replacement for Argument 2. There are other possible interpretations of the conditional in Argument 2a; but in every case the premise is either false or unknowable, or else the resulting argument is invalid. In no case is Argument 2a acceptable as a replacement for Argument 2.[3]

The problem with deductivism suggests that logical accounts of good arguments should be modified to allow as good arguments those arguments that are "inductively cogent." These are arguments that are deductively invalid, but whose premises make probable their conclusion. Argument 2 is a paradigm example. We might formulate inductivism as follows:

L2. An argument is a good argument if and only if (i) it is valid or cogent and (ii) it contains true premises.

As I interpret "cogent," all arguments following simple patterns such as

(1) Most *A*s are *B*s.
(2) *x* is an *A*.
(3) *x* is a *B*.

are cogent. Cogent arguments can fail to be good arguments if they have false premises or if they are "defeated." (I will discuss what defeats a cogent argument later in this chapter.)

When we turn to more complex arguments, evaluation of arguments for cogency gets more difficult. It may seem that two arguments can have the same form, yet one is cogent and the other isn't. This would make cogency not simply a matter of the form or pattern of the argument. Consider Argument 3:

Argument 3
(1) All graduates got a job.
(2) Most job getters can afford a car.
(3) M. Ployd is a graduate.
(4) M. Ployd can afford a car.

This argument seems to be a good one, assuming all is well with its premises. Its pattern is as follows:

(1) All *A*s are *B*s.
(2) Most *B*s are *C*s.
(3) *y* is an *A*.
(4) *x* is a *C*.

But now consider Argument 4:

Argument 4
(1) All grandmothers are females.
(2) Most females are not grandmothers.
(3) x is a grandmother.
(4) x is not a grandmother.

The temptation to say that this argument is not cogent is strong.[4] Indeed, the truth of its premises guarantees that its conclusion is false, so it is hard to see how we can also say that the premises make the conclusion probable. So, it isn't cogent. But if Arguments 3 and 4 have the same structure and one is cogent and the other isn't, then cogency isn't a matter of structure or form.

While some may think that this sort of example reveals an insurmountable problem with the notion of cogency, I think that such a conclusion is premature. I think that the best response admits that Argument 3, and all arguments following its pattern, are not cogent. Our inclination to think that it is a cogent argument can be accommodated by noting that it breaks down into two simpler arguments:

Argument 3a
(1) All graduates got a job.
(2) M. Ployd is a graduate.
(3) M. Ployd got a job.

Argument 3b
(1) Most job getters can afford a car.
(2) M. Ployd is a job getter.
(3) M. Ployd can afford a car.

The first of these is valid. The second is cogent. They can both be good arguments.

Argument 4 also breaks down into two simpler arguments, 4a and 4b, of the same structure as 3a and 3b. Argument 4a will be valid, and Argument 4b cogent. However, as noted, cogent arguments can be "defeated" by background evidence. Argument 4b will be defeated for anyone who knows about Argument 4a. In this respect it is unlike Argument 3b. So, unlike Argument 3, Argument 4 cannot be replaced by a pair of good arguments (according to a standard that recognizes the need for good arguments to be undefeated).

Thus, we can respond to the puzzle by saying that complex arguments such Arguments 3 and 4 are not cogent, and only the first of these can be broken down into two good arguments. The puzzle will recur only if there can be arguments having the same structure as Argument 3b that can differ with respect to cogency. I doubt that there can be arguments like that.

Although there are difficult residual issues about the notion of cogency, I think that it can play a useful role in the evaluation of arguments. There is no problem in saying that arguments such as Arguments 2, 3b, and 4b are cogent. Other arguments are plainly not cogent. There may be remaining cases that only can be classified after developing a more comprehensive theory—something I won't attempt here. I will assume that we have a clear enough idea of cogency to go on.

The main problem with logical accounts of good arguments is that they fail to recognize the epistemological dimension of argument evaluation. Good arguments are arguments that provide people with reason to believe their conclusions. However, arguments can be valid or cogent and have true premises, yet fail to have rational merit. An example should make this point clear.

Suppose I'm on a canoe trip deep in an uninhabited wilderness and I've been completely out of contact with society. Suppose further that I know that there was an election while I was away and that my neighbor voted. However, I have no information about whether she voted for candidate A or candidate B. Now, consider these two arguments:

Argument 5
(1) Either my neighbor voted for A or she voted for B.
(2) She did not vote for A.
(3) Therefore, she voted for B.

Argument 6
(1) Either my neighbor voted for A or she voted for B.
(2) She did not vote for B.
(3) Therefore, she voted for A.

Both these arguments are valid. One of them has true premises. So, one of them satisfies the logical conditions (both versions) for being a good argument, but neither is a good argument.[5] After considering these arguments, I have no reason to accept either conclusion. These arguments have no rational merit. Or, if being valid gives them *some* merit, they share that virtue. Neither is any better than the other, even though one in fact has true premises. Hence, the logical conditions for being a good argument are not sufficient.[6]

The claim that neither of these arguments is a good argument in this context is crucial to the argument of this chapter. I believe that it is clearly correct. The reason that neither is a good argument in this context is that neither provides me with any reason to believe its conclusion. As a result of consideration of these arguments, I have no reason to believe either conclusion. If I had a group of students with me and I were teaching them to evaluate arguments during the slow moments of the canoe trip, I would tell them to conclude that neither of these arguments is a good one.

Defenders of logical accounts may reply that one or the other of the arguments above is a good argument, but that in the situation described I am simply not in a position to figure out which one it is. It's not clear to me that there is much more than tradition to support this contention. It seems clear to me that as *arguments* both are failures. That is because, as I see it, the point of arguments, or at least the point of thinking about arguments, has something to do with figuring out what to believe. (A similar view is defended in Meiland [1989].) These arguments contribute nothing to that enterprise. If someone wants to insist that there is some sense of "good argument" in which one of these is a good argument, I suppose that the point can be conceded. What must also be conceded is that there is some sense of "good argument" in which neither of them is a good argument. That this sense has to do with the epistemic status of the premises is quite clear. It is this sense that I am trying to spell out in this chapter.

Reasoning similar to the foregoing suggests another objection to logical accounts, namely, that good arguments need not have true premises. Suppose that I have a good inductive argument for some conclusion. I then produce an argument using that conclusion and other known truths to deduce correctly some further proposition. This second argument can be a good one, even if one of its premises—the inductively supported conclusion of the first argument—is in fact false.

These considerations are designed to provide motivation for looking for a more epistemological notion of what a good argument is. That is what I will do in the remainder of this chapter.

II

Arguments undoubtedly play an important social role. Some philosophers have drawn on ideas from social epistemology to develop accounts of good arguments. Social theories of good arguments derive their plausibility from the fact that arguments are characteristically things people use in communication with one another. They are instruments of persuasion and components of a collective search for the truth. Social theories of good arguments bring consideration of these matters into their accounts. They make the way arguments affect, or should affect, their intended audience an essential determinant of their quality.

It is unclear whether it is best to regard social theories of good arguments as rivals of the logical accounts discussed in section I or as accounts of a different sense of the phrase "good argument." At least one advocate of a social theory, Alvin Goldman, makes it clear that he thinks that there are two distinct notions of what an argument is, and a sense of "good argument" to go with each. Although in one sense an argument is an abstract set of sentences or propositions, he says,

> In another sense, however, an argument is a complex speech act in which a speaker presents a thesis to a listener or audience, and defends this thesis with reasons or premises. . . . [This is] an interpersonal or social sense of "argument," quite different from the abstract sense; and it seems quite likely that criteria or norms of goodness for this sense of "argument" differ from the criteria cited above. This social sense of "argument" is what I will call *argumentation.* (Goldman 1994)

Thus, Goldman does not see his view as a rival of a logical account of good arguments. Rather, it is an account of what makes for good argumentation. In this section, I will examine the possibility of analyzing the core notion of "good arguments" under discussion in this chapter in terms of the concepts upon which social theorists focus. Since social theorists such as Goldman may have been attempting to analyze a different notion than I am, my comments may apply only to adaptations of their proposals to the current topic.

Persuasiveness

Arguments are often used to persuade people of things. One argues for something in an effort to persuade one's audience of it. In general, if we use things of a certain kind for a certain purpose, then something is a good instance of that kind if it accomplishes that purpose. This suggests the following social formula:

S1. An argument is a good argument if and only if it is persuasive.

Although S1 will win few converts, it is worth spending a moment to identify its flaws.

Since an argument may persuade some people but not others, to understand the implications of S1 we need to know to whom an argument must be persuasive to be good. There are many possibilities, none of them particularly plausible. We might try this one:

> S2. An argument is a good argument if and only if it is persuasive to its intended audience.

S2 makes the quality of an argument dependent in part upon the gullibility or stubbornness of its intended audience. Stubborn people can fail to be persuaded by good arguments. Gullible people can be persuaded by bad arguments. To persuade one's audience is to be rhetorically effective, so S2 confuses rhetorically effective arguments with good arguments.

Thinking carefully about what we teach our students when we teach argument evaluation makes it clear that there is a difference between rhetorical effectiveness and good argumentation. To evaluate the rhetorical effectiveness of an argument we would see whether it persuades us and others. Statistical analysis of the persuasiveness of an argument would be the ideal way to determine its merit. Surely that is not what anyone teaches students to look for when they evaluate arguments in critical thinking or other philosophy classes. Persuasiveness is simply not what we are after.

Variations on the persuasiveness view expressed in S2 are open to similar objections. One might require that a good argument be persuasive to the person who gives the argument or to "average" listeners or to anyone else. One might also consider the idea that the quality of an argument is proportional to the percentage of its actual, intended, or potential audience to whom it would be persuasive. This also makes the merits of an argument too dependent upon contingent factors about its (potential) audience. And it is not what we teach our students to look for.

There may be a sense of "good argument" for which S2, or something like it, is correct. Imagine a politician and her advisers discussing which argument she should use in an upcoming speech. She might say, "That's a good argument. It will persuade lots of people." Even if this is right, however, it is clear that this isn't the notion of "good argument" we have in mind when we attempt to teach our students about reasoning. It is this latter sense that is under discussion here. In this sense, good arguments are arguments with rational, rather than rhetorical, merit.

Audience Acceptability

Another social theory of good argument begins with the observation that there isn't much point in giving an argument whose premises are not acceptable, in some sense, to its intended audience. In a recent paper (1992), Trudy Govier discusses and gives somewhat hedged support to such a theory. Govier formulates the view as follows:

> S3. An argument is a good argument if and only if (i) its premises are acceptable to the audience to whom it is addressed, (ii) its premises are relevant to its conclusion, and (iii) its premises, considered together, offer sufficient grounds for its conclusion. (Govier 1992, p. 394)[7]

Govier's view is in key respects similar to one Alvin Goldman defends. Goldman proposes a set of rules or norms that govern good argumentation. They include the following:

1. A speaker should assert a conclusion only if she believes it.
2. A speaker should assert a premise only if she believes it.
3. A speaker should assert a premise only if she is justified in believing it.
4. A speaker should affirm a conclusion on the basis of stated premises only if (a) those premises, together with unstated premises justifiably believed by the speaker, strongly support the conclusion, (b) she believes that they strongly support it, and (c) she is justified in believing that they strongly support it.
5. A speaker is not allowed to assert any proposition with the primary intention of inducing her audience to infer a further proposition which she herself believes to be false.
6. Ceteris paribus, an argument presented by speaker *S* to audience *H* is better (qua specimen of argumentation) to the extent that *H* is disposed to (A) find the asserted premises credible, (B) share any premises unasserted but presupposed by *S*, and (C) recognize that the premises provide strong support for the conclusion. (Goldman 1994)

I want to focus here on the audience acceptability requirement included in condition 6. It is obviously similar to the conditions Govier mentions. Of course, Govier does not include conditions such as 1-5, which set the conditions the elements of the argument must satisfy relative to the person who presents the argument.

Conditions 1-5 may well set suitable constraints on when a speaker should assert or defend an argument, and thus may be part of a good account of argumentation. However, our goal here is an analysis of the notion of "good argument" that we typically have in mind when we evaluate arguments and when we teach students to evaluate them. Including conditions 1-5 in such an analysis would have strikingly odd results. Suppose you give an argument with premises that I know to be true, but for which you lack justification (and I know you lack justification). Suppose further that these premises imply a conclusion and I hadn't previously realized the connection between these premises and the conclusion. As a result, I now see that the conclusion is true. However, if good arguments must satisfy conditions 1-5, then I should conclude that the argument is no good since *you* lack justification for the premises. This result is extremely odd. In my evaluation of the argument, the status the premises have for you is of no consequence. The argument provides me with good reason to believe the conclusion. It is, for me at least, a good argument. Let's focus, then, on condition 6, concerning audience acceptability. More specifically, let's focus on the status of the premises themselves and not worry for now about the premise/conclusion connection.

Govier requires that the premises be "acceptable" to the audience and Goldman requires that the audience "find the asserted premises credible." It is possible to take these words to express the requirement that the audience merely believe the premises of the argument. This view has incorrect results similar to those of views that emphasize persuasiveness. Arguments could turn out to be good because their intended audience unreasonably accepts their premises or bad because their audience unreasonably rejects their premises. The rational merit of the argument is thus ignored.

Requiring that audiences accept the premises of an argument makes some sense if one is assuming that good arguments must be persuasive. This is because one is more apt to persuade an audience by making use of premises they accept. Once one separates the rational merit of an argument from its persuasiveness, it becomes less clear why audiences must accept an argument's premises for it to be good.

Govier clarifies her view by saying, "Acceptability means rational acceptability for the audience; not everything accepted is in this sense acceptable" (1992, p. 407). Goldman does not say anything directly about this issue, but I suspect that he would welcome a revision or interpretation of his account to require that the audience's beliefs about the argument be reasonable.

It's unclear to me whether Govier intends to require that a good argument have premises that are both accepted by and rational for the audience or merely to require that the premises be ones that it is rational for the audience to accept. The difference is that one view requires that the audience actually accept the premises and be rational in so doing, while the other requires only that it be rational for the audience to accept them. The former requirement has the consequence that if an audience irrationally rejects the premises of an argument, then that argument is no good. That seems to me to be a mistake. If I give an argument using premises that are reasonable for you to believe, I don't think my argument should be deemed a failure because you unreasonably reject those premises. To think otherwise, I believe, is to reintroduce factors concerning persuasiveness into argument evaluation.

A more plausible view, then, is that a good argument must contain premises that are reasonable for its audience to believe, whether they actually believe them or not. Thus, as I am understanding it, the audience acceptability account of good arguments is something like this:

> S4. An argument is a good argument if and only if (i) it contains premises that it is reasonable for its audience to believe, and (ii) its premises provide adequate support for its conclusion.[8]

I will leave open for now just what clause (ii) amounts to.

I will turn now to a series of problems and puzzles for the view just described. I think that the points that follow, while not entirely decisive, make it desirable to look for a somewhat different account of what a good argument is.

One set of problems for this theory arises from the fact that different members of an audience may have different bodies of evidence and thus have different propositions justified for them. It is unclear how to apply the theory to such cases. Should we say that the premises must be justified for all audience members, most audience members, some members of the audience? Depending upon just what view is taken, it could have the effect of making good arguments into bad ones if there are lots of ignorant or misinformed potential audiences for them. It's also hard to see how any such specification of a fraction of the audience for whom the premises must be reasonable could yield a remotely plausible requirement.

Another sort of problem for the audience acceptability theory is that many arguments don't have any definite intended audience. There is a range of cases here. Sometimes someone formulates an argument as a way of thinking something out for himself or herself. Perhaps we should say that the arguer is also the audience in this case. But even when an argument isn't formulated just for oneself, there may be no definite intended audience, or the audience may be so diverse that it is clear that no relevant set of premises will be justified for any significant fraction of that audience. For example, when writing for a widely circulated book or periodical, one knows that no set of premises will be acceptable to everyone. Still, one can formulate one's argument and it could be a good one.

The underlying problem here is that the audience acceptability view tries to give each argument (or perhaps each presentation of an argument structure) a unique assignment of value, depending in large part on how it fares for its audience. A more plausible view, I think, is one that relativizes argument goodness to individuals or groups. Thus, an argument may be good for one person or group, but not for another person or group. On this view, there is no such thing as the simple quality of an argument. Instead, there is its merit relative to different individuals. I'll return to this idea in section III.

There is an important respect in which S4, as well as other social accounts discussed in this section, overemphasize social factors in argument evaluation. They fail to address the questions reasonable people actually consider when they evaluate arguments. This discrepancy between what social theories call attention to and what people actually consider can best be brought out by an example in which one evaluates an argument without knowing its intended audience. For example, if I walk into a classroom and see an argument written on the blackboard, I can evaluate it without knowing for whom it was intended. I won't ask, "Are these premises justified for the intended audience?" Instead, I consider the merits of the premises and their connection to the conclusion.

Consider also a case in which you come across an argument in a publication such as the local newspaper. You know that most readers of the paper are not justified in accepting some of the premises, although you also know that the premises are in fact true. Suppose, further, that the premises do support the conclusion and that you hadn't realized previously that these premises do support that conclusion. You'd be forced to say, using the audience acceptability theory, that the argument is no good. It seems clear to me, however, that it would be a mistake simply to leave one's evaluation at that. If you know that the premises are true and that they support the conclusion, then there is surely something good about the argument, even if its intended audience lacks this knowledge.

These last couple of examples show, I believe, that the audience acceptability theory does not capture how we actually go about argument evaluation. It does not capture what we teach our students when we teach them to evaluate arguments. What we do, and teach, is to evaluate the premises and their connection to the conclusion in the light of whatever information we have. We don't worry so much about what others would or should think of the premises of the argument. We worry about what *we* should think of them. I will spell out the details of this idea in the next section.

In thinking about the intuitive appeal of the audience acceptability view, it is helpful to separate questions about the usefulness or value or appropriateness of giving a particular argument in a particular context from the quality of the argument itself. It may be that principles such as S4 and Goldman's norms correctly state the conditions under which it is appropriate to give an argument. It may even be that we sometimes use the phrase "good argument" to describe arguments satisfying these conditions. However, they don't get at the fundamental notion of a good argument.

Rational Persuasiveness

Anthony Blair and Ralph Johnson (1987) propose a variation on the audience acceptability account of good arguments that meets some of the objections raised in the previous subsection. Their account draws on some elements of the persuasiveness account, some elements of the audience acceptability account, and adds some factors concerning rationality.

Blair and Johnson begin with the observations that "argument is dialectical" and that its purpose is "to get [another] . . . person to accept as true some proposition which he or she does not currently accept" (1987, p. 48). However, they realize that merely requiring that an argument be persuasive to be good would lead to unacceptable results similar to those described previously. Specifically, they assume that a simple persuasiveness account would require of the premises of a good argument only that they be accepted by its audience. They reject the "relativistic implication . . . that any proposition whatever that is accepted by an audience . . . should be regarded as thereby worthy of acceptance" (p. 49).

To avoid the objectionable implication just described, Blair and Johnson suggest instead that a good argument must be persuasive to a "community of interlocutors who . . . exhibit certain traits of reasonableness" (p. 50). Among the traits they mention are being knowledgeable about the topic of the argument, reflective, open to new ideas, and dialectically astute. Blair and Johnson go on:

> In general, then, we are proposing that a premise in an argument is acceptable without defense just in case a person following the methods and embodying the traits of the pertinent community of ideal interlocutors would fail to raise a question or doubt about it. (Blair and Johnson, 1987, p. 53)

They also require that the premise/conclusion connection of the argument meet some dialectical conditions determined by the attitudes of model interlocutors. Among the conditions included here are that the premises provide sufficient support for the conclusion by properly dealing with the sorts of objections that ideal interlocutors might raise.

Blair and Johnson's account suffers from a significant unclarity. (Goldman [1994] makes a similar point) We have little idea what model interlocutors are supposed to know about a topic. To see the problem, consider first an argument about a relatively private matter. Suppose I give an argument to my wife about where it would be best for us to go to dinner tonight. Are we to assume that model interlocutors would know about our food preferences? We might think they wouldn't, on the grounds that this is not generally known in our community. If this is right, then a perfectly good argument would be ruled no good by this theory. If, on the other hand, the model interlocutors do know our food preferences, it is difficult to see just what limits we are to place on what they know. Perhaps they know where it would be best for us to eat, thereby being in a position to reject any argument with a false conclusion. Another possibility is that they know approximately what we know. Blair and Johnson provide no guidance on this. This makes it impossible to determine what implications their theory has for many arguments.

Similar problems arise with respect to arguments about more widely discussed topics. Experts, when they argue among themselves, may give arguments containing premises of which the general public is ignorant. Would model interlocutors know of this specialized information? If so, then perhaps the experts can give good arguments. But then nonexperts can give the same arguments, and they'd count as good arguments, even if the nonexperts lack the expertise to know the premises. If, on the other hand, model interlocutors lack specialized information, then the experts' arguments automatically turn out to be no good. Neither alternative is acceptable.[9]

Even if Blair and Johnson could adequately explain what model interlocutors are supposed to know, I believe that their theory would still be open to a serious objection. I will make this point briefly. I believe that the notion of a model interlocutor is best understood in terms of an independent notion of a good argument. That is, a model interlocutor is a person who accepts all and only good arguments. I don't believe that we have any independent grasp of the notion of a model interlocutor. As a result, their theory suffers from a kind of circularity.[10]

Finally, I think that Blair and Johnson overemphasize the significance of persuasiveness in argument evaluation. Consider again what you would tell a student who is about to evaluate an argument. You would not tell the student to reject an argument whose premises the student knows to be true because a "model interlocutor" would raise a doubt about those premises. If those premises, which the student knows, adequately support the conclusion, surely you'd tell the student to accept the argument, no matter what "model interlocutors" would say about the premises. The reason you would tell students to accept such arguments is that they make belief in their conclusions reasonable for the student. The argument thus helps the student form a reasonable belief. What is crucial to the student is not whether the argument would persuade some obscure model interlocutors, but whether it gives the student good reason to believe its conclusion.

The underlying point here is that Blair and Johnson's account is, in a certain respect, at odds with their own view about the purpose of argument. As noted, they say that the purpose of argument is "to get [another] . . . person to accept as true some proposition which he or she does not currently accept" (Blair and Johnson, 1987, p. 48). Although this may be one purpose of giving an argument, I think it is not the fundamental one and surely is not the one that is the focus of the typical critical thinking or philosophy course. That other purpose, as Jack Meiland (1989) has argued, is to aid in inquiry, to help us figure out what to believe. Meiland notes that if persuasion really is the goal, then the contention that good arguments must satisfy some rational standards is "gratuitous" (1989, p. 194). If the purpose is persuasion, then good arguments are the ones that persuade. Period.

Once you see arguments as instruments of inquiry—that is, as a means of figuring out what it is reasonable to believe—a different account of what a good argument is emerges. I will begin to develop that account in section III.

III

In this section I will develop an epistemological conception of good arguments. The general idea behind this view is that a good argument is in certain important ways analogous to a justified belief. Epistemic justification is a relation between an individual and a proposition. The relation obtains when the person's evidence supports the proposition.[11] The fundamental contention of the epistemic account of good arguments is that a good argument is one that provides good reasons for its conclusion, one that makes belief in its conclusion justified. Thus, a good argument is, roughly, one with premises that are justified and with a justified premise/conclusion connection.

Because of differences in evidence, a proposition may be justified for one person but not another and may be justified for one person at one time but not at another time. Similarly, according to the epistemic account of good arguments, being a good argument is a relation between a person and an argument. What is a good argument for, or relative to, one person may fail to be a good argument for, or relative to, another person. Furthermore, an argument may be a good argument for a person at one time but fail to be a good argument for that person at another time. What determines the status of an argument for a person is largely the evidence the person has at the time. I will discuss this relativistic implication of the epistemic theory later in this section.

As a first attempt to formulate the epistemic view precisely, we might propose the following:

E1. An argument is a good argument for *S* if and only if (i) *S* is justified in believing the conjunction of all the premises of the argument and (ii) the argument is valid.

Notice that E1 requires that the conjunction of all the premises be justified, not just that the premises be individually justified. Whether this makes any difference depends upon whether a conjunction rule for justified belief is correct. If it is, then the premises will be jointly justified whenever they are individually justified. But if the rule is not correct, then there may be cases in which the premises are individually justified for someone but their conjunction is not. Clearly, in that case the argument is not a good one. An argument's conclusion is justified by its premises only if those premises are jointly justified.[12] Notice also that E1 does not require that a person actually believe the conjunction of the premises of an argument that is good for him or her, or even that the person believe the premises individually. It requires only that the conjunction be justified.

In the discussion in section I of logical accounts of good arguments, I argued that to demand validity of an argument for it to be good is to demand too much. One of the main issues in working out the details of an epistemological account of good arguments therefore focuses on how to revise clause (ii) of E1. The obvious response to the problem with the deductive requirement is to weaken the requirement to an inductive one. Thus, we might propose the following:

> E2. An argument is a good argument for *S* if and only if (i) *S* is justified in believing the conjunction of all the premises of the argument and (ii) the argument is either valid or cogent.

E2 is open to objections as well. The most serious problem with E2 is that it overlooks the role of background knowledge in the evaluation of cogent arguments. A cogent argument can fail to be a good argument for a person even if the person knows that its premises are true. This is because the argument can be defeated by background evidence. Reconsider Argument 2:

Argument 2
(1) Almost all professional basketball players are over six feet tall.
(2) The guest speaker is a professional basketball player.
(3) The guest speaker is over six feet tall.

While in some contexts this may be a good argument, consider its merits in a situation in which I know that the title of the speaker's lecture is "Even Short People Can Make It in the NBA: My Personal Story." Somehow, knowing this turns Argument 2 into a bad argument for me. It defeats the argument. This possibility must be acknowledged by our account of good arguments.

We can state conditions under which one's background evidence defeats a cogent argument for a person. This occurs when the conjunction of that evidence and the premises of the argument does not provide good reason for the conclusion. More precisely, when an argument is cogent, it is defeated for a person when the argument formed by adding the person's relevant background evidence to the premises of the argument, and leaving the conclusion unchanged, results in an argument that is not cogent.

We thus should modify E2 by adding the requirement that the argument is undefeated for *S*.

> E3. An argument is a good argument for *S* if and only if (i) *S* is justified in believing the conjunction of all the premises of the argument, (ii) the argument is either valid or cogent, and (iii) the argument is undefeated for *S*.

A central question about E3 concerns the premise/conclusion connection. Validity and cogency are objective relations that may or may not hold between a set of premises and a conclusion. They can hold even when an individual is completely ignorant of this fact. This leads to a problem for E3, best seen by consideration of an example. Suppose a beginning logic student is considering an argument whose premises he knows to be true. Suppose that the argument is valid, although this is something far beyond the student's understanding. The derivation, we may suppose, is complex. Indeed, it could be so complex as to be beyond even sophisticated logicians. It is clear that in these circumstances the argument is not a good argument for the student; it doesn't make belief in its conclusion reasonable for him. Yet, the conditions of E3 are apparently satisfied. A similar point arises for cogent arguments. If cogency is an objective probabilistic relation, arguments can be cogent without a person's having any reason to think that they are.

These considerations make it clear that the premise/conclusion connection in good arguments must satisfy some epistemological condition. There are at least two ways in which one might attempt to spell this out. One possibility appeals to a notion of an "immediate consequence." According to this idea, one proposition can be an immediate consequence of another *for a person.* Thus, for an experienced logician who is simply able to "see" logical connections others can't, the conclusion of an argument might be an immediate consequence of the conjunction of its premises. That same conclusion might not be an immediate consequence of the conjunction of those premises for a novice. A plausible account, making use of this notion, seems possible to me.

Another possibility makes use of meta-level considerations. It holds that an argument is good for a person only if the person is justified in believing that the argument is valid or cogent. We should be cautious in formulating this condition. To require explicit belief that the connection is suitable is to overintellectualize matters. Ordinary reasoners may not have clearly articulated conceptions of validity or cogency. They may at best have some relatively vague notion of good reason, support, or the like. What's required, I think, is justification for thinking that this relation obtains.

I won't attempt to develop either of these accounts of the premise/conclusion connection in more detail here. Nor will I attempt to argue for the preferability of one over the other. I will assume that some such view can be worked out and I will say that when the premises and the conclusion of an argument have the relation in question, they are "properly connected."

Thus, the revised account is as follows:

E4. An argument is a good argument for person *S* if and only if (i) *S* is justified in believing the conjunction of all the premises of the argument, (ii) *S* is justified in believing that the premises are "properly connected" to the conclusion, and (iii) the argument is not defeated for *S*.

The use of the phrase "properly connected" in clause (ii) of E4 obviously masks some perplexing issues not yet mentioned. One of them has to do with enthymemes. As noted earlier, on my view, arguments with missing premises are typically no good. It is only when their missing premises are stated that they become good. Lots of arguments that we are inclined regularly to accept are no good on my account. That's because they are enthymemes. If one wishes to modify the account of "proper connection" to allow that the premises and conclusions of such arguments can be properly connected, I won't object strenuously. However, I think it is simpler to say that such arguments are not, as stated, good, but that they are incomplete versions of good arguments. In fact, it seems to me, that's exactly what they are.[13]

Social Factors and Good Arguments

One crucial difference between the epistemological account defended in this section and the social accounts discussed in the previous section is that the latter theories attempted to arrive at a unique evaluation of each argument. In contrast, E4 assigns an evaluation of an argument relative to each person, that evaluation depending upon the evidence of the person. While the epistemological account does not explicitly build social factors into the conditions of a good argument, it does provide a way to express many of the considerations important to social theorists.

It is plausible to think that, often, when a person defends an argument, the person thinks that it is a good argument for those to whom it is presented. Of course, given differences in the evidence of different members of the audience, it may not be possible to give an argument that is good for all of one's audience. When evaluating the argument relative to its audience, one will consider the merits of the premises, the status of the premise/conclusion connection, and the effects of background evidence for the audience. This will require consideration of many factors emphasized by social theorists. One can also imagine a model interlocutor, if one likes, and attempt to determine the status of the argument relative to such an individual. What the epistemic theory implies is that there is no such thing as *the* real status of the argument. It is not the case that its merits relative to the audience, the speaker, or a model interlocutor somehow identifies its real merit. It just is a good argument, or a bad argument, for various individuals.

I believe that the strength of the epistemic account of good arguments can best be appreciated by thinking about the reasons for which we propose, and evaluate, arguments. There are, of course, many reasons. Sometimes we try to persuade others, sometimes we try to show off our intellectual talents, sometimes we argue for a living, and sometimes we attempt to get at the truth. As noted, to the extent that an argument is designed to persuade, it is good to the extent that it is persuasive (perhaps to those it is designed to persuade). Considerations concerning rationality have no necessary connection with an argument's persuasiveness.

Another central reason we give and think about arguments is to share ideas and enter into a collective search for the truth. (See Meiland 1989 for further discussion.) One reason people give arguments is that they think the arguments may provide good reason to believe a conclusion of some general interest. Sharing that argument with others interested in the truth value of the conclusion is of some value. We can learn from their responses. Arguments are thus part of a collective search for the truth.

Although the idea that arguments serve as instruments in a search for the truth is one that defenders of social theories are apt to accept, emphasizing this role of arguments leads to the epistemic account of good arguments. Thus, given this goal, there is nothing wrong with presenting an argument whose premises one has doubt about or whose conclusion one disbelieves. The point of giving such an argument can be to reflect on it, perhaps with the result that one's beliefs will change. One hasn't violated any linguistic convention by presenting an argument one doesn't believe to be a good argument. Contrary to what Blair and Johnson say, the point of giving an argument need not be to persuade—even rationally persuade—anyone.[14]

The epistemic account of good arguments also fits well with our typical aims when we evaluate arguments. It sometimes seems as if people analyze arguments to decide whether the argument would, or should, persuade an "opponent" or to see if the author of the argument has committed some particular error. Some texts seem to emphasize these interpersonal aims. However, one can also approach arguments with the question, "What should I believe now?" Here, the focus is on the epistemic merit of the argument for oneself. Of course, one can also ask whether the argument has merit for others, though that question is of only marginal interest in one's own pursuit of the truth.

Problems for the Epistemic Account

Justified Premises, Good Arguments, and Relativism

As noted, epistemological accounts of good arguments make the status of an argument relative to an individual. Although there are many doctrines that go by the name of "relativism" that I find quite unacceptable, I don't believe that the sort of relativism introduced by an epistemological account of good arguments is in any way objectionable.

While some philosophers may welcome relativism in this domain, others oppose it. Consider the following passage from a paper by Harvey Siegel:

> This kind of dispute raises the spectre of relativism. For it suggests that what counts as a reason is relative to persons, frameworks or perspectives: telescopic observation provided good reason for Galileo but not his opponents; the writings of Aristotle provided good reason for his opponents but not for Galileo. Thus a candidate reason's status as a (good) reason depends on who is doing the judging.
>
> Such a relativism of reasons is incompatible with education for critical thinking. In such education our aim is (in part) to help students to develop the ability to evaluate arguments and the probative force which putative reasons have, and to encourage students to believe and act on the basis of reasons—to be *appropriately moved by reasons.* This presupposes that reasons have probative force, and that it is possible to misevaluate reasons. . . . If reasons are relative, then we cannot say that one assessment of an argument is better than another; in particular, we cannot legitimately think that our argument assessment rules and criteria

> are superior to our students' untutored rules and criteria (or denial of such). Thus there would be no cogent rationale for teaching students how to assess reasons and arguments; no motivation for the critical thinking course. (Siegel 1989, pp. 133-134)

The relativism Siegel has in mind is indeed something to avoid. It may well have the bleak implications he mentions. However, the relativism of good arguments endorsed here has no such implications. Consider first the relativism of justified belief. If two people have different evidence concerning some statement, it may well be that one of them is entirely reasonable (or justified) in believing the statement and the other not justified in believing it. These can be objective facts about their epistemic situation. The one who is not justified in believing the statement could mistakenly believe that his evidence does support it and that he is justified in believing it. The relativism here is simply a consequence of the fact that different people can be in different epistemic situations. It does not imply that any belief is just as well justified as any other. It does not imply that your belief is justified if you think it is. It is not something to be feared.

The relativism implied by an epistemological account of good arguments is similarly acceptable. It does not imply that any evaluation of an argument is just as good as any other. It does not imply that an argument is a good one for you simply because you think it is. Suppose you and I are evaluating an argument that we both know to be valid. You know that the premises are true, and I have no reason to believe that they are true. You will come to the conclusion that the argument is a good one, and I will come to the conclusion that it isn't. The epistemic account has the implication that the conclusions we reach are correct. The argument *is* a good one for you, but *is not* a good one for me. This strikes me as exactly the right result. The argument does provide you, but not me, with good reason to believe its conclusion. These are objective facts about us and the argument. Acknowledging that whether an argument is a good one is relative to a person's evidence does not imply the sort of mindless relativism and subjectivism so widely abhorred by philosophy instructors and so commonly endorsed by their students.

Apart from any general considerations about relativism, there are good reasons to think that the quality of an argument can vary from one person to another. One reason is the fact that the epistemic merit of an argument's premises can vary from one individual to another. Furthermore, if there are good nondeductive arguments, then it is (almost) inevitable that we make argument goodness relative to individuals. This is because background knowledge must play some role in the evaluation of such arguments, and such knowledge obviously varies from one person to another. Consider a simple example. Suppose I am teaching a class with one hundred students equally divided among freshmen, sophomores, juniors, and seniors. I know that eighty-five of the students in the class have grades of C or better and that the fifteen students with grades below C are all freshmen. My teaching assistant and I see one of the students in the class as we are walking across campus. Now, suppose I formulate the following simple argument:

Argument 7
(1) Most of the students in my class have a grade of C or better.
(2) That person is a student in my class.
(3) That person has a grade of C or better in my class.

On my view, this is a good argument *for me*. I'm justified in believing the premises, I know that they are properly connected to the conclusion, and the argument isn't defeated for me. Now, suppose my TA knows that the student we see is a freshman and that most of the freshmen have lower grades. This additional information defeats the argument for her. Thus, on my view, Argument 7 is not a good argument for her.

To avoid this relativistic conclusion, one must say that Argument 7 is either simply a good argument or simply a bad argument. Neither answer is plausible. Suppose we say that it is a good argument. Presumably, my TA could know this. For her to regard this as a good argument, yet reasonably reject its conclusion, is absurd. Suppose we say that it is a bad argument. Then my contention that it is a good argument is mistaken. Yet surely I am being reasonable in accepting its conclusion on the basis of this argument. Furthermore, on what basis could we decide that Argument 7 is a bad argument? Is it that, in fact, its conclusion is false? This seems to make the notion of good nondeductive argument useless. A cogent argument is then good if and only if its conclusion is true. If we can only correctly judge that the argument is good when we correctly judge that the conclusion is true, there is little point in evaluating the argument itself. We can confine our discussion to the truth value of the conclusion.

I conclude that the relativism introduced by the epistemic account is far from a defect. It is, in fact, a required feature of any adequate account of good arguments.

Circular Arguments

Suppose you come across the following argument:

Argument 8
(1) George Washington was the first president of the United States.
(2) George Washington was the first president of the United States.

This doesn't look like a very good argument. Yet it is likely to satisfy the conditions of E4 for you. Its premise is justified, the connection is proper (since it's obviously a valid argument), and it is undefeated. This appears to be a counterexample to E4.

Defenders of epistemic accounts of good arguments have two basic lines of reply to this objection. The first possibility is to accept the result that Argument 8 is a good argument. They could add that it is a *pointless* argument, since it does not provide reason to believe anything new. They can correctly say that it's not a defective argument either. It's not as if you shouldn't believe its conclusion if its premise is justified. Moreover, it is noteworthy that many of the allegedly circular arguments we encounter do come out to be bad arguments according to E4. This is because, in the typical case of a troublesome circular argument, the premise (as well as the conclusion) is an unjustified and highly controversial claim. Such arguments will be bad arguments according to E4.

A second possible response is to revise E4. As a first step, defenders of epistemic accounts of good arguments might say that the premises and conclusion of a good argument are not properly connected when the conclusion is identical with one of the premises. They might go on to add something such as that the person be justified in believing the premises "independently" of his or her justification for believing the conclusion. If this notion of independent justification can be made sufficiently clear, this modification of E4 may prove to be a good one.

Since I generally find the charge of circularity quite obscure, I regard the first of these two responses adequate. That is, I am willing to admit that some trivial arguments with justified premises are good, but pointless, arguments, just as some trivial beliefs are justified but pointless. However, I would welcome a well-worked-out version of the second response.

Argument Evaluation Is Impersonal

We sometimes evaluate arguments in a way that seemingly implies that there is an impersonal nonrelative standard of goodness. Consider, for example, philosophical discussions of skepticism or the existence of God. In their discussions of the Ontological Argument (or particular versions of it), philosophers don't discuss whether the argument is good relative to one person or another. They simply discuss whether the argument is a good one. An adequate defense of the relativized epistemic account should explain the role of such talk.

I believe that this seemingly impersonal notion of a good argument can be explained adequately within the framework of the epistemic account developed here. It is probably best to think of these evaluations of arguments as similar to seemingly impersonal epistemic evaluations such as this:

> A. It is not reasonable to believe that astrological forecasts are accurate.

I've said above that the fundamental notion of rational (or justified) belief is individually relative. Yet, people do make seemingly impersonal belief statements such as the one expressed in A.

The existence of this seemingly impersonal notion of rational belief does not undermine the idea that the fundamental notion of rational belief is individually relative. This is because A is best understood in terms of that individually relative notion. Thus, what people use A to express is almost surely something along the lines of the following:

> A′. It would not be reasonable for a person having commonly held evidence about astrology to believe that astrological forecasts are accurate.

Of course, in different contexts the kind of evidence that determines the truth value of the impersonal epistemic judgment may be different. In some contexts, the relevant evidence may be that of experts about the topic in question. In other contexts it may be the model inquirers of whom Blair and Johnson speak. There is, I suspect, no limit to the sort of person one might have in mind here. What's crucial to my purpose in this chapter is the claim that seemingly impersonal statements such as A are disguised personal statements such as A′. It is not part of my task here to provide any systematic formula for translating the impersonal statements into personal ones.

I think that something similar is true of impersonal assessments of the merits of arguments. The seemingly impersonal and nonrelative statement that an argument is good is best taken to be about its status relative to some particular sort of person or body of evidence. When we say that, for example, a particular argument concerning skepticism or the existence of God is a good one, I suspect that what we are trying to convey is that the argument is good relative to some pertinent sort of person—in this case, probably a well-informed philosopher. Again, there is nearly limitless variation in the possibility for the intended person. If this is correct, these impersonal judgments are best understood in terms of personal judgments analyzed in the way defended above. As a result, they do not undermine the epistemic analysis.

Finally, it seems to me that these impersonal epistemic judgments are extraordinarily vague. Consider again statement A. Suppose a considerable number of "average" people have evidence that includes testimonial support for the accuracy of astrological predictions. Perhaps, as a result of the selectivity of their memories, they seem to remember quite a few accurate forecasts they've read and relatively few inaccurate forecasts. Assume that many of these people are ignorant of the widespread, though not universal, dismissal of astrology among well-regarded scientists. As a result, the evidence immediately available to them offers some endorsement of astrology. Does this make A false? Or suppose that some experts have concealed evidence of the accuracy of astrology. Would that make A false? I confess that I don't know.

I find equally puzzling most impersonal assessments of arguments. For example, in papers, books, and chapters with titles such as "The Rationality of Belief in God," one encounters discussion of complex arguments never previously (or subsequently) considered by the vast majority of people. When some such argument is found to be a good argument, I'm not at all sure what implication the result could have concerning the rationality of the typical person's belief in the existence of God. Whatever bearing these arguments have on the rational merit of ordinary beliefs, I think it is best to regard the judgments made in such cases as judgments about whether the argument is good for the person making the judgment, for well-informed philosophers, or some other sort of person. Once again, then, I don't think that the existence of seemingly impersonal evaluations of arguments undermines the idea that our fundamental notion of argument evaluation is an individually relative epistemic one.

I conclude that E4 can be adequately defended from the three objections raised here. No doubt there are additional objections to consider and additional details to spell out. Nevertheless, I think that the epistemic account of good arguments provides an explanation of the core sense of the phrase "good argument" as it is used in standard contexts. While there may also be logical and social senses of "good argument," I believe that the central sense of the term is epistemic.[15]

Notes

1. One might agree that Argument 1 is invalid, but contend that it is still a good argument. Presumably, it would be a good argument because its unstated premise, (2) in Argument 1a, has some favorable status. However, it is extraordinarily difficult to say what that favorable status is. As far as I can tell, nothing worthwhile is lost by saying that Argument 1 is simply no good, although it is an incomplete version of Argument 1a, which is good.

2. That is, we can restate arguments in English patterns that easily and naturally translate into patterns valid in standard formal systems.

3. I take up this topic in Feldman (forthcoming). Trudy Govier (1992, pp. 393-409) discusses a similar proposal. She attributes the proposal to David Hitchcock in "Methodological Deductivism," presented at the 1986 Eastern Division Meeting of the American Philosophical Association.

4. Strong enough to have induced James Cain and Scott Brophy to say to me that it (or others like it) are not cogent.

5. Perhaps it is possible that she voted for a write-in candidate. If you want to consider that possibility, then construct a more complex set of arguments with this possibility as a third option in the first premise. The next two premises would then eliminate two of the options and conclude that the third is true. There would be three such arguments. My comments about them would be exactly analogous to my comments about the two arguments presented here.

6. A similar point can also be made with respect to cogent arguments. One can construct pairs of cogent arguments of which exactly one must have true premises though it is not known which it is. Such arguments do not justify belief in their conclusions any more than the arguments just considered do. But one of them would be a good argument, according to logical accounts.

7. A key feature of Govier's view is that good arguments go beyond valid and inductively cogent ones. She contends that there are other patterns of good argument. Clauses (ii) and (iii) are intended to be sufficiently inclusive to count such arguments as good. I will set this issue aside for now.

8. A condition requiring that the audience actually believe the premises could be added to S4 without substantially altering the points that follow.

9. It is not clear which alternative Blair and Johnson would opt for. They say that in some cases, "the community [of model interlocutors] will consist of model experts" (Blair and Johnson 1987, pp. 52-53), but in other cases "the community of model interlocutors will consist of model 'ordinary people'" (p. 52). It is not clear to me what determines the character of the model interlocutors in any particular case.

10. My point here is analogous to the one raised by Socrates about the definition of piety in the *Euthyphro*. I realize that I have not established that there is no independent means of understanding what a model interlocutor is.

11. This is my own view about the nature of epistemic justification. It is defended in Feldman and Conee (1985). Much of what's said in the rest of this chapter is consistent with other views about epistemic justification.

12. I assume here that all the premises are essential to the argument.

13. There are additional issues concerning proper connections. Trudy Govier and others have argued that there are good arguments that are neither valid nor cogent, at least on any standard reading of "cogent." For defense of this view, see Govier (1987, ch. 3).

14. This is not to say that one can't also believe that the arguments one gives are sound or have the intention of persuading one's audience. The point here is just that one needn't have that goal.

15. I am grateful to Fred Schmitt for extremely helpful comments on an earlier draft of this chapter.

9

Accuracy in Journalism: An Economic Approach

James C. Cox and Alvin I. Goldman

THE CONCEPTION OF SOCIAL EPISTEMOLOGY

This chapter is part of a larger project to define and develop a certain nontraditional sector of epistemology—a sector dubbed "social epistemology." As traditionally pursued by philosophers, epistemology is the attempt to study, analyze, or guide the efforts of isolated cognizers, each of whom has the task of deciding, without fundamental dependence on others, what to believe about the world. The individualistic tradition in epistemology received its initial impetus from Descartes, who identified self-knowledge as the starting point of all knowledge. But even epistemologists who reject Descartes's starting point have typically agreed with Descartes in viewing epistemology as the theory of isolated, independent cognizers, each pursuing truth on the basis of evidence available to him or her as an individual. This individualistic conception does not wholly exclude other cognitive agents. The target agent can legitimately consider evidence gleaned from the utterances or speech acts of other people. Nonetheless, the perspective of traditional epistemology is emphatically individualistic: it studies almost exclusively the sorts of reasoning procedures available to the individual agent, with the aim of selecting the best of these procedures.

How might social epistemology differ from traditional, individual epistemology? One of the present authors (Goldman 1987b, also see 1986, 1987a, 1991a, 1994) has proposed the following conception of social epistemology. In addition to the reasoning and other psychological processes that influence agents in deciding what to believe, there are various group processes and institutional arrangements that also influence belief formation. The proper domain of social epistemology, then, is the social processes and institutional provisions that standardly affect belief formation. Furthermore, just as it is widely held that individual epistemology should evaluate candidate reasoning procedures in terms of their tendency to lead reasoners to *true* rather than *false* beliefs, similarly social epistemology should evaluate various social processes and institutional arrangements in terms of their promotion of true rather than false beliefs. With the possible exception of pure science, there may not be any existing social processes or practices that are *exclusively* dedicated to the pursuit of truth, independent of other types of social values. But whatever the relative importance of true belief as compared with other kinds of social values, and whatever weight is placed on true belief by our current institutions, the distinctive role of social *epistemology* (as contrasted with social theory generally) is the assessment of the truth-conducive properties of sundry social practices. The pursuit of truth is not the be-all or end-all of social life, but it is the special proprietary interest of social epistemology.

SOME EXAMPLES

Some simple examples of social epistemology may help put some flesh on this rather abstract skeleton. As a first example, consider true or false judgments that are the product of group decision-making. For instance, committees can judge (or try to judge) what is the most efficient plan for achieving a specified institutional end. Or they can judge which of various candidates would turn in the best performance on a specified job, or in a certain course of study (e.g., a doctoral program). In some of these cases it may be problematic whether judgments have definite truth values. So consider a case where this is relatively unproblematic: weather prediction. A prediction today that it will ran in Tucson tomorrow has a definite truth value, although its truth will not be known with certainty until tomorrow. We ignore here borderline cases such as mist, and also the problem of whether there is a truth value *today* about tomorrow's weather. At least we can say, once tomorrow has gone, that today's prediction of rain either came out true or came out false. Admittedly, many weather predictions nowadays are made with probabilistic qualifiers, e.g., "There is a 20 percent chance of rain tomorrow." It is problematic whether such predictions can turn out either true or false. Assume, then, that weather predictions are made categorically, e.g., "It will rain tomorrow," or, "The high tomorrow will be in the mid-80s [i.e., between 83 and 87])." Such predictions certainly qualify as true or false. Now, most weather forecasting is done by single weather forecasters. But consider a television station that assembles a team of weather experts and assigns them the task of collectively producing a local weather forecast. Supposing that they have different degrees of competence or expertise, ascertainable by looking at their individual past track records, how should the opinions of these several experts be pooled or weighted to arrive at the most accurate group judgment? This is one sort of problem in social epistemology.

This problem, in fact, is quite tractable. As Shapley and Grofman (1984) show, if individual judgments are mutually independent, and if each of the two choices (in our case, rain or nonrain) is a priori equally likely, then the best way to maximize the probability of the team's making an accurate prediction is to assign certain weights to each expert as a function of his or her individual competence. In other words, the most truth-conducive scheme is not majority rule with equal weights, nor dictatorial rule by the most competent expert (if a single forecaster has the highest competence), but a rule that assigns weights w_i in proportion to $\log(p_i/(1 - p_i))$, where p_i represents the probability that member i individually makes a true prediction. Suppose, for example, that there is a five-member team whose individual probabilities of correctness are: .9, .9, .6, .6, and .6, respectively. Then one way of assigning weights in conformity with this rule is: .392, .392, .072, .072, and .072. Assigning these weights and determining a group judgment by weighted voting would then generate a group competence (expected truthfulness) of .927. This is higher than the individual competence of any single member who might be chosen as dictator, but also higher than unweighted majority rule, which has a group probability of only .877. Thus, adoption of this sort of group judgmental practice might be a recommendation of social epistemology. (Its preferability, however, depends on the feasibility of determining accurately the individual competences of all members.)

A second set of examples will be drawn from judicial practices. Juries are prime examples of committees assigned the task of arriving at a group judgment, and presumably a principal desideratum of jury judgments is accuracy, e.g., judging an accused man to be guilty if and only if he is truly (genuinely) guilty of the charge(s) in question. Accuracy or truth is not the only desideratum of trial proceedings, but it is an important one and the one that interests social epistemology. Now, there are many institutional aspects of trial proceedings that seem to be dedicated, at least in part, to obtaining accurate verdicts. Among these are evidenciary rules governing the admission or exclusion of evidence. The rationale for these rules is stated in Rule 102 of the Federal Rules of Evidence, which explicitly mentions the goal of truth: "These rules shall be construed to secure fairness in administration, elimination of unjustifiable expense and delay, and promotion of growth and development of the law of evidence *to the end that the truth may be ascertained* and proceedings justly determined" (emphasis added). One of the evidenciary rules, Rule 403, states in part: "evidence may be excluded if its probative value is substantially outweighed by the danger of unfair prejudice, confusion of the issues, or misleading the jury." If this rule is indeed rationalized by reference to the aim of truth (see Goldman 1991a), then it is appropriate for social epistemology to inquire whether such a rule actually promotes accuracy just as well as competing rules that might be substituted in its place. This is an example of how social epistemology is concerned with institutional provisions that bear on truth acquisition. Other such examples in the law might include rules for jury selection, the privileged attorney-client relationship and advocacy responsibilities, and so forth.

A third example of the domain of social epistemology concerns the topic of argumentation. Goldman (1994) defends the view that social argumentation is governed by tacit rules that are dedicated to the goal of advancing true belief, either for the arguers themselves or for their audience. Part of social epistemology is the elucidation of these rules and the examination of them to see whether they are indeed truth conducive. Assuming that they are so conducive, another recommended task for social epistemology is to explore the variables that influence the extent and quality of argumentation, i.e., the frequency or infrequency with which serious disputation takes place in formal or informal contexts, and the quality of such argumentation, i.e., the degree to which the rules of good argumentation are actually instantiated.

This last task is one to which social scientific models, e.g., rational choice models, can make an important contribution. An example of this is the work of Michael MacKuen (1990), who provides a game-theoretic analysis of decisions to engage in face-to-face political argumentation. The paradigmatic situation MacKuen examines is that of a citizen encountering an acquaintance in an elevator during an election campaign. Will our first citizen initiate a political conversation, or will he be deterred by recalling that the last time he made a political comment his interlocutor called his ideas "foolish" and smugly wandered down the hall? The incidence and extent of political interaction—especially argumentation with people of differing opinions—is widely regarded as significant for democracy. But MacKuen's analysis suggests that the strategy of CLAMMING (avoiding political argumentation) is much more likely to be chosen than TALKING (arguing), so MacKuen is highly pessimistic about the prospects of cross-factional political debate. To the extent that cross-factional argumentation is helpful for truth acquisition, a low incidence of such argumentation is (or would be) a matter of concern to social epistemology. And the variables that influence this incidence should also be of concern to social epistemology, from both a theoretical and a policy perspective.

JOURNALISM AND SOCIAL EPISTEMOLOGY

In this chapter we focus on journalism as a special target of social epistemological study. Traditional epistemology would most naturally address journalism solely from the vantage point of the reader: what inferences can or should a reader make from stories in a newspaper? Our perspective will be somewhat different. We shall ask about the variables that affect the truthfulness or accuracy of stories that get printed in newspapers (or presented on television). We recognize, of course, that readers need not believe everything they read or see, but we shall assume that the default procedure, at least, is to believe what one reads (or sees). Hence, people will suffer from erroneous belief, or misinformation, if newspapers in fact present falsehoods (or half-truths). What are the factors, then, that influence the truth value of what is printed in newspapers?

Some other preliminary comments are in order. It goes without saying that newspapers print much that does not fall in the category of "news," and that what motivates readers is not exclusively an interest in truth. Readers often read for entertainment, where the "facts" are immaterial. For purposes of present discussion, however, we restrict attention to news, and to truth-related interests. We do not deny the existence of non-cognitive interests, but we also believe that readers are substantially and sincerely interested in truth. They expect the sports pages to report correctly the outcomes of games, and to provide accurate statistics. They want coverage of crime in their neighborhood to be accurate, and they expect announcements of the times and locations of movies and cultural events to reflect the facts. They would be quite unhappy with faulty stock market reports, and similarly for other news of business developments. Even when it comes to official corruption or the sexual escapades of political figures, they are not interested in sheer fantasy. Though they may prefer titillating stories to less colorful items, they would not be (so) interested if the stories were known to be spun out of whole cloth. There may be some kinds of things that readers prefer not to know about, but they read newspapers in large part with the hope of learning selected facts. Notice that our claim of a substantial interest in truth is not essential to social epistemology. Social epistemology could conduct an inquiry into the factors affecting the accuracy or objectivity of journalism even if readers themselves had little or no concern for truth. But in this chapter we shall assume that truth acquisition is a major goal of readers.

Admittedly, the concepts of truthfulness and objectivity, especially concerning the news, are concepts very much in dispute. Although it would be impossible to allay all relevant worries about these concepts, some remarks may help defuse some of these worries. At a minimum we can identify where we stand (or at least where the philosopher-author, A.G., stands) on these issues. One set of worries about the concept of truth is abstractly philosophical. Is the concept of truth to be defined or understood independently of the possibility of human verification, or does it depend essentially on verificational possibilities? We take a "realist" position on this issue. The concept of truth allows for the possibility of certain propositions being true—in other terminology, of there being certain "facts"—even if these facts are in principle unknowable or unverifiable by human beings. For example, there may be facts beyond our ken because they concern matters at some distant corner of the universe, spatio-temporally too far removed from human detection during the whole of humankind's sojourn at this corner of the universe. In addition to distinguishing truth from the *possibility* of human detection, it is particularly important to distinguish truth from *actual* human detection. There are presumably many truths that are *unknown* to any human beings. These may include, for example, what particular kinds of fish, if any, are swimming at a particular spot in the ocean depths at a particular time. Such a fact may indeed be unknown to any human, but that doesn't mean that it isn't a truth. It is important to separate the concept of truth from the concept of knowledge because the acknowledged difficulties in settling when people have knowledge should not be allowed to undermine the concept of truth itself. When people disagree, and when evidence conflicts, it is difficult to *tell*, or *know*, where the truth lies. But that does not imply that there is no truth of the matter, however uncertain, or subject to dispute it may be. Of course, not every factual-looking sentence may be the kind of sentence that has a truth value (i.e., truth or falsity). Sentences concerning morals and normative politics are prime examples of sentences often said to lack a truth value. We take no stand on this issue. What we do assume is that many of the matters reported in news stories *do* have truth values, and it is their truth values that we shall be addressing. The full range of truth-valuable sentences need not be settled here.

In point of fact, we are not just interested in the truth values of the sentences actually printed in news stories (or reported on television or radio). Even if all such sentences are true, they may be (seriously) *misleading* in the sense that they lead large segments of the readership or audience to infer *other* statements that are false. To take a simple example, a news story may report: "Yesterday official *O* asserted *p*." If *O* is a highly credible source for most of the readership, they will infer not only that *O* asserted *p* but that *p* is true. Suppose, however, that *p* is false. Since the story does not assert *p*, it does not literally contain anything false. But it does promote a false belief in (much of) its readership, and in that sense is misleading. (In the sense used here, obviously, misleadingness need not be deliberate.) Similarly, an incomplete and/or slanted news story may *distort* the facts not in the sense that it says literally false things but in the sense that it leads readers to draw further conclusions that are false. The accuracy of journalism should be measured not simply by the truth of the sentences it prints, but by the degree of its misleadingness or nonmisleadingness.

Many, perhaps most, academic treatments of journalism take a very skeptical or cynical view of the media's capacity or disposition to depict reality accurately. This is clearly reflected in numerous book titles dealing with the news, e.g., *The News: The Politics of Illusion* (Bennett 1983), *Making News: A Study in the Construction of Reality* (Tuchman 1978), *Inventing Reality: The Politics of the Mass Media* (Parenti 1985), and *The Manufacture of News* (Cohen and Young 1981). A pervasive theme in media analysis is that the media are engaged in "constructing" reality, which strongly intimates that they cannot be "reporting the truth." It is essential, however, to distinguish two senses of reality "construction." In one sense, constructing reality might consist in literal fabrication or invention of news, i.e., the reportage of items that never occurred, or never occurred in the manner described. This sense of construction or fabrication straightforwardly implies falsity. A second sense of "reality construction," however, merely refers to the *selection* or *choice* of events to report from a vast flux of daily occurrences. It refers partly to the fact that media managers have categories they regard as important, newsworthy, or appealing to their audience, and they choose events and design media presentations in conformity with these categories and criteria. This second sense of reality construction, however, does not straightforwardly imply falsity. The selection of bits of reality from a welter of alternatives does not necessarily involve untruths or distortion, unless such selection is misleading in the sense specified earlier. So even if we grant that media managers "construct" reality in the second sense, we need not necessarily despair of truthfulness in the news.

Let us now turn to some of the practices and institutional structures in journalism that invite treatment from social epistemology. It may help to introduce some of this material with the help of an infamous journalistic incident.

> Jimmy is 8 years old and a third-generation heroin addict, a precocious little boy with sandy hair, velvety brown eyes and needle marks freckling the baby-smooth skin of his thin brown arms. . . . His hands are clasped behind his head, fancy running shoes adorn his feet and a striped Izod T-shirt hangs over his thin frame. "Bad, ain't it," he boasts to a reporter visiting recently. "I got me six of these."

So began an article by Janet Cooke on the front page of *The Washington Post* on Sunday, September 28, 1980. (See Goldstein 1985, pp. 215 ff., for details.) The reporter Cooke was promoted from a weekly suburban section to the far more prestigious metropolitan section. Washington Mayor Marion Barry, Jr., ordered police and social service agencies to find the boy. When police threatened to subpoena Cooke in an effort to force her to reveal the names and addresses of her sources, the *Post* supported her in resisting the issuance of the subpoena. Red flags were subsequently hoisted within the *Post* itself, as Cooke seemed to be unacquainted with the neighborhood where Jimmy was supposed to live. Nonetheless, the editors submitted the story for the Pulitzer Prize, which it won the following April. Unfortunately, things started to unravel soon thereafter. It turned out that Cooke had falsified her credentials on her resumé. She said she was an honors graduate of Vassar; in fact, she had dropped out after a year and finished up college at the University of Toledo. After Cooke confessed about this lie, she was interrogated by *Post* editors for several hours and finally admitted that she had fabricated the Jimmy story as well as her resumé. In a survey done three years after the Janet Cooke scandal, the ethics committee of the American Society of Newspaper Editors found it had become a general rule among newspapers that a reporter must share with an editor the identity of a confidential source.

This story conveniently introduces four principal types of agents or actors that are relevant in the analysis of journalism: (1) readers, (2) reporters, (3) editors, and (4) sources. Readers read stories in newspapers to acquire new knowledge or information, i.e., new truths. Their success in this endeavor, however, depends on the stories' they read being true.

However, one of the principal actors in the construction of such stories, viz. reporters, have some incentives for fabrication. Obviously, not all stories are of equal interest to the readership, nor of equal interest, therefore, to editors. Stories that are highly "newsworthy" (whatever exactly that amounts to) are of greater interest to the readership, and are therefore of greater value to reporters, since their production can lead to promotions, higher pay, and even Pulitzer Prizes. Editors also have an interest in publishing highly "newsworthy" stories, but they can also suffer if their newspaper earns a reputation for fabrication or exaggeration. Thus, they have a professional interest in ensuring the accuracy of their reporters' stories.

The fourth type of actor, the source, is purely imaginary in the Janet Cooke incident. But most stories (especially those involving politics) typically involve a source or informant as the reporter's basis of the story. Here too we have two actors with frequently divergent interests. The source may want the public or some other actors on the political scene to believe certain things which in fact are untrue, or only a partial truth. Thus, what he or she tells a reporter has a certain probability of being (wholly or partially) false. In other language, the source may wish to get out a story with a certain "spin" that is favorable to his or her political interests. The reporter, on the other hand, does not wish to publish a story (under his or her byline) that will subsequently be revealed as erroneous or misleading. Yet the reporter may need to cooperate with the source, at least to some extent, if he or she is going to continue to receive stories from that source. Some sources are extremely valuable to a reporter by virtue of their position and "inside" knowledge. Thereby arise some noncoinciding interests between sources and reporters, which affect what sources tell reporters and what stories reporters subsequently write.

AN ECONOMIC APPROACH TO INFORMATION ASYMMETRIES IN JOURNALISM

Much of modern economic theory is concerned with developing models that include information asymmetries. The appeal of this type of model is obvious: it will often be the case that some important kinds of information are inherently private, not public information. Some illustrative examples would be these: the quality of a used car may be known by the prospective seller but not known by the prospective buyer; the productivity of a prospective new employee may be known by the worker but not known by the employer; the risk attitude of one's opponent in a game of strategy may be known by the opponent but not known by oneself; and the limit price of the other party in a wage or price bargaining game may be known by the other party but not known by oneself. It seems natural to explore the possibility that adaptations and/or extensions of economic models of information asymmetries might be applicable to some questions that arise in studying journalism. The present chapter begins that exploration.

There appear to be various information asymmetries in journalism. One type of information asymmetry would seem to be a necessary condition for the very existence of journalism: if journalists cannot credibly claim to know some things that are not common knowledge, then they have nothing to sell. We shall explain that other, more subtle information asymmetries can be important determinants of the truthfulness or accuracy of stories that get reported by journalists.

Two simple models are developed in the next two sections of the chapter. One model analyzes the role that editors might play in establishing accuracy standards in journalism. This model focuses on the implications of readers' not being able to know individual reporters by their reputations for accuracy. In that case, what are the implications of there being low-accuracy and high-accuracy reporters in journalism? Will there be a *pooling equilibrium* in which readers do not know whether they are buying low- or high-accuracy stories? Or will there be a Gresham's Law for journalism in which low-accuracy reporters drive high-accuracy reporters out of the business, with the result that readers are only able to buy low-accuracy stories? Or will there be a *separating equilibrium* in which low-accuracy and high-accuracy reporters self-select into a two-tier journalistic market in which readers can knowingly choose to buy low-accuracy or high-accuracy stories? What role might editors play in this reporter self-selection process? As we shall see in the next section, the answer is that editors can establish editorial standards that make a separating equilibrium feasible.

The second model is concerned with the relationship between sources and reporters. It focuses on the case of a single source and a single reporter. A question of central interest in studying truthfulness in reporting is identifying conditions under which the source can control how the reporter writes the story after the source gives his or her information to the reporter. If the source has no ability to reward or punish the reporter, then the source has no control. Suppose, instead, that the source can reward or punish the reporter by, say, granting or withholding future favors. Then, if the source can observe the reporter's choice of action, the outcome is transparent. If the source can offer the reporter sufficient reward, and prefers to do so, then the source can control how the reporter chooses to write the story. This case is analytically trivial. The interesting case is one in which the source cannot observe the reporter's choice of action. Suppose that the source can read the story and learn whether it is relatively favorable or unfavorable to his or her interests, but that the source cannot know whether the favorable or unfavorable content resulted from the reporter's choices or from decisions made by the editor, the publisher, or some other actor. Under what conditions would the source be able to control the reporter's action even without observing it? The answer, provided by the model developed in the section on sources and reporters, involves a concept from statistics known as the "monotone likelihood ratio property." As we shall see, if the likelihood that the reporter chose an action favorable to the source's interests is a monotone-increasing function of the source's utility payoff from the story, then there exists a system of rewards that would make it possible for the source to control the reporter's choice of action even without observing that choice. This outcome can be problematic for accuracy in journalism because it makes a reporter's choice between more truthful and less truthful reporting subject to control by the source.

EDITORS AND REPORTERS[1]

Assume, for simplicity, that there are two types of reporters. One type of reporter produces high-accuracy stories, each of which has value v_h to readers. The other type of reporter produces low-accuracy stories, each of which has value v_l to readers. We assume that low-accuracy stories have positive value and that high-accuracy stories have higher value: $v_h > v_l > 0$.

Assume that there are so many reporters that readers cannot know them individually by reputation. In that case, a reader cannot know at the time of purchase whether an individual story has high or low accuracy. Let π_h be the proportion of high-accuracy reporters in the population of reporters. Also assume, for simplicity, that all reporters write the same number of stories; hence π_h is also the proportion of high-accuracy stories in the population of stories so long as high-accuracy reporters remain active.

If both high- and low-accuracy reporters are active, then the expected value of a story is

(1) $\bar{v} = \pi_h v_h + (1 - \pi h) v_l$.

Thus, so long as readers cannot know the reputations for accuracy of individual reporters, the *most* that they will be willing to pay for an individual story is $\bar{v}$ (unless they are risk preferring). If stories sell for $\bar{v}$, then the high-accuracy reporters will be paid less than the value of their stories and the low-accuracy reporters will be paid more than the value of their stories. Furthermore, no reader can ever be assured in advance that a particular story has high accuracy. Finally, this outcome is the best of the possible outcomes for the present case because it is based on the assumption that high-accuracy reporters are willing to sell stories that are worth v_h for a price of (at most) $\bar{v} < v_h$. However, if high-accuracy reporters can earn v_o in their best alternative employment, and if $\bar{v} < v_o$, then high-accuracy reporters will exit. In that case, all available stories will be low-accuracy ones with value $v_l < \bar{v}$.

We now introduce a third type of agent, known as an "editor." We assume that there are few enough editors so that readers can know individual editors by their reputations. Reporters can work with editors that impose various editorial standards. The function of editors is to certify to readers the editorial standard for accuracy, e, that is met by stories written by their reporters. We assume that editors cannot check every (alleged) fact in every story for accuracy, but that they can check on the procedures followed by their reporters and certify that the procedures are appropriate for an editorial standard e.

Let c_l be the constant marginal effort cost per story to a low-accuracy reporter of meeting editorial standard e, where $e \geq 0$, Similarly, let c_h be the marginal effort cost per story to a high-accuracy reporter of meeting editorial standard e. Assume that it requires more effort for a low-accuracy reporter to meet any editorial standard than it does for a high-accuracy reporter to meet the same standard; i.e., assume that

(2) $c_l > c_h > 0$, for all $e \geq 0$.

Finally, let θ be the amount that an editor deducts from the value of a story before paying a wage to a reporter; that is, θ is the compensation of editors for their services.

We will identify conditions under which there exists a separating equilibrium. Let $\alpha > 0$, and consider the following wage scale for reporters:

$$(3) \qquad w(e) = \alpha \begin{cases} v_h - \theta \text{ for } e \geq e* \\ v_l - \theta \text{ for } 0 < e < e* \\ v_l \qquad \text{for } e = 0. \end{cases}$$

Under this wage scale, any reporter who works with an editor that certifies an editorial standard of e* or higher will be paid a wage that is proportional to the value of a high-accuracy story less the editor's compensation. The proportionality factor, α, is the average number of stories per unit of time that a reporter writes. Similarly, reporters who work with editors that certify positive editorial standards below e* will be paid a wage that is proportional to the value of a low-accuracy story less the editor's compensation. Finally, reporters who do not work with editors will be paid a wage that is proportional to the value of a low-accuracy story.

Next, assume that

$$(4) \quad 0 < \theta < v_h - v_l ,$$

and recall that $v_h > v_l$. Let e* be some positive real number such that

$$(5) \quad \frac{v_h - v_l - \theta}{c_h} > e* > \frac{v_h - v_l - \theta}{c_l}.$$

We know that such an e* exists because $c_l > c_h > 0$ and $v_h - v_l - \theta > 0$. We will show that statements (3)-(5) imply the following equilibrium editorial standards for low- and high-accuracy reporters:

$$(6) \quad e_l = 0; e_h = e*.$$

There exists a separating equilibrium if each type of reporter prefers its own wage and editorial standard to the wage and editorial standard preferred by the other type of reporter. But this follows immediately from statements (3)-(6) because

$$(7) \quad \begin{aligned} & e* > \frac{v_h - v_l - \theta}{c_l} \rightarrow c_l\, e* > v_h - v_l - \theta \\ & \rightarrow v_l > v_h - \theta - c_l\, e* \\ & \rightarrow w(0) - \alpha c_l 0 > w(e*) - \alpha c_l\, e* \end{aligned}$$

and

$$(8) \quad \frac{v_h - v_l - \theta}{c_h} > e* \rightarrow v_h - v_l - \theta > c_h e*$$

$$\rightarrow v_h - \theta - c_h e* > v_l$$

$$\rightarrow w(e^*) - \alpha c_h e^* > w(0) - \alpha c_h\, 0.$$

Therefore, reporters can self-select in the following way. High-accuracy reporters can choose to work for newspapers that impose editorial standard e*; these reporters will be paid a wage of $w(e^*) = \alpha(v_h - \theta)$. Low-accuracy reporters can choose editorial standard 0; these reporters will be paid a wage of $w(0) = \alpha v_l$.

Under what conditions can such a separating equilibrium be attained? It is necessary that each type of reporter prefers its own wage and editorial standard to the one preferred by the other type of reporter. Statements (7) and (8) show that these necessary conditions are satisfied by the wage scale (3) and the editorial standards $e_l = 0$ and $e_h = e^*$ if statement (4) is satisfied. Statement (4) places an upper limit on the compensation, θ, that is paid to editors: $\theta < v_h - v_l$; i.e., an editor cannot be paid more per story than the difference in value between high- and low-accuracy stories. Two other necessary conditions are as follows:

$$(9) \quad \frac{1}{\alpha} w(e^*) - c_h e^* = v_h - \theta - c_h e^* \geq \bar{v}; \text{ and}$$

$$(10) \quad \frac{1}{\alpha} w(e^*) - c_h e^* = v_h - \theta - c_h e^* \geq \bar{v}_0.$$

Condition (9) is necessary because, if it is not satisfied, then high-accuracy reporters prefer not to work with editors and, instead, sell their stories at the average story-accuracy price, $\bar{v}$. Condition (10) is necessary because, if it is not satisfied, then high-accuracy reporters prefer not to work with editors and, instead, exit from reporting. Both (9) and (10) place restrictions on the amount of compensation, θ, that can be received by editors.

The separating equilibrium in editorial standards realizes the consumer and producer surplus from transactions in high-accuracy stories; however, it produces less social surplus than would be attainable if readers could know individual reporters by their reputations for high or low accuracy. The reason for this is that editors must be paid part of the value of high-accuracy stories even though they neither write stories nor add to the quality of high-accuracy stories. The only role that editors play is in establishing editorial standards that make it feasible for high- and low-accuracy reporters to self-select into a two-tier journalistic market.

SOURCES AND REPORTERS

We have noted above that a reporter may not always be interested in truthful reporting because a story that contains some false information or some half-truths may be more newsworthy than a factually more accurate story. We have also noted that reporters may differ in their individual capacities for accuracy. These questions will not be discussed in this section. In order to focus on analyzing conditions under which sources can control how stories are reported, we will here assume that reporters are only interested in truthful reporting.

Reporting of political news is often dependent on information provided by sources with insider information. Such sources are often not simply interested in making information public but, instead, have an interest in having the information that they provide reported in ways that promote the source's objectives. Such reporting may or may not be truthful. Analysis of the relationship between sources and reporters is trivial in the case where both types of agents want all valid information to be accurately reported. In contrast, the case where reporters are interested in truthful reporting, but sources are interested in having readers misled in certain ways, is an interesting one to analyze. Our analysis will focus on the basic question of identifying conditions under which it is possible for a source to control how the reporter uses the information provided by the source.

There are many aspects to the informal contractual relationship between sources and reporters. For some types of news, there may be many sources competing with each other; for other types of news, there may be a single source with a monopoly on the relevant insider information. Analogously, there may sometimes be a single reporter, and at other times many reporters competing for the same source or sources. We will here analyze one of the possible relationships between a source (or sources) and a reporter (or reporters). We will study the relationship between a single source (with a monopoly on the relevant insider information) and a single reporter (with a monopoly on reporting this specific information). A famous example of this type of relationship is provided by the Deepthroat source in the Watergate scandal, and the reporter Bob Woodward.

A question of central interest in analyzing the bilateral monopoly relationship between a single source and a single reporter is identifying the conditions under which the source can control how the information is reported after it has been revealed to the reporter. Consider the case where, after obtaining the information from the source, the reporter can choose between writing a story that is more truthful (taking action m) and writing a story that is less truthful (taking action l). An example of a reporter's "more truthful" action is one in which the reporter not only writes up what the source says but, in addition, seeks "balance" or "objectivity" by reporting related information.

The action chosen by the reporter does not completely determine the payoffs from the newspaper article to either the source or the reporter. There are several reasons for this. One reason is that the content of the article may be affected by actions chosen by the editor in addition to the reporter's action. The editor may insist on modifying the reporter's initial draft in certain ways, e.g., by adding or interpolating material that disputes or contradicts the source's statements. Another route to the same effect is to publish conflicting material either in another story on the same page or on the editorial page. Such decisions are in the hands of the editor, rather than the (initial) reporter. The payoffs also depend on what statements have been publicly or privately made by other credible principals during the same time period, which is outside the control of either the reporter or the editor. The payoffs from the reporter's article may also depend on whether it appears on page one or on some other page. Other things which may affect the impact of an article, and hence the payoffs to the source and to the reporter, include day of the week and season of the year in which it appears, whether or not Congress is in session, and so on.

Since the reporter's action does not completely determine the payoffs to the source, an important consideration in determining the source's ability to influence the reporter's choice of action is whether or not the source can observe that choice. Subsequent analysis will be divided into two parts which differ in terms of an assumption that the source either can or cannot observe whether the reporter chose to write a more truthful or a less truthful story. As we shall see, the source's ability to influence the reporter's choice without observing it depends on the existence of a regularity condition from the literature on statistical hypothesis testing.

An example that illustrates some of the preceding points is provided by a 1965 story by Tom Wicker in the *New York Times* that was published during the period in which the U.S. government was beginning to increase the level of troop commitment in Vietnam. Wicker's story contained the following:

> President Johnson does not now intend either to halt the United States air attacks on North Vietnam or to move American combat troops into the forefront of a stepped-up antiguerrilla war in South Vietnam. . . .
>
> Despite widespread speculation that many more American soldiers would soon be shipped to Vietnam, high officials here insist that no decision along those lines has been made. (Quoted from Hallin 1986, p. 96)

Obviously the second quoted paragraph undercuts the statement of the official source (Robert McNamara), though it says nothing about the basis of the "widespread speculation." Inclusion of the second paragraph produced a story that was more truthful than a story that excluded this paragraph. If the second paragraph was included because of a decision made by the reporter, this would provide an example of a reporter's choosing to write a more truthful rather than a less truthful story. Presumably, the source was not pleased by the inclusion of the second paragraph. But could the source know whether the inclusion of this paragraph resulted from the reporter's choice or from a choice made by the editor?

The effect on payoffs of the many things that neither the source nor the reporter can control is represented by a random component in payoffs. Thus the action chosen by the reporter does not determine certain payoffs; instead, the reporter's action determines probability distributions of returns for the source and the reporter. Let u_i be the utility payoff for the source if state of the world i occurs, where $i = 1, 2, \ldots n$. Similarly, let v_i be the utility payoff for the reporter if state i occurs. A "state of the world" is defined by a specification of all outcomes from reporting a story that matter to the source and the reporter, including the reactions of readers, voters, professional peers, employers, and so on.

Define p_{im} as the probabilities that the states occur if the reporter chooses action m. The probabilities that the states occur if the reporter chooses action l are denoted by p_{il}. Assume that the state probabilities have the usual properties of probabilities: $p_{im} \geq 0$, $p_{il} \geq 0$, $i = 1, 2, \ldots n$, and

$$\sum_{i=1}^{n} p_{im} = \sum_{i=1}^{n} p_{il} = 1.$$

From the assumption that the reporter prefers more truthful reporting, one has

$$(11) \quad \sum_{i=1}^{n} p_{im} v_i > \sum_{i=1}^{n} p_{il} v_i.$$

If action m is also preferred by the source, then there is no reason for the source to attempt to control the reporter's action. We will analyze the case where the source prefers that the reporter choose action l and the reporter prefers action m.

Assuming that the source prefers action l to action m means

$$(12) \quad \sum_{i=1}^{n} p_{il} u_i > \sum_{i=1}^{n} p_{im} u_i.$$

If the source has no ability to reward or punish the reporter after giving information to the reporter, then statement (11) implies that the reporter will write a more truthful article (choose action m). We will consider the situation where the source does have the ability to reward or punish the reporter. There are two cases to consider, depending on whether the source can or cannot observe the action chosen by the reporter.

Suppose that the source can observe the reporter's choice of action and has the ability to reward the reporter. In that case, the choice of action by the source is transparent. The source can simply incur a utility cost c to provide the reward ψ (c) to the reporter (where ψ $(\cdot)$ is a strictly increasing function) such that

$$(13) \quad \sum_{i=1}^{n} p_{il} v_i + \psi(c) = \sum_{i=1}^{n} p_{im} v_i.$$

Any reward slightly larger than ψ (c) will cause the reporter strictly to prefer action l to action m. The source may not choose to reward the reporter sufficiently to induce the reporter to take action l, even given the ability to do so. If

(14) $$\sum_{i=1}^{n} p_{il} u_i - c < \sum_{i=1}^{n} p_{im} u_i,$$

then the source would prefer the reporter's more truthful report to the combination of the reporter's less truthful report and the cost of the minimun reward needed to induce the reporter to choose action l. Given (12)-(14), the source's decision would depend on the size of the payoff from the best alternative to dealing with the reporter, as represented by the source's reservation utility, $\bar{u}$. If

(15) $$\sum_{i=1}^{n} p_{im} u_i < \bar{u},$$

then the source would prefer to withhold the information from the reporter. On the other hand, if

(16) $$\sum_{i=1}^{n} p_{il} ui - c > \sum_{i=1}^{n} p_{im} u_i$$

and

(17) $$\sum_{i=1}^{n} p_{il} u_i - c > \bar{u},$$

then the source would prefer to incur a cost of c, or slightly higher, in order to induce the reporter to choose action l.

The really interesting case to examine is the one where the source cannot observe the reporter's choice of action. Thus we here assume that the source can read the article and judge whether its content is relatively favorable or unfavorable, but that the source cannot observe whether the article's contents have resulted from decisions made by the reporter or by the editor. We also here assume that the source cannot observe the reporter's influence over other things that affect the source's utility payoffs from the article, such as the page on which it appears and the location and content of other related articles that could influence the source's payoffs. Thus we here assume that the source can only attempt to infer the reporter's choice of action from the payoffs that the source obtains from the article. If that is the case, then under what conditions is it possible for the source to implement a reward plan (informal contractual arrangement) that can influence the reporter's choice of action? We will next analyze this question.

Let c_i be the source's cost of rewarding the reporter in the amount $\phi(c_i)$ if state of the world i occurs. Assume that $\phi(c_i) > 0$ if $c_i > 0$, and that $\phi(\cdot)$ is strictly increasing and strictly concave; that is, assume that the source can reward the reporter at a cost to the source, and that the source can always increase the reward to the reporter by incurring more cost but that there are diminishing returns to this reward/transfer activity. Also assume that the source seeks to influence the reporter to choose action 1 with a set of rewards that minimize the source's cost. Thus, the source wants to identify c_i^*, where i = 1, 2, . . . n, that solve the following constrained maximization problem:

$$(18) \quad \max_{c_1,\ldots,c_n} \sum_{i=1}^{n} p_{il} (u_i - c_i)$$

subject to

$$\sum_{i=1}^{n} p_{il} (v_i + \phi(c_i)) \geq \sum_{i=1}^{n} p_{im} (v_i + \phi(c_i)).$$

The Kuhn-Tucker first-order conditions for maximization problem (18) include

$$(19) \quad \frac{1}{\phi'(c_i^*)} = \lambda* \left[1 - \frac{p_{im}}{p_{il}} \right], \ i=1,2,\ldots,n,$$

where $\phi'(c_i^*)$ is the first derivative of $\phi(\cdot)$ evaluated at the optimal cost for state i, c_i^*, and λ^* is the optimal value of a Lagrangian multiplier for the constraint. The assumptions that the reporter prefers action m (see statement (11)), and that $\phi(\cdot)$ is strictly increasing, imply that the constraint will be binding and hence that $\lambda^* > 0$. The regularity properties of $\phi(\cdot)$ and the conditions of statement (19) imply that c_i^* varies inversely with p_{im}/p_{il}. Thus, if we consider two states, i = s and i = k, then statement (19), strict positive monotonicity and strict concavity of $\phi(\cdot)$, and $\phi(c_i) > 0$ for $c_i > 0$ give us the following result:

(20) $$\frac{p_{sm}}{p_{sl}} > \frac{p_{km}}{p_{kl}} \rightarrow - \frac{p_{sm}}{p_{sl}} < - \frac{p_{km}}{p_{kl}}$$

$$\rightarrow [1 - \frac{p_{sm}}{p_{sl}}] < [1 - \frac{p_{km}}{p_{kl}}]$$

$$\rightarrow \frac{1}{\phi'(c_s^*)} < \frac{1}{\phi'(c_k^*)}$$

$$\rightarrow \phi'(c_k^*) < \phi'(c_s^*)$$

$$\rightarrow c_k^* > c_s^* \rightarrow c_s^* < c_k^*.$$

Statement (20) gives us the key insight needed to understand the conditions under which the source can implement an implicit contract that will induce the reporter to choose action l even though the source cannot observe the chosen action, as we will now explain.

An expression of the form p_{im}/p_{il} is known in the statistics literature as a *likelihood ratio*. It gives us the ratio of the likelihood of observing (outcomes from) state i given that the reporter chose action m, to the likelihood of observing (outcomes from) state i given that the reporter chose action l. If state i occurs, then a high value of p_{im}/p_{il}, is evidence that favors the inference that the reporter chose action m. Similarly, if state i occurs, then a low value of p_{im}/p_{il} provides support for the inference that the reporter chose action l.

The appearance of the likelihood ratio in the necessary conditions of statement (19) suggests that the source's ability to implement a system of rewards that will induce the reporter to choose the action favored by the source is formally related to problems of statistical inference. A common regularity condition that is used for such inference is known as the *monotone likelihood ratio property* (MLRP).[2] In the present context, the MLRP implies that p_{il}/p_{im} is a monotone-increasing function of u_i. This means that the higher the utility payoff to the source, the more likely it is that the reporter chose the action that is favorable to the source. If the MLRP is satisfied, then the source's contracting problem is relatively simple. In order to induce the reporter to choose action l, all the source needs to do is to make a credible promise to the reporter of a sufficiently generous plan to share the payoffs in a monotone-increasing way by adopting a rule such as this: if $u_k > u_s$, then $c_k > c_s$ and $\phi(c_k) > \phi(c_s)$.

The MLRP makes it possible for the source to offer the reporter an implicit contract that will induce the reporter to choose to write a less truthful story. Whether or not the source would choose to offer the reporter such a contract depends on how high the reporter's "price" (the c_i^*) is, the source's relative evaluations of the reporter's actions (m and l), and the source's utility from the best alternative to dealing with the reporter. Thus, analogously to statements (16) and (17), we now have the necessary conditions,

$$(21) \quad \sum_{i=1}^{n} p_{il} (u_i - c_i^*) > \sum_{i=1}^{n} p_{im} u_i$$

and

$$(22) \quad \sum_{i=1}^{n} p_{il} (u_i - c_i^*) > \bar{u} .$$

Condition (21) means that the source would be willing to incur an expected cost of

$$\sum_{i=1}^{n} p_{il} c_i^* ,$$

or slightly higher, in order to induce the reporter to choose action l rather than action m. Condition (22) means that the source would prefer to incur this expected cost rather than withhold information from the reporter and receive the utility payoff, $\bar{u}$, from the best alternative to dealing with the reporter.

We have identified conditions under which it would be possible for a single source to induce a single reporter to choose to write a less truthful rather than a more truthful story. To the extent that these conditions are in fact satisfied, the *existence* of a bilateral monopoly (i.e., single source, single reporter) relationship in journalism will foster inaccuracy. Competition among multiple sources and/or multiple reporters would check this cause of inaccuracy. Thus the existence of multiple sources, with intersecting sets of insider information, would allow even a single reporter to "play off" each source against others as the sources competed to put their preferred "spins" on the reported news. Furthermore, the existence of multiple reporters would make it difficult or impossible for even a single source to induce reporters to choose less truthful over more truthful reporting. The reason for this is that the reward (or punishment) actions that are available to a source operating within a free-press political environment are essentially limited to granting (or not granting) future access to insider information. Such a reward (or punishment) action only has significant value (or cost) to a reporter if the access (or lack of access) to the insider information is exclusive.

DIMENSIONS AND DIRECTIONS FOR FUTURE ANALYSIS

Obviously, a more comprehensive analysis of journalism in the spirit of this chapter must take many additional factors or variables into account. We briefly identify some of these factors in this final section.

The preceding section focused on news reports based on "insider" statements. Most news, however, is generated through channels that are open to other reporters, such as official proceedings (trials, election tabulations, and the like), press releases, press conferences, background briefings, and news reports from other news organizations (see Sigal 1973, ch. 6). Such news is available to all reporters, so every reporter (or newspaper) is in competition with the rest of the media in its handling of the story. No reporter can accommodate the source without considering how his or her own story may look to the public or the professionals when compared with competing stories on the same subject.

When multiple sources of information about an event exist, a reporter has two tasks or decisions to make. First, the reporter must discover such sources and what they have said, or actively invite them to comment on the topic in question. Second, in deciding what competing sources to quote in a story, a reporter must decide which of these sources are sufficiently credible to be included. Sources that are wholly noncredible to the readership will presumably be excluded, since their inclusion could impugn the newspaper's reputation. For example, in their handling of the Gulf of Tonkin incident, which precipitated American escalation in Vietnam, the American media simply reported the statements of President Johnson, who spoke of "renewed hostile actions against U.S. ships on the high seas in the Gulf of Tonkin" (quoted in Hallin 1986, p. 19). In fact, there was serious doubt among those involved in the (second) Gulf of Tonkin incident whether any "battle" actually took place, as Johnson claimed. The sonarman on the U.S. ship the *Maddox* had limited experience; and although he thought he detected torpedo after torpedo fired at the ship, many of the crew thought afterwards that he was probably picking up the sound of the ship's own propellers. The *Maddox* had great difficulty finding any targets on its fire control radar. Several hours after the engagement the commander of the task force cabled to Pacific headquarters:

> Review of action makes many reported contacts and torpedoes fired appear doubtful. . . . Freak weather effects and overeager sonarman may have accounted for many reports. No actual visual sightings by *Maddox*. Suggest complete evaluation before any further action. (Quoted in Hallin 1986, p. 17)

Although the media did not have access to this report at the time, they did have access to the denials by the North Vietnamese that the alleged firing on the *Maddox* (in the relevant, "second" incident) actually took place. These denials were reported in *Le Monde*, for example, but the American press obviously regarded the North Vietnamese as noncredible sources. Or at any rate they were unwilling to run the risk of appearing to give any credibility to the North Vietnamese, presumably because of the expected reaction either of the U.S. government or the U.S. public.

The use of multiple sources can help correct distorting or misleading statements by single sources. But accuracy depends, in the end, on the accuracy or reliability of the sources selected. As many researchers indicate (e.g., Entman 1989), reporters typically depend for national news on easily accessible, familiar elites: top officials in the White House and executive branch agencies, members of Congress and powerful congressional staffers, representatives of important interest groups, and some party spokespersons, think-tank experts, former government officials, elder statesmen and stateswomen still involved in politics. Unfortunately, most of these elites are tainted; what they say is heavily influenced by policies they want enacted or privileges they want maintained. Instead of relying on rival elites, reporters can "mediate" a given source's claims by interpolating their own statements, explanations, or interpretations. The problem with this approach is that the *ethos* of journalism requires "balance" and "objectivity," which means that reporters must not themselves appear to be partisan or biased for or against a given source (e.g., a government official). Departures from the accepted journalistic ethos can result in sanctions from one's professional peers (a loss in reputation), sanctions from the public, and/or sanctions from one's boss (the editor or media owner). Nonetheless, explanations and interpretations of a source's statements can go a long way toward helping the audience reach an accurate assessment of the truth of a source's statements.

A vivid example was some television coverage of Richard Nixon's March 1974 appearance before the National Association of Broadcasters, while he was beset by the Watergate investigations. Immediately following the news conference, CBS broadcast live roughly three and a half minutes of instant analysis by correspondents Roger Mudd and Bruce Morton, which focused exclusively on Watergate (though this subject occupied only six of the eighteen questions posed during the news conference) and analyzed the president's appearance in strategic terms. Mudd explained Nixon's purpose as "to be seen as many places before as favorable an audience as he can arrange" and "to clothe the presidency with as much higher responsibility as he can bring to it." A subsequent experimental study of students' reactions showed that those exposed to the instant analysis were greatly influenced by it (see Paletz and Entman 1981, pp. 66-67). Can network correspondents always be so assertive, however? How often can they engage in factual contradiction, judgment, and speculation about a president's remarks? As Paletz and Entman (1981, pp. 69 ff.) emphasize, this is only "economically" feasible (our expression) under special circumstances. When presidential status is high, for example, it may not be feasible. Only during the waning or weakened period of a presidency can correspondents risk the cost of criticisms or sanctions from various quarters for such "bold" interpretations or statements of their own.

This raises questions about the effectiveness of the ethos of "balance" or "objectivity" in helping to secure truth. Ironically, it may be that the very ethos of objectivity is subversive of its own goal: greater truthfulness. The ethos of objectivity may constrain and deter correspondents from engaging in precisely the kind of analysis and interpretation that audiences need in order to get at relevant truths. Perhaps a change in ethos that allowed a more muck-raking or adversarial posture toward official sources (or *any* sources) would actually encourage greater truthfulness (at least more true belief on the part of the audience) than the precepts of reportorial balance and objectivity.

This kind of possibility emerges in a different form in a discussion by Paletz and Entman of the presentational style of network correspondents and anchorpersons. Paletz and Entman (1981, p. 24) point out that correspondents are authoritative and factual, their demeanor unemotional, uninvolved, dispassionate. They do not reveal strong opinions about the events they cover and are hardly ever emotional on camera. This style comports with the ethos of objectivity, and it enhances the credibility of the information and opinions which compose the news. But, observe Paletz and Entman, this presentational product disguises the process of selecting, framing, reconstituting, and reconstructing reality that is actually taking place. The appearance of knowledgeability and impartiality, it may be argued, contributes to credulity as opposed to skepticism on the part of the audience. And ultimately, such credulity may hinder the formation of true belief on the part of that audience.

Two other topics for the economic analysis of the news may be mentioned briefly in conclusion. First, an economic approach should come to terms with earlier models of the news with an economic tenor. Two such models are called by Cohen and Young (1981, p. 13) the "mass manipulative model" and the "market or commercial model." In the manipulative model, those in power use the media to mystify and manipulate the public. The market model argues that there is variety and diversity in information and opinions presented in the mass media and that such variation minimizes the chances of manipulation. Our discussion does not mean to come down squarely on either side of this dispute, but the elements of truth in each contender should be assessed.

Second, there is an element in the market model that is widely endorsed, and we should give it at least passing attention before concluding. This element concerns the nature of the public "demand" for truth. Although we have defended the proposition that truth acquisition is a "major" goal of readers, we certainly concede that truth is not their exclusive interest. One way of putting the point is to say that the public wants *some* but not all kinds of truths. Readers are more interested in dramatic and simple truths, not abstract, dry, or complex truths. A slightly different way of putting the point is not in terms of the truths themselves, but the *modes of presentation* of truths. Audiences for news are said to prefer the dramatic to the drab, the personalized to the impersonalized, the simple to the complex, the unambiguous to the ambiguous, and so forth. This demand shapes what newsmakers consider newsworthy, and hence what ultimately appears on television or is given prominent coverage in the print media. The question is how much this distorts the body of information (or misinformation) available to the citizenry. It is easy to say, of course, that the result is very poor "quality" of information. But it would be good to have a more precise analysis of how audience preferences for certain modes of presentation, and putative dispositions to minimize cognitive effort in assimilating news, result in actual falsity or inaccuracy of belief.[3]

Notes

1. The model developed in this section adapts a type of analysis originated by Akerlof (1970) and Spence (1974).

2. The key role of the MLRP in some models of information asymmetry was prevoiusly demonstrated by Milgrom (1981).

3. Helpful comments and suggestions were provided by participants in the Social Science and Philosophy Workshop at the University of Arizona. Cox's work on this chapter was partially supported by the National Science Foundation (grant number SES-9108888).

10

A More Social Epistemology

Miriam Solomon

SOCIAL EPISTEMOLOGIES

Not long ago, most epistemologists believed that the influences of social processes on thinking are to be avoided when striving for progress, rationality, or truth.[1] This traditional view began in the central philosophical works influencing the Western philosophical tradition: notably in those of Plato, who separated rationality and the emotions, and Descartes, who retreated from the social world to discover truths through the use of his reason alone. It still has several powerful advocates, such as Glymour, Laudan, and Levi. Recently, a number of epistemologists and philosophers of science—including formerly more traditional philosophers such as Giere, Goldman, Kitcher, Kornblith, and Thagard—have come to argue that the influence of social factors on inquiry is not only inevitable but, often, beneficial. Work in science studies starting with Kuhn that discerns the role of social factors in scientific inquiry has persuaded many to take social factors seriously and respond by developing normative accounts that accommodate them.

These new social epistemologies are different from social accounts of knowledge that are in the traditions of American pragmatism or continental philosophy. In these latter traditions, rationality is often taken to be *constituted by*[2] social practices (e.g., Peirce, Wittgenstein, Foucault). This view has been adopted, in stronger and weaker forms, by many sociologists and historians of science (e.g., Barnes, Bloor, Collins, Knorr-Cetina, Latour, Woolgar).

Although some epistemologists and philosophers of science in the Anglo-American tradition have been influenced by these views (e.g., Stich 1985 [but not Stich 1990], Longino, Putnam, Rorty), the majority find them lacking. It is often pointed out (e.g., Giere 1988, ch. 1; Goldman 1992, ch. 10; Kitcher 1993, ch. 6) that, if social practices are conducive to progress, rationality, or truth, it is not because progress, rationality, and truth are socially constructed. Social practices must be *evaluated* for their effectiveness in a variety of domains (e.g., ordinary, judicial, scientific), and this is not a trivial project. Often enough, social processes obstruct progress. Thus, these social epistemologies are not equivalent to social constructivism. Examples of social epistemologies that assess reasoning practices instrumentally are found in Fuller (1988a), Goldman (1992, chs 10 and 11), Kitcher (1993, ch. 6), Stich (1990), and Thagard (1991).

Typically, social epistemologists evaluate social processes favorably if they are *ultimately* conducive to *individual* rational choice. Social processes are condoned when they are an *intermediate* step in the process of *individual* enlightenment. Eventually, it is claimed, with the help of social processes, every (or almost every) scientist champions the most true (or progressive, or explanatory) theory, and does so for good reasons. So, for example, Kitcher (1990) claims that motives of competition can distribute cognitive labor in such a way that all worthwhile alternative theories are developed, and the best theory emerges and then is recognized as such by *each* scientist. Kitcher (1993, chs 2, 6) also claims, along with Goldman (1994), that rhetorical strategies can be used to make arguments more comprehensible and more available to *each* member of the audience. Kornblith (this volume) discusses the conditions under which it is justified for *individuals* to rely on *expert* (also thought of as an individual) opinion.

There are some social epistemologies that are more social than these; but, on closer inspection, even these still assume the operation of individual rationality at some crucial stage. For example, Goldman (1992, ch. 11) argues that it can be epistemically advantageous for a community to allow the experts to control the data available for group decision-making in cases when most people are not capable of making good decisions individually. (This is what he calls "epistemic paternalism.") However, individualism remains in the account of expert decision-making. And, for example, Schmitt (this volume) regards groups as justified in their beliefs when engaged in a joint, often interactive, enterprise in which individuals in the group each reason rationally, through discussion with others, as members of the group. He does not consider cases where the group belief is justified and the individual's unjustified belief contributes to the justification of the group belief.[3] In a somewhat different vein, Laudan and Laudan (1989) and Sarkar (1983) both argue that scientific communities are ideally composed of subgroups working with different methodologies (i.e., different views of what scientific rationality consists in). Relative to the subgroups, however, they hold that individual scientists reason rationally. Even Longino (1990), who regards some social processes as *constitutive* of scientific objectivity (rather than scientifically objective because they are conducive to success), envisages these social processes as practices of criticism that help individual scientists to reason better.

In this chapter, I shall argue for a *more* social epistemology than any of these. I shall argue that *social groups can work to attain and even recognize epistemic goals without individual rationality or individual cognizance of the overall epistemic situation.*[4] I claim, furthermore, that this happens often enough that our normative views should be revised to allow for this manner of attaining scientific success. I will put forward a new normative perspective, called *social empiricism*, which provides the more thoroughgoing social perspective needed.

This is a normative theory that is at odds with entrenched traditional views about the autonomy, self-sufficiency and rationality of individual reason. Not surprisingly, it is also at odds with some entrenched intuitions about rationality and justification that are uncritically accepted in traditional philosophical analyses of these concepts.[5] I shall argue that the traditional framework does not even usefully apply to experts and authorities within the scientific community. It is my claim that where the new social epistemologies have erred, it is by not taking far enough the rejection of traditional Platonic and Cartesian views of reason. In what follows, I shall show the need for a more social epistemology. The new social epistemology I put forward in response to this need is especially applicable to discussion of *scientific* reasoning, but is sometimes useful in other domains.

The strategy of this chapter is to show, through the use of two case studies (the plate tectonics revolution and molecular genetics), that there are cases of scientific change where scientific goals are attained through *individual* reasoning that is not scientifically rational (i.e., scientifically effective and psychologically available). A few scientists may, on occasion, reason with full scientific rationality, but it is not necessary or even desirable that they do so, whether they be experts, authorities, or lesser players. Scientific goals are reached without dependence on individual rationality or individual cognizance of the effective reasoning and decision-making involved. Instead, they are reached through aggregate individual and social processes (epistemic, cognitive, motivational, socio-political) which are, as a whole, adequately responsive to empirical successes.

This finding will be data for a *normative* framework, rather than a descriptive one: sometimes the aggregate of individual and social processes does *not* produce a scientific community adequately responsive to empirical success. Normative frameworks do not condone everything that scientists do: they offer assessments and implementable strategies for improvement.

CASE STUDIES

The plate tectonics revolution of the mid-1960s was, incontestably, a scientific success that ended decades of dispute and disagreement about the geohistory of the earth's crust. It is tempting to think that geologists were each persuaded of continental drift by objective assessment of the implications of new geophysical and paleomagnetic data produced in the 1950s and early 1960s, or, at least, by reliance on experts who made such assessments. Some geologists, historians, and philosophers have already taken this line (see, e.g., Menard 1986; R. Laudan 1978; Giere 1988; and Thagard 1992). However, the historical record does not support this assessment. (I use LeGrand 1988, Menard 1986, and Stewart 1990 as main sources for this history.)

Before the 1960s, there was worldwide dissent on the question of continental drift. Those who worked on southern hemisphere materials, or on orogeny, were most likely to favor Wegener's view that the continents began in one large continent, Pangaea, and drifted apart. Elsewhere (Solomon 1992), I have argued that this dissent was produced in large part by "biasing" cognitive heuristics of the sort discussed by Kahneman, Slovic, and Tversky (1982) and Nisbett and Ross (1980), and that it was beneficial, for future development of theories of the earth's crust, to have the pluralism of views caused by disagreement.[6] When new evidence in favor of drift became available—first, the magnetic data from volcanic rocks; then, the magnetic anomalies over deep sea ridges, then, measurements of shifting plates—geologists made different evaluations. They tended to become convinced of drift for a variety of reasons: the data were their own (not read about) or presented in salient visual fashion at a conference; the results were produced in their own discipline (the order of acceptance tended to be paleomagnetists, then oceanographers, then seismologists, then stratigraphers, then continental geologists); they experienced peer pressure or pressure of people in authority. Geologists tended to resist drift when they had themselves produced experimental results which seemed to tell against drift (e.g., Ewing); when they had a reputation for opposing drift (e.g., Heirtzler, Worzel, Ewing, LePichon); and when their areas of research were far from the areas in which data supporting drift initially appeared (see Solomon 1994).

These patterns of belief change are best explained in terms of psychological and social factors such as cognitive salience and availability, positive self-illusions, peer pressure, belief perseverance, and political power. This does not mean that empirical successes (or other "objective" advantages) of plate tectonics played no role. It means that the role of empirical successes was not played out in terms of individual unbiased evaluations leading to choice of the most empirically successful theory. Consensus took place when plate tectonics had *universal* (in the scientific community) empirical successes, so that even biased evaluations of the importance of some successes led to the same choice of plate tectonics. That consensus was helped along by salient advertising of new results (especially at international conferences showcasing visual presentations) and bandwagon phenomena. I contend that the successes of plate tectonics were necessary for consensus on the theory, but *not* sufficient. *It makes sense to say that the scientific community as a whole selected plate tectonics because of its universal successes, while no individual did so.* Furthermore, the scientific community did so only via mechanisms that are traditionally viewed as "biasing":[7] cognitive salience and availability; motivational biases such as self-interest, pride, and peer pressure; and social factors such as the influence of institutional training and institutional structure.[8]

The development of genetics this century, culminating in the creation of molecular genetics, is another scientific success story. However, judged from the perspective of current work in genetics, some of the decision-making along the way has not resulted in *unqualified* success. The case of the plate tectonics revolution was more clear cut.[9] I am discussing more than one case study in order to provide different kinds, as well as more quantity, of epistemological data. (Main sources for my discussion of the history of genetics are Bowler 1989, Burian 1986, Burian et al. 1988, Olby 1974, and Sapp 1987.)

The beginning of modern genetics is usually associated with the rise of the Morgan school and the creation of the journal *Genetics* in 1916. This school of genetics, often referred to as "Mendelism," had early and continued success in predicting and explaining the phenotypes produced in breeding experiments in *Drosophila* and other organisms. Phenomena such as genetic linkage, crossover, and eventually genetic mutation were discovered. This success, compounded by the political strength and savvy of Morgan and the opportunities for expansion and innovation in the American academic community, resulted in the creation of a new discipline, a large following in the United States, and knowledge of Mendelism worldwide.

There was not, however, consensus that Mendelian genetics was the correct theory of inheritance. Early on, before there was much discovered about mutation and population genetics, many evolutionary biologists dissented. It was not until around 1940 that they generally accepted classical genetics, in a synthesis of Darwinism with Mendelism. Embryologists were especially dissatisfied with Mendelism. Mendelism gives an account of the relations between genotype and phenotype in terms of entities (genes) which are causes of phenotypic properties. Mendelian genes are almost abstract entities: they are identified with portions of the chromosome, but nothing is said about what chromosomes are or how they produce phenotypes. A paradox arose (which Jane Maienschein and Richard Burian have called "Lillie's Paradox," after Frank Rattray Lillie; see Burian 1986). There is no account of embryonic segregation, or, more generally, cellular differentiation: if chromosomes rule cellular processes, how can very different cells within the same organism be produced and controlled by the same chromosomes? Mendelian genetics could not—indeed did not attempt to—answer this question: mechanisms of genetic regulation were not conceived of in classical genetics. Mendelians downplayed or ignored the paradox, but others used it as the basis for alternative programs of genetic research featuring cytoplasmic control and environmental regulation.

Embryologists, and also European biologists as a group, were most likely to dissent from classical genetics. The European reaction was in part because embryology had a strong tradition there and the universities (especially in France and Germany) were tradition bound and thus not open to the creation of genetics as a new discipline. It was also in part a competitive strategy: in France, especially, alternative genetic research (e.g., research on cytoplasmic inheritance and the inheritance of acquired characteristics) was pursued in order to have an audible voice above the dominant American genetics community, and a chance of special national success (Sapp 1987).[10]

Research on cytoplasmic inheritance and the inheritance of acquired characteristics produced a few robust results over the interwar and immediate postwar years, but not the amount of research and applications (agriculture and animal breeding) of the classical genetics program. The major researchers were Sonneborn in the United States and Ephrussi in France. A common, and not implausible, view among these researchers was that cytoplasmically inherited traits are necessary for species viability, and so the genetic variability used in traditional breeding experiments is rarely available to the experimenter. Cytoplasmic genetic variation usually proves fatal. On this view of inheritance, only trivial characteristics, such as height and eye color, are transmitted in Mendelian fashion.

With the discovery of the structure of DNA and the beginnings of molecular genetics in the 1950s, it looked to most as though classical genetics had triumphed and the final material reduction of the gene—to nuclear DNA—had taken place. The discovery of the structure of DNA was, after all, the work of British and American geneticists and molecular biologists. The "master molecule" view of the internal organization of the cell was widespread and disseminated in textbooks and popular writing as well as scholarly journals. This almost-consensus failed to acknowledge two related facts: first, that molecular genetics is not in fact a reduction of classical genetics (i.e., it is not the case that gene = portion of chromosome = length of DNA); and second, that many genetic phenomena cannot be understood on the master molecule view. Work on genetic transposition and cytoplasmic inheritance done in the 1950s and 1960s (e.g., the work of Barbara McClintock and Ruth Sager) had a difficult time gaining acceptance—in part because it was not mainstream American research in genetics; in part because the leading researchers were women. The work of Sonneborn, Ephrussi, and their students, some of which was crucial for understanding the action of genes, and which offered a more accurate (and more complex) view of cellular processes and inheritance than that offered by the master molecule view, was frequently overlooked or unacknowledged. Both Ephrussi and Sonneborn were passed over for Nobel prizes.

It was not until the 1970s that phenomena of genetic transposition and cytoplasmic inheritance (cytoplasmic DNA) were generally accepted—and they were accepted only because evidence for them came directly from molecular biology (rather than from traditional techniques of genetic experimentation). Not all the promising results in non-nuclear genetics have been incorporated, however. Work of Sonneborn on the inheritance of cellular structure via transmission of supramolecular information has been largely ignored, and that research program has faded. The largest current genetics project—the human genome project—both suffers from and exploits (for funding purposes) its description as the cracking of the code of the master molecule in humans.

This brief history of genetics has some similarities with the history of plate tectonics, and some significant differences.[11] The similarities first: patterns of belief change can be explained in terms of the same social and psychological mechanisms. Again, biologists tended to be most influenced by what was happening in their own discipline and, especially, their own laboratories. Those at Columbia, with Morgan, were convinced first; evolutionary biologists were not convinced until the development of population genetics extended the results into their own discipline; embryologists were rarely convinced. The additional influence of work in one's own laboratory and own discipline is caused by both cognitive salience and, probably, motivational factors (e.g., overvaluing of the self). The political power of the Morgan school helped to establish Mendelism in America. Moreover, as Keller (1985) has argued, classical genetics and the later master molecule theory have ideological appeal to those attracted to hierarchical political systems. International competition produced by social, motivational, and political factors, and also international institutional differences, fueled alternative European work in genetics. The distribution of research commitment was fruitful, producing work on both sides that was eventually used in the development of molecular genetics. Even Ephrussi and Sonneborn's student Nanney (but not Sonneborn himself) shifted position in the 1950s toward the overwhelming majority view—recognizing nuclear dominance—when they had results of their own that connected cytoplasmic and nuclear investigations.

Now the differences with plate tectonics: consensus in genetics did not occur in as straightforward and as positive a manner. There was almost complete consensus in the 1950s and 1960s on the master molecule view. Because classical genetics is committed to nuclear dominance, and the discovery of DNA was associated with classical genetics, the "central dogma" of nuclear control of cellular processes continued. When genetic regulation (by cytoplasm and other genes) was discovered, the paradox of cellular differentiation was dissolved. The discovery of the structure of DNA was readily seen as a triumph of molecular biology, and the results accepted along with the theoretical package—master molecule theory—that they came with. While master molecule theory has had many experimental successes, it did not accommodate all the experimental results of the time. The almost complete consensus on the theory proved an obstacle to the acceptance of important ideas and results, and still does, to a lesser extent, today.

Master molecule theory received almost universal support because of an early and enduring distribution of "biasing" factors that more frequently favored Mendelism. Mendelism benefited from Morgan's political effectiveness, institutional support in the United States, support from the eugenics community as well as plant and animal breeders, and widespread attraction to political hierarchies (which translated into adoption of a functional hierarchy within the cell). Non-Mendelians gained only from continued support of embryologists, competitive international strategies, and the conservatism of the European intellectual communities. In addition, non-Mendelians suffered from the politics of the Cold War, lack of institutional support, and anti-Semitism and sexism against prominent researchers. (Sonneborn, Jollos, and Goldschmitt all suffered professionally from anti-Semitism in the United States; McClintock's and Sager's research were not taken seriously because of their sex.) All these factors skewed the consensus in genetics in a direction that, while positive, was not best for science, because it excluded important results.[12]

Individual choices in scientific change are frequently influenced by cognitive, social, or motivational factors that do not reliably select the most successful (or most plausible) theory. In this sense, individual scientists fail to have scientific rationality. If all scientists evaluated in the same way—if they were all influenced by the *same* cognitive, social, and motivational factors, to the same degrees—distribution of research effort would not take place, few theories would be developed, and consensus might take place on an inferior theory. This did not happen (at least, not in an extreme way) in the historical cases discussed because of the *variety* of factors involved in choice and their *distribution* in the involved scientific community. In addition, consensus took place in promising directions because scientific *successes*—not just scientists —were distributed among research groups within the scientific community. As a community, scientists can (although they do not always) select the most successful theory. As individuals, it is more a matter of luck. These case studies show the need for a normative epistemological account that evaluates effectiveness of aggregate decision-making in the scientific community. The account also needs to be substantive enough to distinguish *degrees* of effectiveness in aggregate decision-making (i.e., distinguish the effectiveness of decision-making in geology and genetics, and also other cases). In the next section, I will provide such an account.

A MORE SOCIAL EPISTEMOLOGY: SOCIAL EMPIRICISM

Social empiricism is a normative framework I have designed to assimilate and take advantage of these findings about scientific change. I claim that it can be applied fruitfully to make assessments in other case studies, including contemporary disputes in progress. Five numbered claims summarize the main features of social empiricism; some qualifications, elaborations and explanations follow the list:

1. Scientific decision-making furthers scientific goals, and in this sense is scientifically rational, when empirical successes (see claim 5 below) are produced and maintained.
2. Scientifically rational decision-making is, typically, achieved socially *at all stages* of scientific change, and therefore assessments should be made primarily of communities and only derivatively of individuals.
3. It is appropriate for scientists to adopt different theories when the different theories have different empirical successes, and appropriate for them to agree on a theory only when that theory has *all* the empirical success.
4. When different theories have different empirical successes, social, institutional, political, cognitive, and motivational factors (so-called "biasing" factors) influencing choice should be well distributed among scientists.
5. Empirical successes are engagements with the world which include experimental, observational, predictive, and some technological successes. Thus "empirical" is used much more broadly here than in traditional "logical empiricism."

Social empiricism is a *naturalistic* normative framework. The goals of science set out in claims 1 and 5 are not a priori instructions, but capture the ethos of science since at least the scientific revolution: the realistic goals of scientists qua investigators of the natural world.[13] (I do not include truth here—despite the fact that it is often viewed as part of the scientific ethos—because there is considerable doubt that it is, indeed, a realistic goal of scientists in many scientific domains. I recognize, however, that this is a controversial matter that cannot be discussed here. For those who disagree with me about this, I should point out that the "social" part of "social empiricism" is separable from the "empiricism"; the distinctive features of my social epistemological view can be considered independently of my claims about scientific goals.)

Social empiricism is also a naturalistic framework because, among various possible ways of pursuing scientific goals, it selects feasible, implementable strategies. Assessment of social, rather than individual, change in claim 2 is one example of this. Another example is the treatment of dissent and consensus in claim 3: it is acknowledged that having dissenting subgroups is the realistic way of keeping all empirical successes in the scientific community; but, also, the realistic expectation is (given factors such as competition and peer pressure) that attempts will be made to develop theories in directions that reproduce (and even outdo) empirical successes of competing theories. Thus it is realistic to expect scientists to work to try to make one theory have all the empirical successes.

It should be noted that I do not say that consensus is normatively appropriate when one theory has "most" empirical successes; I take the more extreme view and insist that it be *all* the empirical successes available in the community at that time.[14] (These successes may not be total—theories may be empirically inadequate—but all the successes must be captured.) This is a lesson learned from the history of science: underdog, yet still empirically successful, theories often maintain important connections with the world that later theories build on. (Wegener's theory of continental drift, and cytoplasmic theories of inheritance are examples of this.) And the consequences of suppressing less successful theories (e.g., cytoplasmic theories of inheritance) can be bad for science not only because of the failure to make widely known some empirical successes, but also because the theories suggest directions for development of *other* theories.

The requirement in claim 4 that "biasing factors" be well distributed is quite imprecise as stated. What counts as "well distributed"? Unfortunately, we do not yet have the kind of multifactorial theory that models the factors influencing choice, along with their strengths and interactions with one another. The most we have is knowledge of what these factors are. Thus, an improper linear model (which specifies the factors, and arbitrarily assigns them equal weights) is, currently, the most appropriate one to use. It produces results superior to those produced by global assessments of patterns of bias (see Dawes 1988, ch. 10).[15] I implicitly used such an improper linear model in the above discussion of choices in the plate tectonics revolution and the history of genetics, where I concluded that belief was not as well distributed by "biasing" factors in the history of genetics as in the plate tectonics revolution.

I construe "empirical success" very broadly: it includes observational, predictive, experimental, and technological successes. The notion is intended to capture successful engagements with nature, whether they be human (plus machine) manipulations of parts of the world—in the sense that Hacking (1983) features centrally—or the creation of new opportunities for nature's phenomena to interact with us. Examples of the latter include measurements in fields like geology and astrophysics which are neither passive observations nor manipulations of the objects under study. Often, claims to have empirical success are contested at the time they are produced. Since normative judgments (along the lines of social empiricism) are partly dependent on judgments of empirical success, many disputes cannot be definitively resolved during times where empirical successes are disputed. Full resolution can take place when disagreement is about the import, rather than the existence, of particular empirical successes. And it can sometimes take place when, from a neutral perspective (one uncommitted to the competing theories), a verdict on the existence of empirical success is clear. When this is still not the case, *partial* normative judgments can be made: for example, it can be ascertained whether "biasing" factors are skewed in favor of one theory or well distributed.

Social empiricism is precisely enough characterized that it yields normative judgments for the processes of scientific change in the geological revolution and the history of genetics. Implicitly, I have already made such judgments. I showed how dissent and consensus were influenced by empirical successes via evaluations that were also influenced by social, motivational, ideological, and cognitive factors and how, for the most part, this complex set of causal influences was conducive to scientifically effective decision-making by the community. The various "biasing" factors were not as well distributed among competing genetic theories, and this harmed the progress of genetics.

Social empiricism allows *degrees* of normativity—i.e., of more or less scientifically rational decision-making. The plate tectonics revolution took place especially rationally (according to the normative standards set by social empiricism); the history of genetics somewhat less so. Other cases show low levels of scientific rationality. To take a brief example:

at the beginning of the recent debate over cold fusion, much interest and research effort went into trying to duplicate reported phenomena of excess heat and radiation in electrolytic cells. This might never have happened without the competitiveness among the first experimenters (Pons and Fleischman at Utah versus Jones at Brigham Young) and the attention and interference they received from grant institutions, educational institutions, state government, and media. However, in my view, what went wrong was *not* the operation of these so-called external, "biasing" factors per se (as, e.g., Taubes 1993 argues), but that they operated in the absence of empirical successes. Thus, cold fusion received much more attention than it deserved; "biasing" factors were not well distributed.[16] In my view, "biasing" factors are necessary for scientific progress; but not all distributions of bias are progressive.

CONCLUSIONS

Social, motivational, ideological, and cognitive factors have pervasive effects on scientific decision-making. These factors are caused by situations and conditions outside of the scientific enterprise, traditionally construed. Among many historians and sociologists of science (e.g., Collins, Pinch, Woolgar), the temptation has been to conclude that, since both successful and unsuccessful science have been produced by the same factors, there is no useful distinction to be drawn between good science and bad science. Among philosophers (e.g., Kitcher, Thagard) and some historians (e.g., Sapp), the temptation has been to claim that good science has *fewer* "biasing" factors, biasing factors that have limited effects, or "biasing factors" that are internal to the politics of scientific communities rather than due to more general political or ideological influences. I deny all of these views. I claim that what matters is the *distribution* of "biasing" factors and not their strength (compared to "epistemic factors"), source, or pervasiveness. With this, and the resultant normative framework of social empiricism, I claim that I have a substantive normative framework that can be applied to yield verdicts about scientific rationality of choice in scientific communities.

Scientifically literate observers or historians of scientific disputes are often in an epistemically more neutral position than scientists themselves. They rarely have prior theoretical commitments; they are not subject to the particular peer and authority pressures in the community; and their professional rewards are not usually bound up in the outcome of particular scientific disputes. They are in more of a position to evaluate claims of empirical success, since they are less likely to reason with confirmation bias, motivational factors, and so on. (This is still a matter of degree; other kinds of partiality, such as ideological biases, may remain.) They also have the leisure (unlike scientists) to investigate and determine the particular cognitive, motivational, social, and institutional factors influencing the scientific debates under study. For this reason, scientifically educated observers may be better placed to make normative recommendations such as suggesting additional incentives to pursue theories that will better balance the distribution of "biasing" factors. There are, of course, no "God's eye" points of view that are free of partiality of one kind or another: empirical investigation can tell us more about the biases in any particular case, and, in particular, about the various biases of scientists, observers, and critics of science relevant to the disputes under consideration.[17] We do the best we can in making normative assessments, just as we do the best we can in any other empirical endeavor.

It would be misleading to conclude that I tolerate "biasing" factors when they cancel one another out and allow scientific decision-making to be conducted with discussion of epistemic merits alone. The effects of "biasing factors" are essential for scientific progress and internal to scientific disputes. It is rather that social empiricism encourages such factors when they magnify and transmit the effects produced by empirical successes and stimulate the production of more empirical successes.

Social empiricism differs from traditional accounts of rationality in being both thoroughgoingly *social* and thoroughgoingly *external* (to individual intuitive awareness). Scientific decision-making can be scientifically effective without any individual's having to reason effectively on her or his own, or even recognizing that the community reasons effectively. It is not my intent that this replace all uses of "rationality"—merely those in which scientific effectiveness (rather than, e.g., individual cognitive responsibility) is at issue.[18]

Notes

1. "Social processes" or "social factors" are phrases often misleadingly used (by both philosophers and psychologists) to encompass *both* social and motivational factors. Strictly speaking, motivational factors are individual (as are cognitive factors). However, they are often evoked in social context, e.g., feelings of competitiveness, fear of disapproval of others, peer pressures.

(Cognitive factors are sometimes also evoked in social contexts—e.g., anchoring phenomena in group reasoning—which is why the usual terminology is especially misleading.) I go with the misleading terminology for *description* of scientific change, because this causes the least confusion, and because the issue is not directly relevant to this chapter. When developing a normative perspective, however, I shall distinguish analyses at the individual and at the social level more carefully.

2. Sometimes this is called "social relativism." I avoid this terminology because I want to leave open the possibility that the rationality of reasoning practices is relative to the contexts in which they are practiced. (Different strategies work better in different situations, including different social situations.) "Social constructivism" is the position that what *makes* practices rational is the process of their creation (construction) in particular social structures.

3. Schmitt's framework does not exclude this possibility. But it does not explicitly consider it, either. (The same is true for Goldman's and Kitcher's views.)

4. Of course, there are normative standards that apply to individual scientists. But these are *derivative* of (i.e., secondary to) the standards that apply to scientific communities and, moreover, end up requiring *less* of individual scientists than is intuitively thought to be good judgment of scientific issues.

5. I am with Goldman (1992, ch. 9) in advocating moderate openness to reform of ordinary epistemic concepts and principles.

6. I use scare quotes around "biasing" throughout this chapter because, although the results of "biasing" cognitive, motivational, and social factors do not coincide with the application of logic, probability theory, and confirmation theory (traditionally thought of as unbiased reasoning), they are not ipso facto undesirable for scientific reasoning. Indeed, the purpose of the chapter is to explore how they contribute to the progress of science.

7. Again, the quotation marks indicate that I do not think that this bias is always negative; the word "bias" is the one traditionally used for mechanisms that depart from traditional probability, logic, or confirmation theory in their conclusions; I use the word to mark these mechanisms, but do not draw immediate epistemological conclusions.

8. Thus I disagree with Laudan and Laudan's (1989) claim that groups of geologists differed in their judgments on the plausibility of continental drift because they had different scientific methodologies (and, therefore, were all reasoning rationally, in accordance with their particular methodologies).

Individual differences in prior belief, salience of data, exposure to peer pressure, etc. are not different methodologies.

9. Actually, it was not quite as clear cut as I suggest, but taking it to be so makes for a clearer, and hardly misleading, discussion. For the record: Le Grand (1988) has, I think rightly, urged that expansionism was rejected earlier than it should have been; it dropped out of consideration in the early 1960s, before the evidence that distinguished it from plate tectonics was produced. So the success of consensus on plate tectonics was, in this respect, good luck. (It was not good luck that plate tectonics was chosen over permanentism, and this has been the main focus of my discussion.)

10. Here is a case where Goldman's (1992) and Kitcher's (1990) suggestions that cognitive labor is distributed by individuals or groups in bids for professional rewards applies.

11. See Solomon (forthcoming) for fuller discussion of this case study.

12. I have tallied the factors for and against nuclear models of inheritance without consideration of their relative importance. I have done this because I have no information about relative importance. Indeed, what I have constructed is an improper linear model of the factors influencing choice. This is a crude but, in fact, quite effective method of modeling complex phenomena, as has been argued in Dawes (1988). I shall discuss this further below.

13. In other words, I set aside their goals qua credit-seeking individuals, employment-seeking individuals, ideologically bound individuals, etc. Although these goals may strongly influence choices when doing science, scientists would deny that such goals are part of the ethos of the scientific enterprise.

14. This is a change from my earlier view (Solomon 1994).

15. Historians, who tell the history of scientific change by using narratives, are most susceptible to the sort of error produced by global assessments. As Dawes (1988) documents, global assessments frequently proceed by unwittingly giving undue weight to single factors and ignoring others.

16. Some of this may have been well-founded error. It was not possible for the scientific community to tell, from the reports of Pons, Fleischman, and Jones, whether or not anomalous heat or radiation had been produced. This is a case where, at the time, it is difficult to tell how much empirical success a theory has. In such conditions of ignorance, individuals may be doing the best they can (and thus, in another sense of the word, are rational), but still they are not deciding in a scientifically effective way.

17. I take this phrase from Donna Haraway (1991, ch. 9).

18. I am grateful to Dick Burian, Chuck Dyke, Gary Ebbs, Ron Giere, Mark Kaplan, Philip Kitcher, Alan Richardson, Bob Richardson, and Marya Schechtman for discussions related to this material. Special thanks to Fred Schmitt for reading a draft of this chapter and giving detailed criticisms and suggestions.

11

Remarks on Collective Belief

Margaret Gilbert

INTRODUCTION

> Listen, Alexey Fyodorovitch. Isn't there in all our analysis—I mean your analysis . . . no, better call it ours—aren't we showing contempt for him, for that poor man—in analysing his soul like this, as it were, from above, eh? In deciding so certainly that he will take the money? (Doestoevsky, *The Brothers Karamazov*, 1943, p. 257)

In daily life, people often say things like, "We decided that he would take the money," "In our view Jones would make a poor chairman," "We believe she is wrong." What is it for *us* to believe that such-and-such, according to our everyday understanding?

It is common to answer this question with some form of "summative" account. For *us* to believe that *p* is for all or most of us to believe that *p*.[1] Or perhaps a "common knowledge" condition may be added: for *us* to believe that *p* is for all or most of us to believe that *p*, while this is common knowledge among us.[2] Whatever the precise account given, the core of it is a number of individuals who personally believe that *p*.[3] Our belief is thus said to be constituted in large part by a "sum" of individual beliefs with the content in question. As I have argued elsewhere, there is another interpretation of such belief ascriptions—one I take to be quite standard—which connects them with a quite different phenomenon, a phenomenon of great practical importance.[4] I shall attempt to clarify further the nature of the phenomenon in question. I shall refer to it as *collective belief.*

I begin—in the next section—with an observation about the way in which some expressions of opinion are greeted with a certain special kind of shocked surprise. Those who know when to expect this type of shocked surprise are likely to be strongly affected by that knowledge. In particular, they are likely to censor their expressions of opinion. In the long run, the growth of human knowledge at both the collective and the individual level is likely to be affected. How does this shocked surprise response come about? Can it be avoided, or is it an inevitable part of human life? I go on to articulate my conception of collective belief and argue that the shocked surprise response is predictable given its presence.

OBSERVATION: THE "SHOCKED SURPRISE" RESPONSE

Sometimes one will express an opinion and it will be met with a special kind of shocked surprise. This is not directed at epistemic qualities of the opinion itself such as its obvious falsity, its absurdity, its lack of known substantiation. It is, rather, directed at the speaker who expressed this opinion. It is directed at the speaker in the light of certain apparently nonepistemic facts about him or her. That is, the relevant facts do not relate to the speaker's perceived capacity to discern truths or reach justified beliefs in the relevant domain. The shocked surprise is not a matter of the observer's finding the speaker oddly obtuse, for instance, or, confused. Before I attempt a more positive characterization of the relevant shocked surprise response, some examples will be helpful.

(1) A group of acquaintances have been discussing a man they know, Jake Robins, and they have reached the conclusion that Jake is an unpleasant character. Greg, one of their number, subsequently remarks without special preamble, "Jake Robins is so *nice.*" Now, there could of course be a kind of shocked surprise here at Greg's apparent and unexpected lack of judgment or simple ignorance. But there is in any case likely to be a significantly different kind of shocked surprise—the kind I am concerned with here. This is in some way a matter of Greg's participation in the conversational group that reached the conclusion that Jake Robins was an unpleasant character. One of the others might think, "How could Greg say that now, after what we've been saying?"

This example comes from an informal everyday context, and may seem relatively trivial. Apparently similar things happen in more formal contexts, however, such as the conduct of education, science, and politics. Here are two examples that relate to education and science, respectively.

(2) A class of students has been told by their teacher that modern science has a "masculine" bias. The existence of such a bias has subsequently been taken for granted in class discussions and tests. Towards the end of the semester Jessie raises her hand in class discussion and says, "You know, there's really no good evidence that modern science has a masculine bias." There could be shocked surprise here stemming from wonderment on the part of the students and the teacher that Jessie could be so ignorant, as she may indeed seem to be in their eyes. But a kind of shocked surprise with a different edge is in any case predictable: this stems in some way from the fact that Jessie has participated in the life of the class up to this point.

(3) A group of physicists are working together on some problems in string theory. One day in the course of a working lunch, Alphonse—one of their number—says, "String theory just isn't going anywhere!" Here again, there could be shocked surprise coming from the conviction that Alphonse is wrong, or from what is perceived as Alphonse's unexpectedly misguided thought. But a different target of such a response is also predictable: one of the group might perhaps think to himself, "How can he say that—he's one of us!"

Let us pause for a moment and consider what precisely this attitude of shocked surprise may amount to. I take it that, at a minimum, people who are shocked are "put out" in some way. They are "taken aback." They believe that something has gone wrong. This may or may not be true of all forms of surprise (see below). In any case, the type of surprise at issue here is indeed "shocked" at least in the minimal sense that the surprised person believes that something has—to some extent or in some respect—gone wrong.

Now there is more than this to the particular kind of shocked surprise I am concerned with, but it is worth considering this aspect of it in isolation for a moment.

The anticipation that one's utterance is likely to provoke the reaction "Something has gone wrong!" could be enough to prevent certain utterances from being made. In any case, more than the simple provocation of this particular negative *attitude* is likely to be at issue, given that it is provoked. It is clear enough that shocked surprise of this type is not something people tend to enjoy experiencing. They can therefore be expected not to deal entirely kindly with those who provoke it. They may frown at them, ridicule them, or shun them. In extreme cases those who provoke this response could lose their jobs or social positions. Fear of such losses would clearly be enough to explain the desire not to provoke shocked surprise in the first place. Thus someone may be moved not to express an honest well-thought-out opinion—even something they take to be certain knowledge, and something it is important to know.

So far I have characterized shocked surprise as (at the least) a negative attitude to the effect that "Something has gone wrong!" which could lead to behavior unpleasant or even disastrous to the person who provokes it. The particular type of shocked surprise at issue here can give rise to a special type of reaction which will help us to characterize it more precisely.

Some typical expressions associated with this shocked surprise are, "How can you say that?" and "*What* did you say?" or just plain "*What*?" With these expressions (uttered in the appropriate tone), one clearly expressed one's sense that the original speaker has behaved wrongly. One does more than this, however. One is not simply saying, "As I see it, it was wrong of you to say that!" Nor simply (in a less subjective vein), "It was wrong of you to say that!"

Observe that in the first of these cases, the original speaker could appropriately reply, "I regret that you think it was wrong of me to say that!" In the second case, the original speaker could appropriately reply, "Perhaps you are right!" or "That is unfortunate." As I shall explain, all of these replies would be inadequate in the context of the shocked surprise response at issue here.

The special reaction to which the shocked surprise response can give rise may in the first place be referred to as a *rebuke*. A rebuke—as I understand it—is, in the first instance, more than the simple communication to a person of a negative evaluation of that person's behavior. When one says, "It was wrong of you to do that," one is not necessarily rebuking the other person. Consider that statements like the following seem to be in order: "It was wrong of you to do that. I can't reproach you for it, of course. I've done the same thing many times myself. God knows the temptation is great."; or "You did something wrong! I'm so glad! You were beginning to seem too perfect!"

What is it, then, to rebuke someone or to communicate a criticism in a rebuking way? What distinguishes remarking on a person's error to that person (or saying that there seems to have been an error) from *telling a person off*?

Let me return to the particular phenomenon of shocked surprise with which I am here concerned. What is involved when someone expresses this shocked surprise by saying *"What?"* in the relevant way?

One aspect of this reaction is that it would be appropriately answered with some sort of explanation. More particularly, it would be appropriately answered with an explanation intended to defuse the reaction, that is, with an excuse. Thus the original speaker might suggest that he was not fully responsible for what he did: "Honestly, I don't know what came over me." Or he might, as we say, explain it away: "I just wanted to see what happened if I said that! Of course I wasn't *serious*." He is quite likely to speak apologetically or to make an explicit apology, perhaps at the same time taking back the offending remark: "I'm sorry, I don't know why I said that! Of course string theory is going somewhere!" Such responses are clearly appropriate answers to *"What?"* and the like.

Other types of response are possible also. The original speaker might, for instance, defiantly repeat what was said before. For now, I want to focus on the appropriateness of apologetic excuses. Even a defiant repetition may well be preceded by such an excuse, as in, "I'm sorry, but that's the *truth*. String theory just isn't going anywhere!"

Those who say *"What?"* suggest, it seems, that some kind of *offense* has been committed against *them*. Their shock, then, is by no means simply a matter of sensing an error or flaw somewhere. It involves a sense of offense: of being offended against. Their cry has in part the following ring: "Why are you doing this to me?" Or rather "to *us*?" For, importantly, any member of the relevant group might say *"What?"*—and, indeed, they might even say it in unison. They all lean forward: *"What???"* There is, indeed, something apparently impersonal about the offense. I, this person, am offended, but I am offended in my capacity as a member of this group.

A suggestion of offense suggests also that excuse and apology are in place. In contrast, if people simply point out to you that you have made some kind of error, they do not imply that it is appropriate for you to provide any kind of explanation, let alone an apology. (That is not to deny that many individuals would apologize in such circumstances, or that some cultural practices encourage this.)

Those who have been offended against by a person's action were, we may say, entitled at least to the absence of the action in question—a right that has been violated by the offender. This puts them in a special position in relation to the offender. They now have a basis for approaching the offender in a variety of related ways. They may engage in some kind of punitive behavior. They may demand restitution or recompense. An excuse is fitted to defuse the idea that such approaches are in order. An apology is fitted to defuse the idea that they are needed: the offender acknowledges the offense, and regrets it. Someone who, as we say, "takes something back" effects a kind of restitution.

I return now to the question of what a rebuke amounts to. I have observed that a rebuke is more than the noting of an error. In addition, it appears to have something punitive about it. The rebuking speaker, we may say, verbally chastises the hearer for a presumed wrong. One who issues a rebuke implicitly claims, then, to be entitled to chastise the rebuked person—verbally at least.

Perhaps not all rebukes imply that the rebuked person has somehow directly offended against the person issuing the rebuke. It may be that one's standing to issue a rebuke can sometimes derive from other sources. I shall not pursue that issue here. In the case with which I am concerned, there appears to be a rebuke in the minimal sense just noted, coupled with a sense of offense on the part of the person who rebukes. Presumably it is this sense of offense that justifies the rebuke in his or her own eyes. In case there are other sorts of rebuke, we may reserve for a rebuke which stems from a sense of offense the label "offended rebuke."

Talk of offenders, entitlements, and the like may call to mind the law and serious harms. Yet it seems to me that if we are to do justice to what is going on in the kinds of informal interchanges with which I am concerned, we need to bring in such concepts, or we cannot begin to see what is going on.

An offended rebuke clearly constitutes a form of pressure on the offender. The offender is called to account, and put on notice that any similar behavior may provoke further chastisement. The kinds of contexts at issue here tend to call out other kinds of pressure also, such as attempts to silence a speaker before the offending words are altogether spoken, attempts to shout them down, and so on.

In sum, the shocked surprise response in question here involves a sense of offense such that the surprised person will feel justified in uttering. We can add that the recipient of an offended rebuke may be expected to understand its basis. It will be understood (at some level) to be in order. These observations require explanation.

We now have a number of questions. On what grounds are people critical of certain expressions of belief when their criticism does not (as it seems) have epistemic grounds? In particular, it is neither a matter of the presumed epistemic unacceptability of what is believed nor some presumed epistemic flaw in the speaker. On what grounds do people feel entitled to communicate their sense of error to the person concerned? In particular, on what grounds do they feel entitled to issue a rebuke, where to rebuke is to chastise verbally for a presumed error? Given that the rebuke is an offended rebuke, whence comes the sense of offense?

These are questions of great practical relevance. An offended rebuke is both penalty and pressure. Such pressure (and its anticipation) can have grave consequences for the growth of knowledge in society, not to speak of the effects of self-repression on individual people.[5] One might indeed wonder how such practices of criticism and pressure could ever be defended.

APPROACHING COLLECTIVE BELIEF

Allusions to What *We Believe* in the Context of the Shocked Surprise Response

What might explain the complex shocked surprise response at issue here? Let us look back at the examples presented in the previous section. We had various speakers saying something which evoked the shocked surprise response.

In the first example, the offending utterance was, "Jake Robins is so *nice*." As I have noted, the shocked surprise response might prod a listener to comment starkly, "*What*?" or "What do you *mean*?" and so on. There is, however, another familiar type of comment to which this response may give rise. In the Jake Robins case, someone might object, "But we decided that Jake was *unpleasant*!" In the case of the class discussing science, one can imagine someone responding, "But we know there *is* a masculine bias in science!" In the case of the apparently skeptical string theorist, one of the group might burst out, "But *we* don't think that!"

In short, sentences beginning "But we think that . . . ," "But we know that . . . ," "But we decided that . . . ," and the like might well be uttered in such contexts. Here beliefs, conclusions, knowledge, and so on are ascribed to "us." I shall call statements which do this *collective belief* statements.[6] The question of their interpretation, of course, remains.

Since utterances beginning "But we think . . ." and the like are liable to occur in the context of the shocked surprise response, it is a reasonable conjecture that at least some occasions of that response are situations in which, according to those who are shocked, one of "us" has denied the truth of one of "our" beliefs, either explicitly or implicitly. In other words, they are situations involving a collective belief.

More, it appears that in at least some of these situations the existence of a particular collective belief, as such, is taken to merit an offended rebuke. The implication is that the original speakers erred in saying what they said simply by virtue of the fact that they expressed a belief contrary to "our" belief. The form of words used—"But we think . . ." and so on—suggests this. That is, it suggests that the simple fact of our thinking that such and such is enough to ground a rebuke, the rebuke itself being signalled by the "But . . . ."

In interpreting collective belief statements it is reasonable, therefore, to raise again the question raised earlier of the shocked surprise response. What could justify the response? What rational basis could it have?

It could, of course, have no justifying basis. It could be a response which occurs spontaneously in certain contexts without any rational warrant. This possibility is no reason to abandon the search for a rational basis. So let us ask: what could justify the shocked surprise response? In particular, on what account of collective belief would the expression of a belief contrary to the collective one justify this response?

Two Summative Accounts of Collective Belief and the Shocked Surprise Response

Before proceeding to my positive answer I return briefly to the two summative accounts of "our belief" mentioned earlier. Consider the more complex one. This invokes a belief which is widespread in a certain population, where it is common knowledge that the belief is indeed widespread. Now suppose that it is common knowledge in a certain small community that most members believe that it is desirable to leave home on vacation in summer. One member, Claire, says to another, Dan, "You know, there is really little point in going out of town in summer." Is this enough to justify an offended rebuke on Dan's part, all else being equal?

Someone may argue that Dan is likely to be *surprised* at Claire's statement, knowing that most of their number think differently. Dan will then have some reason to be upset by it, since surprise can be seen as a reflection on the quality or efficacy of one's reasoning capacities. It is reasonable to assume that all this is common knowledge in the community in question. Claire will then have known that she was liable to upset Dan to some degree when she spoke as she did, and Dan will know this.

Suppose that for the sake of argument we accept these points. It is by no means obvious that both Dan and Claire will immediately understand that Dan is now justified in approaching Claire with an offended rebuke. The basis for the rebuke, given this argument, would presumably be that Claire did something she knew was liable to upset Dan to some degree. But to what degree? Suppose it were common knowledge between Dan and Claire that Dan was extremely sensitive to the epistemic implications of surprise: surprising him was always on a par with inflicting severe mental distress. An offended rebuke from Dan might then be in order. But in the world as we know it, most people are not like this.

In any case it appears that the appropriateness of the offended rebuke stemming from the existence of a collective belief is not a matter of sensitivities or evaluations that may vary from person to person or culture to culture. The simple fact that *we have a certain belief* provides a basis for rebuking one of our number who says something contrary to the belief.

If it is observed that one who expresses a minority view in a community is doing something *unusual* or *uncommon*, this does not in itself support the idea that Claire is in any way in error in saying what she said, let alone that an offended rebuke from Dan is appropriate. Highly conventional people may think that uncommon behavior is bad, but those who thrive on variety will find it delightful.

To say that a given belief is widespread in a particular community, then, or to say that this is so and that it is common knowledge in the community, is not in any obvious way to show that members of that community will have grounds for an offended rebuke if one member gainsays the belief in question. So, if this particular type of response is sometimes based on the existence of a collective belief, as there is reason to think, it is not based on collective belief according to the complex summative account, nor according to the simple summative account. This of course suggests that these accounts do not adequately describe what people mean when they refer to what *we* believe. If they sometimes intend these phrases in a summative sense, it appears that this is at least not *always* so.

Plural Subjects

In common parlance one hears frequent references not only to what we believe, but also to what we like, what we prefer, what we are doing, what we intend, to our principles and our purposes, and so on. My book *On Social Facts* (1989) constitutes a lengthy argument to the effect that analysis of such references discovers for us an important family of everyday concepts. I have labelled these concepts the "plural subject" concepts.

If the concept of collective belief is construed as a plural subject concept, the existence of a collective belief will be enough to justify the shocked surprise response, as I shall show. I first say something about the plural subject concepts in general, before focusing on the case of belief.

I should stress that the phrase "plural subject" is a technical one: it applies (as I use it) only to those who are connected in a way I shall specify. Meanwhile the phrase itself is intended to convey the underlying perspective of these concepts: the idea that a plurality of persons may in certain special contexts be seen as constituting the subject (as opposed to the subjects) of a certain psychological attribute.

For present purposes, I shall focus on the following account of plural subjecthood:

> For persons *A* and *B* and psychological attribute *X*, *A* and *B* form a *plural subject* of *X*-ing if and only if *A* and *B* are jointly committed to *X*-ing as a body, or, if you like, as a single person.

Some explanation of the terms of this account must be given.

(i) What is the idea behind the alternative formulations "*X*-ing as a body" or "*X*-ing as a single person"? The way to convey this idea that is perhaps most entrenched in English is "*X*-ing together." However, this has its own ambiguity. "*X*-ing together" can be interpreted as "*X*-ing side by side" or "in close proximity." It can also connote the "*X*-ing as a body" or "as a single person" idea. Thus, "Jane and Sally are travelling together" could mean that they are travelling on the same train or whatever (though perhaps even unaware of each other). It could also mean that they are travelling "as a single body" ("as a single person").[7]

An important aspect of the idea of *X*-ing as a body is this: from the mere understanding that for some psychological attribute *X*, *A* and *B* are *X*-ing as a body, we cannot infer that *A* personally *X*-es or that *B* personally *X*-es. Consider the case of *A* and *B* building a house together. Normally when people build a house together there is some division of labor. One person puts in the windows, say, and another lays the roof. Thus people may succeed in building a house together without any one of them doing anything that would count, on its own, as building a house.

There are, of course, more positive aspects of *X*-ing as a body. I shall not attempt to specify what these are for the general case here, but will rely on intuitive understandings. I will leave discussion of specific cases until I turn to the case of collective belief.

(ii) Membership in a plural subject of psychological attributes clearly requires an understanding of the nature of the attribute in question. I do not say that it requires the concept of an individual human being who *X*-es. There is no need here to preempt an answer to the question whether plural subject concepts are in some way parasitic upon or secondary to our conceptions of the psychological attributes of individual human beings. In any case, one must have the concept of *X*-ing in order to enter a joint commitment to *X* as a body.

(iii) I must now say more about what is perhaps the key concept in my account of plural subjects: the concept of *joint commitment.*[8] I use the term "joint commitment" as a technical phrase—though, of course, one chosen for its appropriateness to its intended content.[9]

A fair amount can be said about joint commitment and its structure. One thing to stress is that the existence of any joint commitment is a function of the participants' conception of their situation. Roughly speaking, people become jointly committed by mutually expressing their willingness *to be jointly committed*, in conditions of common knowledge. One cannot be a party to a joint commitment, then, without having the concept of a joint commitment.

As the parties to a joint commitment understand, they are "individually committed" in the sense that each one is subject to a commitment. Yet the commitment they are subject to is seen as a joint one. This way of seeing things has two central aspects.

First, the "individual commitments" in question bear a special relationship to one another: they are radically *interdependent* with respect to both their generation and their persistence. They *cannot exist* apart. In seeing themselves as party to a joint commitment, people understand themselves to be committed in this way. They understand, therefore, that their commitments through the joint commitment arise simultaneously. Moreover, one of these commitments cannot survive the end of the other.

If one party deliberately breaks faith, the constraints of commitment are lifted from the other.

Second, the parties understand that mutual consent is required to rescind the commitment. One does not hold sway over one's "individual commitment" here as one does over one's personal decisions, say, or one's own intentions. Given an intention of my own, if I want to change my mind, I can. I can rescind my own decision and abrogate my own intention. I may be unwise or capricious or unstable to do so, but I have that option: my own decision is *mine to change.* A joint commitment in which I take part is understood not to be mine to change: it is ours, rather, and only we together can rescind it.

It is true that one party can deliberately violate or break a joint commitment with the result that it is henceforth no longer there to impose constraints on anyone. But the constraints the commitment creates exist in full force right up to the break.

I have sometimes referred to the entry into a joint commitment as involving the expression of a "conditional commitment." This phrase is open to various interpretations. The rather delicate point I have intended should by now be fairly clear. One must evidently be "ready for joint commitment" as far as one's own will is concerned, yet (as one understands) only if a certain condition is fulfilled *can* one be committed as a function of a joint commitment. This is what each party must express to the relevant others. Each individual's participation in the joint commitment requires a similar expression of willingness on every other individual's part. Thus, a man who says, "Shall we dance?" indicates that, in effect, he will be committed to dancing if (and only if) his question is answered appropriately. His ensuing commitment to dance will be a function of the joint commitment then, and only then created.

I have now elaborated up to a certain point the general nature of the plural subject concepts that I take to inform much of our everyday discourse. I take such concepts to be implicit, that is, in much if not most talk of what we prefer, what we think, what our goal is, and so on. More could be said, but for present purposes this should be sufficient.[10]

Joint Commitment and Obligation

Before focusing particularly on the topic of *our belief,* I want to connect the concept of joint commitment with the concepts of obligation and entitlement. I believe that understanding the concept of joint commitment helps us, indeed, to understand better what obligation is.

I propose that joint commitments, given what they are, generate a special and central form of obligation. I have argued this at some length elsewhere, but since it is highly relevant to my present concerns, I must say something about it here.[11]

Suppose that June is party to a joint commitment. As she understands, the source of the commitment she is now personally subject to is not an act of her own mind or will alone, and she is not in a position to rescind that commitment by an act of her own mind or will alone. For it takes at least two to make or rescind a joint commitment.

Now, June's commitment gives her a reason for acting.[12] This is a reason that she is not in a position to remove by simply changing her mind. Nor, indeed, will a change in her external circumstances remove it. However justified she is from one point of view or another in acting against the commitment, she cannot remove it without the concurrence of the other parties to the commitment. We can thus pointfully say that the parties to a joint commitment are *bound or obligated to one another*. They have a reason for acting which will press upon them unless and until the parties decide otherwise as a body.

My hypothesis about obligation, then, is that a central use of the term "obligation" is to refer to a reason for acting such that the person who has it (whom we may call the "obligee") is beholden to another or others (the "obligors") for its eradication by virtue of the participation of both obligee and obligors in a joint commitment.[13]

Apparently we can talk of rights and entitlements here, also. It seems natural to say that, unless they have consented otherwise, the obligors are entitled to certain behaviors from the obligees. If these behaviors do not occur, the rights of the obligors have been violated.

It is important to note that what I shall now refer to as the *obligations* of joint commitment have certain special features that distinguish them from at least one other familiar form of (so-called) obligation. In other words, the obligations of joint commitment are obligations of a special kind or in a special sense.[14]

First, in order to establish these obligations, each party must be willing to be jointly committed. The "willingness" at issue here might also be referred to as "readiness" or "preparedness." There is no obvious necessity for coercion to be absent from the situation. In other words, it looks as if it is possible to enter a joint commitment in coercive conditions. "So we're travelling together?" Doris says, menacing Al with a gun. Al might well say "Sure" in such circumstances, and do so sincerely. He may not mind travelling with Doris, but he would not have said he would do so unless Doris had threatened him. He has been coerced into travelling with Doris.

Now, if he has indeed entered into a joint commitment, he has the ensuing obligations, for these flow as a matter of logic from the joint commitment. One cannot be party to a joint commitment without having obligations of joint commitment.

According to many people, there is a sense in which Al "has no obligation" to go through the motions of travelling with Doris if Doris coerced him into agreeing to travel with her. If there is a sense in which this is so, then it corresponds to a type of obligation that is distinct from the obligations of joint commitment. Now, many would say that what Al does *not* have here is a "moral" obligation to go along with Doris. In that case, the obligations of joint commitment are not moral obligations.

It is not necessary here to debate the best way to delimit morality or moral obligation. One practically relevant aspect of the point about coercion is that joint commitments and their obligations can flourish in a wide variety of conditions, including conditions of intimidation and coercion. Someone who *is* coerced into a joint commitment experiences a double constraint: coerced into the commitment, Al understands that he will have a reason to do what he committed himself to do unless parties release him from the commitment.

A second aspect of the obligations of joint commitment is that they persist whatever the countervailing factors. Given a joint commitment to travel with Doris, even if Al subsequently has good reason to default on his commitment, his obligations to Doris will persist. For only with Doris's concurrence can the joint commitment be dissolved. If he does default, it would be appropriate for him to apologize to Doris for failing to fulfil an obligation he has to her. Given that Doris coerced him in the first place, he may of course decide not to apologize.

A final aspect of the obligations of joint commitment is that we can expect parties to a joint commitment to understand that they are obligated and entitled accordingly.

Rather than press the relatively obscure proposal that the obligations of joint commitment are not moral obligations, I shall rest with these three points about them: (1) they can arise in coercive conditions; (2) they persist in the presence of facts that justify not fulfilling them; and (3) they can be expected to be known to those who have them.

COLLECTIVE BELIEF

Plural Subjects of Belief

If we follow the schema for analyzing plural subject concepts presented above, we get the following result for believing that *p*:

> *A* and *B* form *a plural subject of believing* that *p* if and only if *A* and *B* are jointly committed to believing that *p* as a body.

Some comments are in order. First, let me spell out some implications of this account which should be clear given the discussion in the previous section. Given this account, if Anne and Betty form a plural subject of believing that *p*, *each of them is obligated to the other* to do her part in believing that *p* as a body. Should Anne or Betty not act accordingly, she has defaulted on an obligation to the other, and the other's corresponding right to her performance has been violated. Both Anne and Betty will understand this. We see, then, that if they form a plural subject of believing that *p*, Anne and Betty will understand that *they have a basis for rebuking one another should the appropriate behavior not occur.*

Second, what precisely is the behavior appropriate to members of a plural subject of belief? What are their obligations? In this connection it must be noted that plural subjecthood, both in the case of belief and more generally, appears to be susceptible of various forms of contextualization. This has implications for the extent of the obligations generated in a given case. A few rough pointers must suffice here on a topic of some interest, importance, and delicacy.

Suppose that George and Mary have to decide how late their son Johnnie can stay out tonight. Mary thinks he should be home by ten, George thinks that he should stay out as long as he pleases. They discuss the matter for a while, and can't agree. George: "Look, we've got to tell the boy something!" Mary: "Suppose we say midnight?" George: "Well, that's better than ten, anyhow!" At this point George might well go to Johnnie and say to him quite sincerely, "We think you should be home by midnight."

It appears at this juncture that George and Mary will understand themselves to be jointly committed to believing as a body that Johnnie should be home by midnight *at least insofar as they are dealing with*

Johnnie. Now suppose that, in the privacy of their bedroom, George says, "I still don't see why the boy shouldn't be home at three if he wants to." Given that their joint commitment had the contextualized content suggested, we can expect Mary to hear this without any sense that an obligation to herself has been violated.

Things would be different if their discussion had proceeded as follows. Mary: "I think Johnnie should be home by ten." George: "Really? That's a bit early! He is sixteen, you know! I don't see why he shouldn't stay out as long as he pleases!" Mary: "Oh really, George, be reasonable! He has to go to school!" George: "Hmm. That's true. . . . Midnight's a bit more like it, though!" Mary: "That's okay, I suppose." At this point George might go and talk to Johnnie as before. However, back in the bedroom, it would surely be harder now for George to sit down and say, "I still don't see why the boy shouldn't stay out till three if he wants to." For, among other things, the dialogue in this instance suggests a closure of discussion of the subject *between George and Mary.* For George to say this to Mary "without preamble" is for him to take their previous discussion in vain, so to speak.[15]

The latter hypothetical situation represents perhaps the simplest and purest type of plural subjecthood. It might be dubbed the "simple interpersonal" type. One or more people have had a conversation and reached a conclusion. Their dominant sense of the proceedings is that they are these individuals discussing this issue. In such cases, it appears that if in personal conversation immediately after the close of the conversation one of the parties bluntly denies the conclusion to the other, he or she is not keeping to their bargain.

What would *keeping faith* with the joint commitment amount to in this case? I shall not attempt to explore all aspects of this here. One can at least say that, all else being equal, it would be appropriate for George and Mary to conduct their own subsequent conversations as if it were true that Johnnie should be home by midnight. They do not, of course, have to keep expressing this view. It will, rather, "go without saying." But if it is to go without saying, then it must not be gainsaid—or not without some delicate preamble. (I say more about this shortly.)[16]

Quite generally, the precise understandings between the parties is what determines the extent of their obligations in each case. Sometimes what understandings there are may be relatively vague, with perhaps a clear core. These understandings can, of course, change over time. They may become more or less definite; they may change radically. Sometimes, violation of the relevant obligations, as currently understood, may lead to settling on a different understanding.

Third, there are ways of talking that appear to allow people to affirm that not-*p* although they are members of a plural subject of believing that *p* in a situation where the blunt denial of *p* is out of order. One may say, for instance, "Look, *I personally do not believe* that *p*. . . ." Or, "Speaking personally, . . ." One seems to differentiate oneself *as an individual* from—what? Oneself as a member of the relevant plural subject, perhaps. The fact that we have this way of speaking suggests that, in general, participating in *believing that p as a body* does not require *personally believing that p*. This accords, of course, with what was said earlier about the general idea of several persons "*X*-ing as a body": this does not entail, for every *X*, that each of the parties individually *X*.[17]

That is perhaps a surprising result, since it suggests that the summative views discussed earlier are completely on the wrong track. It is not even a *necessary condition* of our believing that *p* that each or most of us believe that *p* personally.

But perhaps I get ahead of myself. Is what people refer to when they speak of what "we believe" the belief of a plural subject constituted by each of "us"? There is reason to think that, at least sometimes, references to what we believe do have this meaning.

Collective Belief

Recall my discussion of the shocked surprise response. I noted that this might well be expressed in terms of what *we believe* or what *we think* and so on: "But we know that science has a masculine bias!"; "But we concluded Jake was quite unpleasant!"; "But we don't think string theory isn't going anywhere. On the contrary!"

If our believing something is a matter of our being the parties to a joint commitment to believe as a body, we have an explanation of how our believing something can lead to the shocked surprise response and of why that response should issue in "But we think . . ." and so on. For the speaker who provokes the response violates an obligation to his hearers. The three example cases can be interpreted along these lines, given the amount of description already provided. That gives us some reason to accept the following account of collective belief:

> There is a *collective belief* that *p* if some persons constitute the plural subject of a belief that *p*. Such persons *collectively believe* that *p*.

I write "if," rather than "if and only if": I have argued elsewhere that the type of collective belief characterized here may be the basic type, from our understanding of which other types attract the same label.[18]

I regard this account as essentially the same as a variety of rather different formulations I have used in other places. A note should be added here on one aspect of these other formulations, given that I have elsewhere referred to my account of collective belief as the "joint acceptance" account (Gilbert 1987, p. 194; 1989, pp. 298ff).

I have written, in this connection, of a joint commitment to "accept that *p* as a body" or to "jointly accept that *p*" (Gilbert 1987, 1989). This was something that I did spontaneously, without questioning why I did not, rather, write of a commitment to "believe that *p* . . . ."

A number of philosophers have recently made distinctions between "belief" and "acceptance" such that there is a real distinction between the two (Stalnaker 1984, p. 74f., Van Fraassen 1980, p. 88). However, a look through a number of dictionaries suggests that there is a sense of "accepts that *p*" and "believes that *p*" such that these are virtually synonymous. I think it likely that when I originally wrote of "joint acceptance" I was not consciously meaning to introduce a concept distinct from that of belief, and that my spontaneous use of "accepts that *p*" may have been guided as much by my sense of euphony as anything else. There is no need to pursue this issue at length here. The following points may be noted, however.

The general schema introduced here for the plural subject concepts seems to me auspicious. It proposes that the plural subject of a psychological predicate "*X*" involves a joint commitment precisely to *X*-ing as a body. Clearly if "*X*" and "*Y*" are synonymous, it will be correct to say that (using the terms in the relevant senses) a plural subject of *X* involves a joint commitment to *Y*-ing as a body. Meanwhile, things will be clearer if we use the same term in both places. Then, if we define collective belief in terms of plural subjecthood, we will define it in terms of joint commitment to *believe* as a body (rather than using the putatively synonymous "accept").

Now it could be that you can only believe that *p* as a body if you also accept that *p* as a body, in some nonsynonymous sense of "accept" such that accepting entails believing. This could be a reason for proposing an account of collectively *X*-ing in terms of a joint commitment to *Y* as a body. I shall not pursue this, or related ideas, here.[19]

What I want to stress is that, as I understand it, the behavior that results from collective belief is driven by *the concept of belief* and *the concept X-ing-as-a-body*. It is as if the participants ask themselves,

"What do I need to do to make it the case that I and these others together believe that *p* as a body?"—and then act accordingly. I have suggested that the answer given by our everyday understanding for the simple interpersonal case is that, among other things, in reasoning together we say things that entail *p* rather than not-*p*, we do not deny that *p* without preamble, and so on. More briefly, we attempt as best we can to make it true that the body we constitute relates to *p* the way any *individual* who believes that *p* relates to *p*.[20]

CONCLUDING REMARKS

Is there a moral here, a practical conclusion? It may well appear that collective beliefs in the sense delineated here are unsavory phenomena. They justify the infliction of pressure by one person on another in the service of beliefs which may be false, and which, indeed, may not be personally accepted by any of the parties. Thus we may well be moved to ask whether collective beliefs are avoidable.

In practice I think they are not. If you are taking part in a conversation you are liable to be faced with expressions of opinion you have to respond to in some way. You will have to accept or reject the opinions, or to express indecision on the matter. If you so much as nod agreement, a collective belief will result, and you are, and know you are, now liable to evoke the shocked surprise response if you deviate from the obligations of the newly formed joint commitment.[21]

If collective beliefs are unavoidable in our situation as interacting, conversing beings, then we may suspect that they have their uses, as of course they do. Apart from the general function of providing individuals with a sense of unity or community with others—a function all joint commitment helps to some degree to fulfil—the collective beliefs evidently provide points from which people can go forward, not forever locked in the back-and-forth of argumentative conflict.[22]

It will be hard to avoid the repressiveness of collective beliefs. Perhaps the best we can do is attempt to assure that the beliefs that become collective among us are beliefs we can live with. For, once they are set, they are powerful forces.[23]

Notes

1. See, for instance, Quinton (1975-76).

2. The term "common knowledge" was introduced into the philosophical literature by Lewis (1969). There is by now a large literature on the subject in both philosophy and economics. To put things in familiar terms, one might say that it is common knowledge (in the relevant sense) that *p* in a certain population if and only if the fact that *p* is completely out in the open in that population. For further discussion of how common knowledge is best defined, see Lewis (1969), Schiffer (1972), Heal (1978), and Gilbert (1989).

3. See Gilbert (1989, ch. 5) for a discussion of these two and a third summative account.

4. The main references are Gilbert (1987 and 1989, especially ch. 5, and also ch. 7). Though this paper is intended to be self-contained, it is not intended as a substitute for these earlier discussions.

There is of course no question that when all or most members of a certain population have a certain belief, this will often be a matter with important consequences. If we all believe that Jones is the best candidate, Jones may be elected as a result. That a general belief is common knowledge will often have its own consequences. If it is common knowledge that we all prefer Jones, we will not waste time arguing in Jones's favor. The consequences in the case I have in mind are, in any case, rather different. See below in the text.

5. Cf. John Stuart Mill's classic text in political philosophy, *On Liberty* (1978).

6. For some purposes one might want to say that only "We believe that. . ." is properly labelled a collective *belief* statement. However, there is clearly quite a large number of other sentences which are understood to ascribe belief or something involving belief, including "We decided that . . . ," "We know that . . . ," "We are convinced that . . . ," "We think that . . . ," "Our opinion is that . . ." and "We concluded that. . . ." among others. For present purposes the category of collective belief statements may be taken to encompass all of these. In focused discussion I shall generally concentrate on "We believe . . ." specifically as an example. An approach to understanding each member of this family individually will be provided. This approach will also apply to related ascriptions such as "We are inclined to think that . . . ," "For present purposes we are assuming that . . . ," and so on.

7. If one pauses to think about it, these ways of describing things have their picturesque side. They bring to mind the well-known figure on the engraved title page to the first edition of Hobbes's *Leviathan*: a vast number of persons making up a vast person. A less picturesque alternative might be "as a unit." This may risk missing something useful in the connotations of the other phrases: the idea of a single "source of action." I have in mind the joint commitment which

constitutes a given plural subject, and which has the power to motivate those involved to act appropriately. Joint commitment is discussed in some detail below in the text.

8. See Gilbert (1989, chs 4ff.).

9. In earlier work, I wrote at one point of being "committed as a body" Gilbert (1987, p. 194). Either phrase could be used to convey the general idea.

10. For discussion of the resemblance between everyday *agreements* and joint commitment phenomena in general, see Gilbert (1993b).

11. See Gilbert (1993a, especially pp. 686-700).

12. On this, see Gilbert (1993a, pp. 686-687, including footnote 13).

13. It is clear from this that, strictly speaking, the obligation one is subject to through a joint commitment is an obligation one has to the parties to the commitment in that capacity. Thus "obligee" June will be obligated to "obligor" Joe in his capacity as party to their joint commitment. She will not, one might say, be obligated to Joe "considered as an individual." She herself, of course, is a member of the group to which she is beholden for release. For present purposes the main point is that she is understood not to be in a position unilaterally to remove the relevant constraint on her behavior. Others—or at least one other—must be called into play.

14. The following discussion draws on that in Gilbert (1993c).

15. Cf. N. Shakespeare (1993), on overhearing his parents in private conversation: "never before had I heard them converse unencumbered by the knowledge and presence of children. Nothing that passed between them was remotely embarrassing or distressing, or even particularly interesting, but, as if for the first time, I was hearing the two of them as man and woman rather than as parents." For some related discussion, see Gilbert (1989, pp. 219-221, 302, 374-375). I thank Fred Schmitt for discussion of the contrast illustrated in the preceding three paragraphs of the text.

16. David Lewis has suggested (personal communication, 3 January 1989) that such ideas fit together well with those of Robert Stalnaker (1973, 1974) on presupposition. As Lewis observed, Stalnaker is primarily interested in the interaction of presupposition and language rather than in the analysis of presupposition itself. See also Lewis (1983).

17. Thus being part of a plural subject of belief allows in principle for one's "freedom of thought" (cf. Cohen 1967). But see Gilbert (1987, p. 198; 1989, pp. 304-6) on the likely influence on individuals of membership in a plural subject of belief. See also Mill (1978, ch. 2). Mill proposes that freedom of thought is closely tied to freedom of expression of opinion.

18. See, for instance, Gilbert (1987, pp. 199-120; 1989, pp. 311, 239-40). See also Gilbert (1994, sec. 2).

19. This paragraph was prompted by some comments from Fred Schmitt.

20. It may be suggested that what we in fact do *individually* in constituting a collective belief that *p* is *accept that p* in a sense in which this is not equivalent to *believe that p*. Rather, each of uses the proposition that *p* as a premiss in his or her reasoning, without necessarily believing it. (Tuomela [1992] appears to suggest this or something similar.) This would be relevant to my account of collective belief as an attempt to give a general account of what it is to do one's part in believing as a body in terms of a specific propositional attitude taken up by the individuals involved. I shall not attempt to evaluate it from this point of view here.

21. See Gilbert (1989, ch. 5, sec. 7.3), which suggests that a conversation can be viewed as the "negotiation" of a jointly accepted view.

22. On the sense of unity aspect of joint commitment see Gilbert (1989, pp. 223-225; 1990). Fred Schmitt discusses uses of collective belief in the sense discussed here in his paper "The Justification of Group Beliefs," this volume.

23. This accords with Emile Durkheim's insistence on the "coercive power" of collective beliefs in *The Rules of Sociological Method* (1982), see especially chapter 1 and the prefaces. See also Gilbert (1989, pp. 243-254; 1994).

An earlier version of this paper was read to the Department of Philosophy, Hamburg University, June 1993. I thank those present for a lively discussion. Thanks also to Fred Schmitt for useful written comments on that version, and to Michael Cook and Saul Kripke for related discussion. The paper is already long enough, but I regret not having been able to address certain queries that have come my way regarding my account of collective belief. I hope to do that in another place.

12

The Justification of Group Beliefs

Frederick F. Schmitt

In current epistemology there is much interest in whether, and in what ways, knowledge and epistemically justified belief (the kind of justified belief necessary for knowledge) might be social. There is one obvious way in which justified belief might be social. It might belong not only to individuals, but to *groups* of individuals—groups being social entities. The claim that there is such social justified belief is not completely trivial. It entails the nontrivial consequences that groups exist, that they have beliefs, and that these beliefs are justified. I will say a bit in defense of these consequences below. The burden of the present chapter, however, is whether justified group belief might be social in a more interesting way, one that goes beyond these consequences. There are those who go so far as to say that all knowledge—even the knowledge possessed by individuals—is ultimately group or communal knowledge, or at least derives from it. This goes too far, though I will defend a limited claim of the primacy of group over individual knowledge in the final section of the chapter. Most of the chapter will explore less extreme, but still quite strong, claims about the sociality of group justification.

It is beyond the scope of this chapter to argue for the existence of groups or group beliefs. I will say something about the nature of group beliefs in the first section below. Here it will suffice to make an intuitive case for the existence of justified group beliefs. Begin with the observation that we routinely ascribe knowledge, perception, and memory to groups. We say such things as, "The Engineering Division of the Ford Motor Corporation knew that the Pinto was explosive," "The crowd that had assembled on the square below could see that the window washer was dangling by his belt," and "This Court will remember counsel's objection during cross-examination." These are, on the face of it, ascriptions of cognitive states to groups. Yet, so interpreted, these ascriptions entail that the groups are justified in their beliefs. It may be tempting to read these claims as attributing cognitive states not to the groups themselves, but to their members (to all or most members, or to designated members). However, I will eventually argue against such a view of group justification.

In the meantime, we may make another intuitive point in favor of the claim that groups are sometimes justified in their beliefs. We say that people succeed in *justifying* propositions to groups. An engineer might justify to a court or a lecture audience the belief that the Pinto is explosive. And in saying this, we do not mean merely that the proposition has been justified to each member of the audience, since we allow that there might be members to whom it has not been justified. The proposition has been justified to the *audience*. Yet if someone justifies a proposition to a subject, it follows that the subject is justified in believing the proposition. Thus, if someone justifies a proposition to a group, it follows that the group is justified in believing the proposition. Indeed, it is plausible that justifying a proposition to a group is simply bringing it about that the group is justified in believing the proposition by providing the group with reason to believe it. A similar point holds for *informing*. Informing an audience that a proposition is true entails that the audience knows and is justified in believing the proposition. Informing a group that a proposition is true is simply bringing it about that the group knows the proposition by saying or otherwise indicating that the proposition is true.

These intuitive points are hardly decisive in favor of the claim that groups can be justified in their beliefs, but perhaps these points will suffice for the moment to motivate a look at the nature of the justification of group beliefs. Before we turn to that topic, however, we must say something about the nature of groups and group beliefs. Our remarks on these topics may add some support to our intuitive case that groups can be justified in their beliefs.

THE NATURE OF GROUPS AND GROUP BELIEFS

Let us begin with the nature of groups. There are two apparently opposing views about the ontological status of groups. According to one view—*ontological individualism*—a group is nothing but the individuals who belong to the group. But according to *ontological holism*, a group is something over and above its members. It is natural, and I think correct, to seek a view of the ontological status of groups that lies between these apparent extremes, or otherwise reconciles them. One wants to say that both parties are right. In a sense a group is its members, but in another sense it is more than its members.

Margaret Gilbert has offered just such an account of groups in her landmark book *On Social Facts* (1989), the richest and clearest exploration of the semantics and ontology of collective notions ever attempted. I regard Gilbert's account as at least on the right track, and certainly preferable to alternatives; I will follow it closely here.

Gilbert proposes conditions under which a set of individuals constitutes a group. Her conditions provide a natural and intuitive way of reconciling ontological individualism and ontological holism. We may introduce Gilbert's account by citing her observation that ontological individualism and ontological holism may each be interpreted in two ways. On one interpretation of ontological individualism, the view says that a group consists of nothing but its members each intending to act on his or her own behalf (or by his or her own lights)—intending to act as a *singular agent*. On this interpretation, ontological individualism is implausible. For a set of singular agents does not constitute a group. What is required for a group is that a set of individuals forms a *plural subject*. The individuals in the set must do more than intend to act each on his or her own behalf or as singular agents. Each must intend to act *jointly* with the others. More precisely, a set of individuals forms a plural subject only if each member of the set openly expresses a willingness to act jointly with the other members of the set. Thus, a group consists of something more than its members each intending to act as a singular agent. It consists of its members each intending to act jointly. So ontological individualism is mistaken if interpreted as claiming that a group consists of its members each intending to act as a singular agent.

However, there is a second interpretation of ontological individualism on which the view is plausible: it claims that a group is nothing but its members each intending to act jointly with the others. Such a view is still individualistic in saying that a group consists of individuals having certain intentions. It meets the *human intentional states requirement* on an account of groups: that "viable sociological collectivity concepts will entail that facts about human collectivities, in particular about their actions, are constituted by facts about the ideas and acts of will of human beings" (Gilbert 1989, p. 417). Admittedly, the account of groups here does not *reduce* the notion of a group to noncollective notions. For the account is formulated in terms of joint action, and the notion of joint action is a collective notion. And there is no obvious way to define the notion of joint action in noncollective terms. Nor is there any obvious way to eliminate all collective notions from the account of groups. Nevertheless, the account of groups vindicates ontological individualism understood as the claim that groups consist of individuals with certain intentions.

Turning now to ontological holism, we may interpret it as saying that a group is not composed of individuals at all, but is something over and above its members. On one view, a group requires a group mind distinct from the minds of members. So interpreted, ontological holism is unwarranted. But ontological holism may be interpreted as claiming that a group is not merely its members each intending to act on his or her own behalf, as a singular agent. A group consists of its members each intending to act jointly with the others (where, for simplicity, we may understand action broadly to include accepting a proposition). On this interpretation, ontological holism is plausible.

We have, so far, a working account of groups: a set of individuals forms a group just in case the members of the set each openly expresses his or her willingness to act jointly with the other members of the set. This account of groups has the advantage of offering a way between ontological individualism and ontological holism. It suggests interpretations of these views on which they are consistent with one another and correct. The account of groups has the advantage of meeting the human intentional states requirement on an account of groups. The account also suggests an account of group action: a group acts only if its members jointly act together. These remarks, brief as they are, will perhaps suffice to explain what we have in mind in the remainder of the chapter when we talk of groups and group actions.

Our next topic is group belief. Antipathy to the claim that groups can have beliefs is quite common. Gilbert attributes this antipathy to the combination of two plausible views. One is *psychologism about belief*: a subject can have a belief only if the subject has a mind. This view follows (nearly enough) from the claim that a belief is a state of mind. The other view is *antipsychologism about groups*: a group does not have a mind. The two views together entail that groups do not have beliefs. To save the claim that groups can have beliefs, we must deny one of these views. In my opinion, it is best to deny psychologism about belief. To see this, we must review some candidates for group beliefs.

It is natural to begin with an account of group belief that identifies it with belief of some sort, though if antipsychologism about groups is to be maintained, group belief cannot be identified with belief understood as a state of mind of the group. Can it then be identified with the beliefs of members of the group?

The simplest account of this sort is a *summative* account, on which group belief is *common* belief in the group:

> A group *G* believes that *p* just in case all or most members of *G* believe that *p*.

Unfortunately the summative account is both too weak and too strong. It is too weak because it is possible for members *all* to believe a proposition without the *group's* believing it. Suppose the members believe it for reasons that have nothing to do with their membership in the group? Surely all members of the Audubon Society believe that the sky is blue, but that does not mean that the *society* believes this. Nor will it help to add the requirement that members recognize that other members hold this belief. For this requirement is satisfied in the present example: each member of the society recognizes that every other member believes that the sky is blue. Yet the group does not believe this proposition.

Gilbert offers a striking example that confirms the point that the summative account is too weak. Two groups may have the same membership, yet differ in their beliefs. The membership of the Library Committee may be identical with that of the Food Committee. Yet the two committees might have very different purposes and accordingly make judgments about quite different issues based on very different kinds of evidence. Every member of the Library Committee might believe that there are a million volumes in the library, and so might the Library Committee itself. Yet the Food Committee holds no such belief. Thus, the summative condition is too weak.

It also seems too strong. Suppose the Library Committee and the Budget Committee must each judge whether last year's library budget is adequate for this year. The Budget Committee judges so, while the Library Committee judges not. Yet their members are the same (and let us suppose, to make matters simple, judge alike). It follows that one of the two committees believes a proposition *p* that no member believes.

These points are enough to cast doubt on a summative account of group belief as common belief in favor of Gilbert's joint account:

> A group G believes that p just in case the members of G jointly accept that p, where the latter happens just in case each member has openly expressed a willingness to let p stand as the view of G, or openly expressed a commitment jointly to accept that p, conditional on a like open expression of commitment by other members of G.

On this account of group belief, the group believes p when members lend their acceptance to p not by believing it, but by expressing a willingness jointly to accept it. (See Tuomela 1992 for a similar account of group belief.) In general—and approximately—when a group believes a proposition, the group is committed to proceeding in future (joint) action and cognition on the assumption that the proposition believed is true. No doubt this needs qualification: the group is committed to proceeding on the assumption that the belief is true, but only as far as the strength of the reasons for the belief warrants.

We have endorsed Gilbert's intuitive case for a joint account of group belief, as well as her particular joint account. This leaves the important question, unaddressed by Gilbert, as to what value the group belief might have on such an account—a question that figures crucially in the value of justified group belief. To make the question tractable, let us restrict our attention to the *instrumental* value of group belief for *group action*. We will leave aside the question of its instrumental value for individual action and belief, as well as its intrinsic value. I will say more about the value of group belief for individual belief in later sections.

To understand the instrumental value of group belief for group action we will do best to contrast the role of group belief in group action with that of *common belief* and of *coordinated belief*. It would seem that group actions require common beliefs of certain kinds. In a group action, each member must believe that he or she belongs to a group, that each member has expressed a willingness to engage in joint action, and that each member is engaged in a joint action. Perhaps the group could get by with mere group belief in these things, or a group belief that each member believes these things, and so on. But the regress has to stop somewhere: at some point there must be common beliefs that there is a group belief in such propositions. For group action is possible only if individuals perform singular actions, and singular actions require individual beliefs. More importantly, unless members believe that others are engaged in a joint action, they will not normally perform their part in the projected group action, since there is normally no point in performing a part in a group action that does not materialize. Beyond this, common beliefs of other kinds no doubt enhance the efficiency with which groups perform actions. When members share beliefs about their environment, the range of actions available to them increases, and this will generally enable them to perform actions more suited to their goals.

Let us turn next to the value of *coordinated* beliefs for group actions. Let us define the coordinated beliefs of group members to be beliefs formed as a result of inquiry assigned a member under a division of cognitive labor among group members. On a train trip the engineer is assigned the task of monitoring the train's speed and fuel, the conductor the task of monitoring the passengers' possession of tickets, and so on. Such a division of labor allows the group to assign certain members tasks of inquiry that may facilitate the members' joint actions even when other members do not undertake such inquiry and do not undertake to form beliefs on the topic of inquiry, and even when other members do not know what a member assigned a task believes on the topic. The conductor need not always know the speed of the train. Coordinated beliefs save group members and others a great deal of effort by dividing the labor of inquiry over group members. They allow the group to assign tasks of inquiry to members who are especially reliable on the relevant topics. And they make group action possible in cases in which the requirement of common belief or joint belief would cause the group to founder for lack of agreement among members. Coordinated beliefs are thus an effort-saving, reliability-promoting, and controversy-sparing device. They enable groups to act in situations where a requirement of common or joint belief might prevent action. Again, coordinated beliefs need not be true to facilitate group action.

Let us turn, finally, to our key question here—the value of group belief on a joint account. Why would there be any need for group beliefs in addition to common beliefs and coordinated beliefs? Group beliefs are needed for three reasons.

First, when group action relies on coordinated beliefs (as it often does), the presence of these coordinated beliefs usually entails subgroup beliefs. That is, in such circumstances, the presence of coordinated beliefs in a group usually entails that some subgroups of the group will have beliefs. For when group action relies on coordinated beliefs, members of the group commit themselves to acting on the beliefs of other members even in the absence of the reasons possessed by those other members. A member *A* is assigned the task of judging whether *p* (e.g., whether the train has enough fuel to get to Memphis). At least one other member *B* receives the information that *p* from *A* and acts as if *p* were true. *B* need not believe *p*—nor, for that matter, need *A*. What is necessary is that *A* and *B* are both committed to acting as if *p* were true.

Usually, the behavior of *A* and *B* may be taken to express openly a willingness jointly to accept *p*. *A* and *B* are openly committed to proceeding in joint action and cognition as if *p* were true. But that entails that *A* and *B* jointly believe *p*. Thus, coordinated belief usually requires some subgroup belief.[1]

Second, there is a need for something in between common beliefs and coordinated belief. The existence of a group entails joint intention, and groups nearly always engage in joint action. Common beliefs and coordinated beliefs facilitate joint intention and action. Common beliefs serve as a basis for members' expectations about each others' actions and joint actions. But common beliefs are not easy to come by. To be sure, there are a great many propositions with which most members of a group, and indeed most human beings, will agree: the sky is blue, the sun is hot, and so on. Some of these serve as a basis for expectations. But they are apt to fall short of all the assumptions on the basis of which members must expect others to act in performing joint actions. Of course one way around the problem of controversy, and accessibility cost as well, is coordinated belief: let individuals specialize to acquire enough information, and let them have responsibility for particular expectations about which others need have no beliefs. But there are limits to this solution to the problem of controversy. For one thing, group action typically, if not always, requires certain shared acceptances—e.g., about what it is permissible, right, or good to do—acceptances that are shared by all members of the group. Yet often the propositions that must be accepted are controversial. Common belief is thus ruled out. Such propositions must be jointly accepted without individual belief. In such cases, group belief secures action and cognition on the assumption that the proposition is true.

Third, there is one more reason why group belief is valuable. It is valuable for group action because it *generates* a basis for expectations of joint action. When members express their willingness jointly to accept *p*, they commit themselves to acting jointly on the assumption that *p*. Thus, members can expect others to honor the jointly accepted proposition in further joint action and cognition.

These points about the value of group belief suggest analogous points about the value of *justified* group belief for group action, to which I will return below. What is important at this point is that we have a joint account of group belief on which group belief is, in an obvious sense, more social than it is on a summative account. We may now ask whether, intuitively, group justification is similarly social.

GROUP JUSTIFICATION: SUMMATIVE OR JOINT?

The following simple summative account of group justification is analogous to the summative account of group belief:

> Group *G* is justified in believing *p* just in case all (or most) members of *G* are justified in believing *p*.

This account will not do, however. Let us return to the case of groups with coextensive membership. Suppose again that the Library Committee and the Food Committee have the same membership, but suppose now that the two committees have very different purposes. They accordingly gather different kinds of evidence and make judgments about different issues based on these different kinds of evidence. Then the Food Committee may fail to be justified in believing that the library holds a million volumes, even though all members of the committee are justified in believing this proposition. This shows that the simple summative account is too weak. It is a somewhat trickier matter whether the condition can be shown to be too strong by such an example—more on this below.

To explain why the Food Committee is not justified in believing the proposition, we must advert to the fact that the *committee* does not have good reason to believe the proposition. The following joint account is suggested:

> A group *G* is justified in believing *p* just in case *G* has good reason to believe *p*,

where

> *G* has a reason *r* to believe *p* just in case all members of *G* would properly express openly a willingness to accept *r* jointly as the group's reason to believe *p*.

Let me make some comments on this account before we proceed. First, this account of having a reason is of course circular, since it employs the concept of group reason in its definiens. However, it is not my purpose to offer a noncircular account—if indeed that is even possible—but rather to contrast joint and summative accounts. Second, what it is for a reason to believe *p* to be *good* is a matter for a substantive theory of group justification, to be discussed in a later section. Third, note that the account of a group's having a reason to believe *p* requires that the members *would properly* express openly a willingness to accept *r* jointly as a reason to believe *p*, and not merely that they *actually do* express openly such a willingness. The reference to what members would *properly* do is needed because the reasons possessed by the group include those that are *available* within and to the group, not merely those the members *actually* jointly accept as reasons. If there is a reason *r* that members would properly accept jointly, then *r* counts as a reason possessed by the group, even if members do not openly express a willingness to accept it jointly as a reason. Of course we need some account of what it is for a joint acceptance of *r* as a reason to be *proper*. But I will not attempt such an account here. Fourth, note that proper joint acceptance of a reason is not the same as the reason's being *good*. Joint acceptance of *r* as a reason may be proper even if the reason is bad.

On the present account, what it is for a group to be justified in virtue of possessing a reason differs significantly from what it is for an individual to be so justified. An individual may be justified in virtue of possessing a reason *r* for believing *p* even if that individual does not accept *r* as a reason to believe *p*. A group must, however, accept *r* as reason to believe *p*. More importantly, an individual possesses a reason only if she or he holds the belief (or has the sensory state) that constitutes the reason. A group may possess a reason *r*, however, even if it does not believe *r*, so long as members would properly accept *r jointly*. The difference arises because for an individual a belief that constitutes a reason is available only if the individual holds the belief; whereas for a group the available reasons outstrip those the group believes and include reasons within the group that would properly become beliefs through an open expression of willingness jointly to accept them.

Before we develop our joint account of group justification, we may further support it with an observation. It seems obvious that, for modes of justification other than the epistemic, group justification must be understood *jointly*, rather than summatively. For example, this is true of the practical justification of approval. The Steering Committee of a political party might be practically justified in approving the expenditure while the Budget Committee is not (though of course both committees cannot have their way). And this may be so despite their possessing and considering the same evidence, having the same concerns, and undertaking the same decisions. And it may be so even if all members of both committees take the same personal attitude (of approval or disapproval) to the expenditure, with practical justification—indeed, even if the membership of the committees is the same. Thus, the practical justification of the Steering Committee's approval cannot be a summative justification defined by the justified approval of the members. But how could one committee be practically justified in its approval or action and another not, despite possessing the same evidence, having the same concerns, and undertaking the same decisions? The answer is that the two committees might have different charges and, in virtue of this, take different considerations as admissible or even available, weigh considerations differently, and use different criteria for deciding what to approve on the basis of the considerations they take into account. In this way, one committee could justifiedly end with approval and the other not. And both committees could be practically justified in their attitudes. This calls for a joint account of the practical justification of group approval. It ought not to be surprising, then, if it turns out that the *epistemic* justification of group beliefs must be understood jointly.

Moreover, we seem to have here an argument for a joint account of *epistemic* group justification. It seems that the Steering Committee is not only practically justified in its approval, but it may also be *epistemically* justified in *believing* that the expenditure is practically justified. For, corresponding to the reasons that make the Steering Committee practically justified in its approval are reasons for believing that the expenditure is practically justified, and these reasons may make the Steering Committee epistemically justified in believing this. The Budget Committee may, for the same reason, be epistemically justified in believing that the expenditure is not practically justified. This seems to show that one group can be epistemically justified in believing a proposition while another with the same members is not.

We have now made some points in favor of a joint account of group justification. I expect there to be some antipathy to the account, and to the claim I have used to support it, that one group might be epistemically justified in a belief while a coextensive group is not. It would therefore be desirable to address a source of antipathy to the latter claim.

This source might be expressed as follows: it is difficult to see how one group could have good reason to believe p and another coextensive group not. First, the reasons possessed by two coextensive groups must be the same. For, whatever the proper joint acceptance of r as a reason may amount to, it seems that the matter of which reasons members would properly accept jointly is determined by the reasons they possess among them, subject only to the requirement that these reasons are available to and admissible for the group. But the matter of which reasons are available or admissible is itself entirely determined by the beliefs and abilities of members. If a reason possessed by some member is not available to or admissible for the group, it is because that member cannot communicate it to other members or because it is not agreed to be a reason by other members. But these are obstacles that exist in virtue of the members, not in virtue of the group itself. Thus, which reasons the group has is determined by the membership of the group and could not differ for coextensive groups.

Second, what counts as a *good* reason for one group must count as a good reason for a coextensive group. A group has a good reason to believe *p* just in case the reasons possessed by members that *ought* to be available to and admissible for the group favor *p*. But which reasons ought to be available and admissible is also determined by the members. Putting this second point together with the first, we reach the conclusion that two coextensive groups must be equally justified or unjustified in believing *p*. Thus, we cannot oppose the summative account of group justification on the ground that coextensive groups can differ in the good reasons they possess.

To spin out the objection in detail, let us focus on the first point: that the reasons members would properly accept jointly as reasons to believe *p* are entirely determined by the members' beliefs and abilities, and these are the reasons *available* to and *admissible* for the group. In the simplest case, these would be the reasons possessed distributively by the members, and in this case coextensive groups have the same reasons. But in more complicated cases, some reasons possessed by members are not accepted jointly as reasons by the group, because they are unavailable to the group—e.g., because the members who possess them are unable to reveal them to the group. Or they are not admissible because they are not accepted as reasons, perhaps because members do not agree that they bear on the issue. Let it also be noted that members may fail jointly to accept *r* as a reason for the group to believe *p* because the reasons fall short of the strength required by a criterion of strength of reasons. But again, it might be said, this matter depends entirely on group members. What is relevant is the criterion of strength employed by the members. The problem, then, is that the admissible and available evidence cannot differ or be weighed differently for two coextensive groups, and the criterion of strength of reasons cannot differ for two coextensive groups. But if all these are the same for the two groups, then they must have the same reasons.

What is needed to rebut this objection is an explanation of how the available or admissible reasons, or the weighing of reasons, or the criterion of strength could differ for two groups with the same members. I will not directly argue that the matter of which reasons members would properly accept jointly is not entirely determined by the members' beliefs and abilities. Rather, I will attempt to cast doubt on the parallel claim that whether the group has a *good* reason to believe *p* is also individualistically determined in this way. To explain this, it will be necessary to make a long detour into a deep, though at first appearances independent, social issue common to group and individual justification. The relevance of this issue will emerge in due time.

ORDINARY VS. SPECIAL STANDARDS OF JUSTIFICATION

David Annis (1978) has claimed that whether an individual is justified in believing *p* on the basis of a set of reasons the individual possesses depends not just on the content and strength of those reasons, but on that individual's social or occupational role. A medical doctor would not be justified in believing that polio is caused by a virus by his or her reading of that fact in the *New York Times* Science Section, even though a layperson would be justified in this belief—for the admissible reasons and the criteria of strength of reasons vary with individuals' social roles. For the doctor, the justification of a medical belief sets higher standards of justification than for a layperson—higher standards of admissible reasons and of strength of reasons. Actually, this claim can appear in a relativistic or a nonrelativistic version. The relativistic version would say that whether our doctor is justified is relative to a context: relative to her personal life, the doctor is justified in her belief about polio; while relative to her medical practice, she is not. The nonrelativistic version says that the doctor is never justified in this belief (so long as it has only an informal basis).

Now, I would agree that the doctor would not be *medically* justified in *stating* the proposition, nor in *acting* on it in her medical practice. I would go so far as to concede that this shows that the doctor would not be justified, *all things considered*, in stating or acting on the proposition in her practice. But it hardly follows that the doctor is not *epistemically* justified in her *belief*. Regarding the relativistic version, I would counter with the observation that in many instances (including the present one), *belief* differs from statements and actions in being a long-standing state of the subject—one not susceptible to rapid addition or retraction. If unjustified belief is *impermissible* belief, then in general it is not plausible to assign justification to a belief on Sunday and deny it to the same belief on Monday. For this reason, the nonrelativistic version is more plausible than the relativistic one. The justification of the belief must remain constant across the doctor's personal and medical practice. However, I see no reason to go along with the nonrelativistic version's claim that the *epistemic* justification of the belief must follow the *medical* justification of stating or acting on the proposition. On the contrary, I find the claim counterintuitive. Intuitively, the doctor is as justified by the newspaper report as a layperson would be. The doctor has as much reason for believing that polio is caused by a virus as the layperson does, and this seems to be enough to entail that her belief is as justified as the layperson's belief. (Of course the doctor may have special knowledge that casts doubt on the newspaper report or special grounds for doubting the testimony of medical reporters; but if so, Annis cannot use the example to show that the standards of justification are higher for the doctor, since the reason the doctor is unjustified has simply to do with defeating background knowledge under the ordinary standards of justification.) I am inclined to say that the standards of epistemic justification of beliefs differ from the standards of medical statements and actions. Moreover, as we will see in a moment, there are theoretical reasons for allowing epistemic and occupational standards to diverge.

To say that the doctor is epistemically justified in her belief is not, however, to absolve her of all epistemic sins. I have argued elsewhere (Schmitt 1987) that occupational and social roles engender *epistemic* and not merely occupational standards of virtue. Our doctor, relying on the newspaper report alone, holds a belief that is in a sense epistemically—as well as occupationally—objectionable, even though her belief is as fully justified epistemically as the layperson's belief. Of course, allowing beliefs to be justified when they fall short of occupational obligation deprives the label "epistemically justified" of any ability to distinguish the beliefs that may serve occupationally from those that may not. One may instead employ the label "epistemically virtuous" to distinguish these.

What is the point, then, of valorizing specialists' beliefs (on occupational topics) as justified when these beliefs fall short of epistemic virtue? There are two possible strategies to discourage specialists from occupational actions premised on assumptions for which they possess no reasons that meet occupational standards. The *strict* strategy is to forbid a specialist from a belief on an occupational topic when the reason for it that she or he possesses falls short of occupational standards. This strategy sets occupational standards for epistemic justification. The *permissive* strategy is to permit such beliefs but, at the same time, place limits on the tasks for which the specialist may rely on the beliefs. This second strategy sets ordinary standards for epistemic justification and imposes restrictions on reliance on these epistemically justified beliefs in occupational activities.

In my view, the permissive strategy is preferable. One point of labelling specialists' beliefs as epistemically justified when they fall short of occupational standards is to permit specialists to hold these beliefs so that they may rely on the beliefs in ordinary, nonoccupational activities. Reliance on such beliefs would seem to be desirable for the conduct of ordinary life. Perhaps specialists could get by in ordinary life without beliefs on occupational topics that fall short of occupational standards. Our doctor could get by without her belief that polio is caused by a virus. But arguably, such beliefs can enrich a doctor's life as much as they do the lives of others. So there is as strong a case for allowing them for the doctor as for the layperson. To be sure, the doctor has more opportunity to misuse these beliefs than a layperson does, and thus there is risk of greater harm. But doctors are trained in the use of knowledge, and for this reason there is less risk of harm than in the case of a layperson dispensing informal medical advice. A doctor is more likely to do damage by relying in medical practice on an unscrutinized nonmedical belief (about the eating habits of the poor, say) than by relying on a medical belief. Nor could we quarantine all beliefs that might be used in making medical judgments; most any belief is potentially relevant. Another point in favor of the permissive strategy is that it allows evaluators to locate reasons for a proposition possessed by specialists, or judge whether there is a preponderance of reasons in favor of a proposition by checking whether the specialists' beliefs are justified. In this way, evaluators may in turn become justified in believing the proposition. One might wonder whether evaluators could not glean this information from specialists' having reasons even if specialists did not and were not permitted to believe when they possessed such reasons. But there are two obstacles to evaluators doing so. One is that it may be more difficult to tell whether a specialist possesses such reasons if she or he does not believe the propositions. An important way of telling whether reasons are present is to infer their presence from belief. And believing is more apt to cause one to reveal reasons for belief. A second and more important obstacle is that making these beliefs impermissible may discourage specialists from acquiring reasons of these sorts. The reasons may not be present to provide evaluators with a basis for their own beliefs. Thus, the permissive strategy seems preferable to the strict.

Specialists' beliefs need meet only a lower, ordinary standard of justification.

I have so far argued that *individual* justification does not impose occupational or other special standards. What I want to consider now is whether matters may be different for *group* justification. If so, then groups—even coextensive ones—may be subject to different standards of justification, depending on their social roles. And if they are subject to different standards of justification, coextensive groups may differ in whether the same reasons are good.

Might the standards of group justification depend on the social role of the group even though the standards of individual justification do not? I am inclined to think they do, at least for a certain important class of groups. For there is a significant difference between individual justification and the justification possessed by groups belonging to this class.

To be sure, there are significant similarities between individual justification and all group justification. Evaluators can evaluate both individual and group beliefs to judge whether the reasons favor the belief, and in this way become justified in the belief. This point favors ascribing justification to group beliefs when everyday standards are met.

There is, however, a countervailing case that, for a certain important class of groups, we should ascribe justification to a group's beliefs only when these beliefs meet standards of justification set by the social or occupational office of the group. When a group's beliefs meet such standards, there is no point in permitting group beliefs that fall short of these standards, as there is in the case of individuals in occupations. I will call groups of the sort I have in mind *chartered groups.*

A chartered group is one founded to perform a particular action or actions of a certain kind. Not all groups are chartered groups. According to the account of groups we have endorsed, a group exists when its members openly express a willingness to act jointly. On this account, there need be no particular action or kind of action the members openly express a willingness to perform in openly expressing their willingness to act jointly. Our Gang, the old comedy group, forms a group in virtue of expressing a willingness to act jointly, to hang out together, without specifying in advance any actions or sorts of actions they intend to perform. However, people often do form a group in virtue of expressing a willingness to perform a certain joint action or kind of joint action. When they do so with the understanding that the group will perform only such actions, the group is a chartered group, and its office is specified by the founding intentions of its members. The U. S. Congress, the Sierra

Club, and perhaps even the mob that stormed the Bastille are chartered groups.

When a group has a charter, it can normally perform only out of the office specified by its charter. To say that the group performs an action out of its office is not to say that the action fulfills that office but that it is directed toward doing so. A chartered group may perform actions that do not fulfill its office, but it seems that the actions it performs must at least aim at fulfilling its office. An army is an example of a chartered group. The office of an army is to be prepared for and engage in land defense and offense in war. But of course an army may fail to fulfill that office. Nevertheless, there would seem to be limits to how far short of fulfilling its office a chartered group may fall. Even when individuals openly express a willingness to engage in a certain kind of joint action, the group they form does not survive unless, when it acts, it aims to fulfill its office. Appointed and ranked individuals may intend to form an army, openly expressing a willingness to defend their country; but they hardly constitute an army if, when they act, they do not at least attempt to make preparation for defense or offense in war.

Chartered groups must function in their offices. This means, minimally, that they must try to fulfill their offices. A chartered group has no life apart from its office, as a specialist individual has a life apart from his or her occupation. A chartered group cannot step out of its office in the way that a specialist can. The Board of Directors of General Motors cannot abdicate its function as board, which is to act as proxy for the stockholders of General Motors, on pain of failing a condition of its existence. It cannot say, "We have decided to abandon the interests of the stockholders," though of course it can unintentionally fall short of acting in (and perhaps even ignore) their interests. Since chartered groups have no unofficial activities, they have no need to rely on group beliefs for ordinary activities. In judging their own beliefs for reliance in their activities, these groups must employ a special standard and have no use for justification under an ordinary standard. Chartered groups must rely in their activities only on beliefs that meet their special standards.

What does this imply for group justification? For the group's purposes in relying on beliefs in its activities, special standards of permissibility must be observed. This suggests that the standards of justification for such groups are special standards. For, as far as the use of beliefs in group action goes, there is no point in permitting beliefs that fall short of special standards. It is true that, for the *evaluator's* purposes in judging whether the reasons favor a belief, an ordinary standard of permissibility may be observed. But this is permissibility for the *evaluator*, not for the group. And presumably, what determines permissibility for the group is what it is desirable or necessary to allow the *group* to believe, not what it is desirable to allow the *evaluator* to believe.

If what I have so far argued is correct, then whether a chartered group is justified in a belief will be governed by special standards of *available* or *admissible* reasons, or of the *weighing* or *strength* of reasons. An example of a special standard of available reasons is the exemption of unrevealed confidences to members from the reasons available to the group. Whether available reasons include or exempt unrevealed confidences may vary depending on the charter of the group. An example of a special standard of admissible reasons is the standard of excluding hearsay in a court of law. This exclusion devolves from the office of a court. The same exclusion may not hold for nonlegal groups. For these groups, a member's possession of hearsay may be admissible. Thus, a nonlegal group may fail to be justified in a belief because a member possesses countervailing hearsay. A court, on the other hand, would not lose its justification merely because a member possesses countervailing hearsay. And this is because in its legal capacity, the court rightly excludes hearsay, and its legal capacity is the only capacity in which it operates. Finally, an example of a special standard of weighing or strength of reasons is the standard of evidence beyond a reasonable doubt in a court of law. This again devolves from the office of a court.

To return at last to our main issue—the case for a joint account of group justification—we must consider the bearing of our most recent conclusion on this issue and, in particular, on the objection to my case for the joint account: that coextensive groups must possess the same reasons. The conclusion gives us a way to answer that objection by explaining how it is possible for coextensive chartered groups to differ in the reasons they possess. Since the standards of justification vary from one chartered group to the next, it can happen that two groups with the same membership—each member justified in believing the same propositions—differ in whether they are justified in a belief. A group might fail to be justified in believing *p* even though each member is justified in believing *p*. The reasons available to members distributively might not be ones they would properly accept jointly as reasons, because these reasons are not available or admissible to the group or do not meet the amount of reasons required by the group's social office. Conversely, the group might be justified in believing *p* even though some members are not justified in believing *p*. For, the group might lack reasons against *p* that are rendered unavailable or inadmissible, even though members possess those reasons. This is enough to defend the joint account of group justification from the objection. We have completed our case for a joint account.

I have offered a joint account of group justification that cuts some slack between group justification and the justification of group members. Not only is the account logically compatible with a group's being justified in believing *p* even though no member is justified in believing *p*, and vice versa, compatible with each member's being justified in believing *p* though the group is not so justified. It is also plausible that for many chartered groups, group justification actually diverges from that of some members.

On the other hand, I want to grant that this slack has its limits—and not merely contingent limits imposed, say, by how talkative people are when they recount their reasons for belief. It had better not often happen that groups are justified in believing *p* when most of their members know better. For the point of group justification (and its evaluation) is the same as the point of individual justification (and its evaluation): to bring about the satisfaction of the characteristic epistemic goal, traditionally taken to be true belief (true individual belief, if not true group belief). But a wide divergence between group justification and the justification of members would prevent group justification and its evaluation from bringing about true individual belief. Individuals would not often come to accept propositions justifiedly believed by groups if members of the groups were not justified in believing those propositions. Certainly, group members would not often come to accept these propositions. And to the extent that others outside the group recognize what members are justified in believing, others would not often come to accept propositions justifiedly believed by the group either. In this way, the slack between group and member justification is limited by the point of group justification.

Having defended a joint account of group justification, I should address the question of whether such joint justification is valuable. I will answer in a way that dovetails with our earlier account of the value of group belief. Regarding the instrumental value of justified group beliefs for group actions, group beliefs understood as joint beliefs enable members to form accurate expectations of other members' actions and joint actions. For propositions jointly believed serve as assumptions in further group action and cognition. Group beliefs can be valuable even if they are not justified or true. Nevertheless, if group beliefs are assumed as premises for group action, then a group is generally better off having true beliefs than false beliefs. (Indeed, it is generally at least as well off in believing the true consequences of a practically useful false proposition as in believing the false proposition itself, since belief in false propositions is generally useful—and arguably always as useful as an information carrier—in virtue of the true consequences of these false propositions.) So, true group belief is especially valuable. If we then understand justified belief in the customary way as belief that in some sense aims at the characteristic epistemic goal of true belief, we see the instrumental value of justified group belief for group action.

Summative justified belief is less advantageous for these purposes. It has the same drawback as common belief: it is hard to come by. For controversy often stands in the way of securing justified belief in a proposition for every member of the group. Justified joint belief is more easily secured. Moreover, for reasons discussed under the first heading, justified coordinated beliefs generally involve the justified joint beliefs of subgroups. These points in favor of the value of group justification are of course entirely derivative from our account of the instrumental value of group belief for group action.

We may add to this two points. One is that justified group belief fosters justified individual belief, since it entails the airing of reasons. The other point, which I will develop in the last section, is that much justified individual belief has significance only as a part or product of an effort to reach justified group belief. The value of justified individual belief, on this view, depends on that of justified group belief, rather than the other way around. These points, too, depend on a joint rather than summative account of justified group belief.

SUBSTANTIVE ACCOUNTS OF GROUP JUSTIFICATION

I have argued for a joint account of group justification. On a joint account, group justification is social in an important and nontrivial way: it is a matter of the *group's* possession of good reason for belief. There remain, however, at least three other nontrivial ways in which group justification might be social. I would like to consider in the rest of this chapter whether group justification is social in any of these other ways.

A second way, then, in which group justification might be social is this. The joint account of group justification is merely a formal account. It tells us what it is for a group to possess reasons, and it tells us that a group is justified in a belief when it possesses a good reason for the belief. But it does not tell us what it is for a group's reason for a belief to be good. That is the job of a substantive account of group justification. Since there are numerous contenders for a substantive account of *individual* justification—an account of what it is for an individual's reason for a belief to be good—it is natural to ask whether any of these accounts applies without great modification to group justification. This brings us to a new way in which group justification might be social: it might be that most plausible substantive accounts of individual justification do not plausibly apply to groups. Of course the failure of accounts of individual justification to apply to groups would only be *symptomatic* of an important difference between group justification and individual justification. It would not tell us just what the difference is. Nevertheless, the failure of accounts of individual justification to apply to groups would mark one way—albeit a weak one—in which group justification is social. A stronger way in which group justification might be social is this: the *correct* account of individual justification might not apply to group justification. That would presumably reveal an even more significant difference between group and individual justification. I wish to argue here that group justification is social in the first, weaker way. I will have to leave it an open question whether it is social in the second, stronger way.

To check whether accounts of individual justification apply to groups, I will consider four plausible substantive accounts of individual justification: perspectivism, accessibility internalism, coherentism, and reliabilism. These accounts hardly exhaust the contending accounts of individual justification, but they cover a wide enough spectrum of views to afford us a conjecture as to whether most plausible accounts of individual justification apply to groups. My question for each account will be whether there are any obstacles to applying the account to groups, *over and above* any obstacles there may be to the account as an account of *individual* justification. Is the account *less* plausible for group justification than it is for individual justification?

According to *perspectivism*, justified belief is belief sanctioned by the subject's epistemic perspective, where a subject's epistemic perspective is, roughly, the subject's views about justification. Perspectivism about individual justification is a popular view in recent epistemology and is held by, among others, BonJour (1985), Foley (1987), Pollock (1986), and Lehrer (1990). As this list of authors indicates, there are broadly and importantly different versions of the view. For purposes of illustration, however, we may employ a simple version of perspectivism. Similar points will carry over to more complicated versions. On the simple version I have in mind,

> a subject *S* is justified in believing *p* just in case *S* is justified in believing that *S* is justified in believing *p*.

This counts as a version of perspectivism if the subject's perspective is the set of beliefs of the form "*S* is justified in believing *p*," and a belief counts as sanctioned by the perspective when it is among those beliefs recognized as justified by the perspective.

It is not hard to see that this simple version of perspectivism runs into trouble when we try to apply it to groups. The problem is that a group may have a justified belief even though it lacks a perspective from which to judge the belief justified. For it might be that the members would not properly accept jointly as a reason any good reason for thinking that the group possesses a good reason to believe *p*. Suppose perspectivism is true for individual justification: whenever a member of a group possesses a good reason to believe *p*, she or he also possesses a good reason to believe that she possesses a good reason to believe *p*. Suppose now that the *group* possesses a good reason *r* to believe *p*. Members might diverge in their reasons for thinking that the group possesses a good reason to believe *p*, in which case the *group* may have no reason for thinking it. Or they might possess such reasons, but these reasons might not be good—this despite the fact that they do jointly accept a good reason to believe *p*, and each possesses a good reason to believe that *she* or *he* is justified in believing *p*. Of course if every reason to believe a proposition possessed by a member were also possessed by the group, then individual perspectivism would (with qualifications) entail group perspectivism. But that condition is exactly what is denied by the joint account of group justification.

To flesh this out with an example, suppose a group of investors has good reason to think that the time has come to invest in bonds (*p*). Then the group is justified in believing *p*. Suppose that each investor has good reason to believe that she has good reason to believe *p*. And suppose each member's reason *r* to believe *p* is the same: that interest rates will decrease in the near future. Suppose that the members would properly jointly accept *r* as a reason to believe *p*. Then the group possesses *r* and is justified in believing *p*. Does it follow that the group has good reason *r′* to believe that the group has a good reason to believe *p*? No. For suppose each member has a different reason for thinking that *r* is a good reason to believe *p*, and these reasons are based on different, controversial economic theories. Suppose that each member has good reason to believe her favorite economic theory, but members' background beliefs about economics are so different that they could never justify their favorite economic theories to the others. Then the members would not properly accept jointly any one economic theory as a reason for thinking that *r* is a good reason to believe *p*. It seems that there is *no* reason *r′* that members would properly accept jointly as a reason for thinking that *r* is a good reason to believe *p*. But then the group is not justified in believing that *r* is a good reason to believe *p*. In this case, perspectivism incorrectly entails that the group is *not* justified in believing *p*. (A similar point applies to the group's possessing a *good* reason to believe that the group possesses a good reason to believe *p*.) So, perspectivism does not plausibly apply to groups. It fails for groups because perspectivism requires enough agreement among members to generate the group's possession of a reason to believe that the group possesses a reason to believe *p*. But there can be group justification without such agreement.

The perspectivist might reply to this example by claiming that there *is* in fact a good reason *r′* that members would properly accept as a reason to believe that *r* is a good reason to believe *p*. For all the economic theories support the proposition *q* that *r* is a good reason to believe *p*. And if all the economic theories support a proposition *q*, then there is a good reason to believe *q*—namely, that all the economic theories support it. Consequently, there is a good reason *r′*, and members properly would jointly accept *r′*. In response, I would not deny the fact that all the economic theories support a proposition *q* is a good reason to believe *q*. I would instead question whether it must be that members properly would jointly accept *r′*. It might happen that one or more members do not accept *r′* as a reason for *q*. For example, these members might doubt whether all the economic theories really support *q*. And as a result it might happen that members would not properly accept *r′* as a reason for *q*. Thus there need be no good reason *r′* that members would properly accept jointly as a reason to believe that *r* is a good reason to believe *p*. But it seems to me that doubts of this sort need not undermine the group's justification for believing *p*. To say that they do courts a very broad skepticism about group justification, given that the background beliefs of the members of typical groups can be expected to diverge at some point in the regress of justification.

I believe, therefore, that the case against perspectivism stands. It is a case that arises from a problem specific to groups—the problem of interpersonal disagreement in background beliefs. Such disagreement sometimes deprives groups of the perspectives needed for justification according to perspectivism. Perspectivism thus imposes too strong a requirement on group justification.

Before we leave perspectivism, it is worth mentioning a substantive view about group justification that is sometimes called "perspectivism." On this view, a group is justified in believing *p* just in case *p* is sanctioned not by the *group*'s perspective, but by the perspective of each member. The relevant perspectives could be epistemic perspectives—views about justification—or they could consist of other background beliefs (Longino 1990 and this volume). This multiperspectival view escapes my objection that there need be no *group* perspective. But it does so at the cost of entailing that group justification does not require that the *group* has a good reason to believe *p*, since all that is required is that *p* is sanctioned by the *member's* perspectives. Thus the multiperspectival view runs afoul of the joint account of group justification. There is a version of the multiperspectival view which does appear to entail the requirement that the group has a good reason to believe *p*—namely, the view that a group is justified in believing *p* only if the belief *p* survives criticism from all perspectives represented in the group. However, this version (and the other versions as well) fails to make group justification parallel to individual justification, since it does not require that justified belief be sanctioned by the *subject's*—the group's—perspective.

Turning now to group *accessibility internalism*, the same objection arises. Accessibility internalism is not exactly a theory of justification, but a constraint on such theories in which

> a subject *S* is justified in believing *p* just in case *S* can tell by reflection alone that *S* is justified in believing *p*.

It is clear that our objection to group perspectivism carries over to group accessibility internalism.

Group *coherentism* faces a similar problem. On coherentism,

> a subject is justified in believing *p* just in case the belief *p* belongs to a coherent system of beliefs (or coheres with a specified set of beliefs).

There are perhaps two fundamentally different forms of coherentism. One is a form on which coherentism derives from perspectivism in virtue of the perspectivist requirement that one is justified in believing *p* only if one is justified in believing that one is justified in believing *p*, or some similar iterativist requirement (BonJour 1985; Lehrer 1990). We have already seen the problem with this view. The other form of coherentism has a better chance of characterizing group justification. On this form, justified belief is belief that is in reflective equilibrium (Goodman 1955). That is,

> *S* is justified in believing *p* just in case the belief *p* belongs to a set of beliefs in reflective equilibrium,

where

> a set of beliefs is in reflective equilibrium just when, as a result of or on reflection, the propositions believed about instances support and are supported by the generalizations believed in virtue of being instances of the generalizations in sufficient numbers.

If this view requires that a justified belief belongs to a set of *actual* group beliefs in reflective equilibrium, then it will not be satisfied by very many group beliefs. Group belief requires that members express their willingness jointly to accept the proposition believed. But there are relatively few propositions for which there is such an open expression. Moreover, it seems that there can be cases in which the group is justified in a belief and there are enough group background beliefs to generate reflective equilibrium, but members' background beliefs differ so much that they would not *properly* accept jointly these background beliefs as reasons. The sort of case I have in mind is similar to our case against group perspectivism. Thus, this version of the reflective equilibrium view sets conditions of justification that are too strong for groups.

The reflective equilibrium view might, on the other hand, be taken to require only that a group is justified in believing *p* just in case the belief *p* would belong to a set of beliefs in equilibrium that the group would hold if it were to reflect on sufficiently many topics. The paucity of actual group beliefs is not a problem for this view. Nevertheless, the view faces nearly the same problem as the preceding view. Each member of a group might be justified in believing *p* in virtue of the reflective equilibrium of that member's beliefs. But members' systems of beliefs might differ so much that, even on reflection, members would not properly accept jointly as reasons enough background beliefs for reflective equilibrium. In the end, a reflective equilibrium version of coherentism fails for reasons similar to those which defeat perspectivism and accessibility internalism. The upshot is that group coherentism fails.

Our observations so far show that a number of contending accounts of individual justification do not plausibly carry over to group justification. These observations reveal some important differences between group justification and individual justification. However, it would be hasty to conclude that no contending account of individual justification can apply to group justification. It remains possible that *reliabilism* applies:

> A group *G* is justified in believing *p* just in case *G* exercises a reliable belief-forming process that yields *G*'s belief that *p*.

I see no argument against group reliabilism. Group reliabilism does not face the objection that besets group perspectivism, accessibility internalism, and coherentism—that members' background beliefs may differ in such a way as to deprive the group of the ability to be justified in all the background beliefs that must be justified if the group is to be justified in believing *p*. Group reliabilism avoids this difficulty because it does not make justification turn on background beliefs in the way these other theories do.

Of course this feature of reliabilism is just what most of its opponents have against it. But this blade has two edges. It may be taken to show that reliabilism has a better chance to characterize group justification than individual justification. Or it may be taken to show, as I am inclined to take it, that background beliefs have less relevance to justification than many suppose. Reasoning this way does, however, deprive one of the point that group justification is social in being characterized by a different account of justification from that which characterizes individual justification.

There are numerous questions that would have to be answered to fill out group reliabilism. Some of these questions concern the nature of the justification-making process. Is the belief-forming process referred to here a *group*-belief-forming process, one that yields only group beliefs as output, or is it an individual-or-group-belief-forming process, one that will yield either individual or group beliefs? Just what does the group-belief-forming process produce? Does it produce the members' willingness to let *p* stand as the group view, or rather the open expression of that willingness? What is the relation between the group-belief-forming process and the public process by which members would properly express openly their willingness to accept a proposition jointly? What serves as input to group-belief-forming processes? Do the experiences and perceptual and cognitive states of the individual serve as inputs to the process, as they do in the case of individual justification? Or are inputs restricted to *public* events such as open expressions of willingness to accept propositions jointly? Is the process in virtue of which a group is justified in a belief necessarily social in involving some contentful dialogue between members, or might it involve only their open expressions of willingness to accept the proposition jointly? Might the process involve individual cognition? Might it involve biased or textbook irrational individual cognition, as Miriam Solomon (this volume) argues (in the context of a social empiricist, rather than a social reliabilist view), or must it involve only rational cognition? These are all difficult questions, but I do not believe that the plausibility of group reliabilism turns on their answers. It suffices to say that group reliabilism is a live option in a way that group perspectivism and other views are not.

THE PRIMACY OF GROUP JUSTIFICATION

There is a fourth and final respect in which group justification might be social. It might have *primacy* over individual justification. The summative account of group justification might be regarded, along with other accounts that reduce group to individual justification, as a claim of the primacy of individual justification over group justification. The joint account, on the other hand, nonreductive though it is, cannot be regarded as the reverse. It does not entail that individual justification is in any way indebted to group justification. There are, however, numerous primacy claims that might be made. I can only give the briefest list here.

An *extreme* thesis of the primacy of communal knowledge over individual knowledge would hold that an individual knows that *p* only if the community to which the individual belongs knows that *p*. The view is to be taken as defining individual knowledge partly in terms of communal knowledge. There are several more moderate theses of the primacy of communal knowledge that I will mention below.

Our joint account of group justification is, in the main, consistent with the extreme primacy thesis. For the joint account does not define group justification in terms of individual justification. In this it differs from the summative account of group justification, which does define group justification in terms of individual justification and is accordingly inconsistent with a view that treats communal justification as prior to individual justification. (However, there is a hitch here. Though I did not discuss the matter, the joint account needs to be qualified, most naturally by requiring common or mutual knowledge that the joint condition is satisfied. Yet common or mutual knowledge is a kind of individual knowledge. So the joint account will, after all, define group justification in terms of individual justification. Perhaps, though, it will be possible to replace the reference to common knowledge in the joint account with a reference to common belief of certain kinds and thus escape employing the notion of individual knowledge. If this can be done without loss of content, then the joint account will be fully consistent with the extreme primacy thesis.) Thus, we have no basis in our joint account for rejecting the extreme primacy thesis.

On the other hand, I see no good reason to accept the extreme primacy thesis. One might appeal to a version of a multiperspectival view of knowledge mentioned earlier. On this version, an individual knows *p* only if the belief *p* survives criticism from all relevant perspectives in the community. If a belief *actually* survives criticism, then, it might be claimed, the belief is the consensus of the community and known by the community. The trouble is, there is no good reason to accept this version of the multiperspectival view as an account of individual knowledge (as opposed to the same version as an account of *group* knowledge).

Let us turn next to some communal primacy theses that are more moderate than the extreme thesis. One claim would be that an individual knows *p* only if the belief *p* conforms to rules approved by the community. This claim is plausible on one interpretation: that any instance of knowledge meets conditions that are recognized by the community—e.g., results from a perceptual or inferential process of a sort the community recognizes to be knowledge producing. One rationale for this pragmatic requirement might be that only under this requirement can there be an efficient communal system of the evaluation of beliefs. But this requirement will be satisfied by any theory of knowledge on which knowledge-making characteristics are generally accessible to knowledge evaluators. My reliability theory of justification (see Schmitt 1992a), for example, satisfies this requirement despite being consistent with individualism. Proponents of a communal primacy thesis must therefore have something more potent than this in mind. It is not easy to formulate a more potent thesis that remains plausible, and I will not try to do so here.

A second moderate communal primacy thesis is that an individual's belief gains the status of knowledge only in virtue of its communal role. For an individual knows *p* only if the belief *p* contains information ready to be used in dealing with nature and in living in society. It is worth reviewing briefly one argument for this thesis, also discussed by Philip

Kitcher (this volume). This argument begins with the observation that there are diverse *embodiments* of knowledge—in books, diagrams, computer programs, works of art, etc. But plausibly, these items count as embodiments of knowledge only because they have a certain communal use. In particular, they counts as embodiments of knowledge because they contain useful information that can be extracted by members of the community. Now the argument is that individual knowledge is analogous to these embodiments of knowledge and so counts as knowledge for an analogous reason. Individual knowledge is, of course, *knowledge*, not merely an embodiment of knowledge. But this difference of status derives merely from the fact that information does not need to be *extracted* from knowledge in order to be used. Knowledge contains information in a form already useful—a form that empowers the subject in dealing with nature and in living in society. Thus, individual knowledge is belief containing information that empowers the subject to deal with nature and society. It is knowledge in virtue of its communal role.

I have no objection to the claim that knowledge is generally useful in dealing with nature and society. But I can see no basis for elevating that to a definition of knowledge. One suspects that the argument gets the order of understanding backwards. It is plausible that embodiments of knowledge count as such because they contain information that can be extracted. But to say this is only to say that *knowledge* can be extracted from them. Thus, embodiments of knowledge count as such because they are designed so that individuals can extract knowledge from them. If so, individual knowledge cannot be analogous, on pain of circularity: a belief cannot count as knowledge because people can extract knowledge from it. Knowledge is therefore rather disanalogous to embodiments of knowledge. The argument concedes this by assigning knowledge direct usefulness, rather than usefulness through the agency of extraction. But now the idea that knowledge is useful bears all the weight, and the role of usefulness was never established for embodiments of knowledge—simply assumed. It is plausible that an embodiment of knowledge contains information that can be extracted. Why assume the information must be useful? But if it need not be useful, then there is no basis for the communal view of knowledge.

I have made enough discouraging remarks about communal primacy theses. I would like to turn now to an important *group* primacy thesis that I think has a very good chance of being true, and one that is now clear enough to admit an attempt at evaluation. The primacy thesis I have in mind is inspired, as so much else in this chapter, by Margaret Gilbert's work on groups. In Gilbert's view, a great part of human life consists of the joint activities of individuals in informal ad hoc groups—two people having a conversation, taking a walk, eating a meal. The activities of these informal groups are the basis of formal groups as well. What is important for our purposes, however, is the idea that many *singular* actions of individuals have a point only as a basis for *group* action or, more immediately, for joint actions performed by those individuals in groups—in much the way that many *basic* individual actions (e.g., moving one's arm up and down) have a point only as a basis for *nonbasic* individual actions (e.g., pumping the well). Something similar may be true of singular actions with respect to their role in group actions. My utterances have a point only as part of my conversation with you; my walking on the left side of the path has a point only as part of my walk with you. The singular gestures I make in talking or walking with you make sense only if we see them as a basis for my joint action of talking or walking with you, and ultimately for the group action of our talking or walking together.

Now our question is whether anything analogous to this might hold for cognition. Could it be that much individual belief has a point only as a basis for group belief, and the pursuit of individual justification makes sense only as a basis for the pursuit of group justification? I can see one way in which this could be so: *coordinated* belief often has a point only as a basis for a *distribution* of information over members of a group. Since it is one key point of this distribution to afford joint and group beliefs, it follows that much coordinated belief has a point only as a basis for whatever joint and hence group beliefs are entailed by coordinated belief. The engineer's coordinated belief that the train has so much fuel has its point as the basis for a group belief that the train will get to Memphis. And for the same reason, the engineer's effort to reach a justified belief has its point as the basis for a justified group belief. We no longer see justified group belief as having instrumental value for justified invidiual belief, but the other way around.

This is a significant primacy thesis, and it seems to me correct. However, we should be cautious about its extent. It makes group belief primary over coordinated belief. But, though coordinated belief is common in everyday life as well as science, it is not as pervasive in human life as joint action is. We should not suppose that we have here an exact analogue of the primacy of joint over singular action. Conversely, on a joint account of group belief, group belief does not require individual belief in the way that group action requires the singular actions of members. So we cannot expect that group beliefs will implicate individual beliefs and give them sense as regularly as group actions give sense to singular actions. We cannot expect a full analogy between the primacy of group actions and the primacy of group beliefs. The joint account of group justification entails at best a limited primacy claim for group justification. In other words, one way in which group justification is social—the joint account of group justification—places limits on another way in which group justification might be social: the primacy of group justification.

We have come to the end of our list of ways in which group justification might be social. We have endorsed three such ways: group justification is joint rather than summative; several viable substantive accounts of individual justification fail to be similarly viable for group justification; and group justification has primacy over coordinated belief. We have also speculated that a reliability account of individual justification might carry over to group justification, in which case there will be a notable commonality between individual and group justification. We have, however, observed limits to the primacy of group justification. Where does this leave us? Despite the hedged results, we are now quite a bit farther along the road toward socializing epistemology than when we started.[2]

Notes

1. The points in this paragraph were suggested to me by Jim Spellman.

2. My thanks to Margaret Gilbert, Alvin Goldman, and Jim Spellman for helpful discussion of this chapter.

Socializing Epistemology: A Bibliography

Frederick F. Schmitt and James Spellman

This bibliography covers works by philosophers on social epistemology. The first section lists historically important works that touch on topics in social epistemology. For extensive and illuminating discussions of the texts, we recommend Coady (1992). The second section lists recent works. We have had to omit relevant work in the sociology, history, economics, and politics of science and knowledge. We have also had to omit relevant work in social psychology, rhetoric, the theory of argumentation, informal logic, critical thinking, educational theory, feminist theory, the law of evidence, and decision theory, and in the philosophy of these subjects, as well as philosophical work on feminist epistemology, relativism, social constructivism, and idealism. For extensive bibliographies of the sociology of science as of 1982, see Mulkay (1982) and Shapin (1982).

HISTORICAL SOURCES

Aquinas, T. (1945) *Summa Theologiae* in *Basic Writings of Saint Thomas Aquinas*, vol. 2, ed. and ann., with intro. Anton C. Pegis, New York: Random House. II-II, qu. 4, art. 1 and qu. 2, art. 1 and 2 xxxi, Faith.

——— (1987) *Commentary on Boethius's De Trinitate*, in *Faith, Reason and Theology: Questions I-IV of his Commentary on the De Trinitate of Boethius*, trans., with intro. and ns, Armand Maurer, Toronto: Pontifical Institute of Mediaeval Studies. Qu. III, art. i, 3.

Augustine (1871-76) *De Trinitate, De Magistro, De Utilitate Credendi, Retractiones* in *The Works of Aurelius Augustinus*, ed. M. Dodds, Edinburgh: T & T Clark. *De Trinitate* XV.xii.21. *De Magistro* 39, *De Utilitate Credendi* 25, *Retractiones*, I. xiii. 3.

——— (1953) *Letter to Paulina* (Letter 147), in *Fathers of the Church* xx, ed. and trans. W. Parsons, New York: Fathers of the Church.
Austin, J. L. (1975) *How to Do Things with Words*, 2nd edn, ed. J. O. Urmson and M. Sbisa, Cambridge, Mass.: Harvard Univerity Press.
——— (1979) "Other minds," in *Philosophical Papers*, 3rd edn, ed. J. O. Urmson and G. J. Warnock, Oxford: Oxford University Press.
Bacon, F. (1857-58) *The Advancement of Learning* and *Novum Organum*, in *The Works of Francis Bacon*, vols 3 and 4, ed. J. Spedding, R. L. Ellis, and D. D. Heath, London: Longman and Co.
Binet, A. (1900) *La Suggestibilite*, Paris: Librairie C. Reinwald, Schleicher Freres.
Bradley, F. H. (1935) "The evidences of spiritualism," in *Collected Essays*, vol. 2, Oxford: Oxford University Press. Essay XXIX.
——— (1969) "The presuppositions of critical history," in *Collected Essays*, vol. 1, Oxford: Clarendon Press.
Campbell, G. (1983) *A Dissertation on Miracles*, ed. L. W. Beck, New York: Garland (Orig. pub. 1762, Edinburgh: Kincaid and Bell).
Clifford, W. K. (1879) "Ethics of belief," in *Lectures and Essays*, vol. 2, ed. L. Stephen and F. Pollock, London: Macmillan.
Collingwood, R. G. (1970) *The Idea of History*, New York: Oxford University Press.
Condillac, E. B. de (1982) *A Treatise on the Sensations*, in *Philosophical Writings of Etienne Bonnot*, Abbe de Condillac, trans. F. Phillip, Hillsdale, N. J.: Erlbaum.
Craig, J. (1964) *Craig's Rules of Historical Evidence* from *Mathematical Principles of Christian Theology*, in *History and Theory*, Beiheft 4 (Orig. pub. 1699, London: T. Child).
Descartes, R. (1984) *Meditations on First Philosophy* in *The Philosophical Writings of Descartes*, vol. 2, ed. J. Cottingham, R. Stoothoff, and D. Murdoch, Cambridge: Cambridge University Press.
Durkheim, E. (1982) *The Rules of Sociological Method*, trans. W. D. Hollis, New York: Free Press.
Hume, D. (1967) *A Treatise of Human Nature*, ed. L. A. Selby-Bigge, Oxford: Oxford University Press.
——— (1975) *An Enquiry Concerning Human Understanding*, in *Hume's Enquiries*, ed. P. H. Nidditch and L. A. Selby-Bigge, Oxford: Oxford University Press. S. 88.
James, W. (1898) "The will to believe," in *The Will to Believe and Other Essays*, New York: Longmans, Green & Co.

Kant, I. (1949) "What is orientation in thinking?" in *Critique of Practical Reason and Other Writings in Moral Philosophy*, ed. and trans. L. W. Beck, Chicago: University of Chicago Press.

——— (1951) *Critique of Judgment*, ed. J. H. Bernard, New York: Hafner.

——— (1970) "What is enlightenment?" in *Kant's Political Writings*, ed. H. Reiss, trans. H. B. Nisbet, Cambridge: Cambridge University Press.

——— (1974) *Logic*, trans. R. Hartmann and W. Schwartz, Indianapolis: Bobbs-Merrill.

Leibniz, G. (1981) *New Essays Concerning Human Understanding*, ed. and trans. P. Remnant and J. Bennett, Cambridge: Cambridge University Press. IV. XV.4

Locke, J. (1959) *An Essay Concerning Human Understanding*, 2 vols, ed. A. C. Fraser, New York: Dover. I, p. 58 and IV, xv and xvi, ss. 10 and 11.

Mannheim, K. (1936) *Ideology and Utopia*, trans. L. Wirth and Edward Shils, New York: Harcourt, Brace.

——— (1952) *Essays on the Sociology of Knowledge*, ed. P. Kecskemeti, Oxford: Oxford University Press.

Mill, J. S. (1978) *On Liberty*, ed. E. Rapaport, Indianapolis: Hackett. Ch. 2.

Plato (1961) *Meno*, in *Collected Dialogues of Plato*, ed. E. Hamilton and H. Cairns, Princeton: Princeton University Press. 97a-b.

——— (1961) *Theaetetus*, in Hamilton and Cairns, 201.

Peirce, C. S. (1955) "The fixation of belief," in *Philosophical Writings of Peirce*, ed. J. Buchler, New York: Dover.

Price, H. H. (1969) *Belief*, New York: Humanities Press. Lect. 5.

Reid, T. (1969) *Essays on the Intellectual Powers of Man*, intro. B. Brody, Cambridge: MIT Press. I, viii and VI, iv and v.

——— (1975) *An Inquiry into the Human Mind on the Principles of Common Sense*, in *Thomas Reid's Inquiry and Essays*, ed. R. Beanblossom and K. Lehrer, Indianapolis: Bobbs-Merrill. VI. xxiv.

Russell, B. (1948) *Human Knowledge: Its Scope and Limits*, New York: G. Allen and Unwin.

Sextus Empiricus (1933) *Outlines of Pyrrhonism* in *Sextus Empiricus*, vol. 1, trans. R. G. Bury, Cambridge: Loeb Classical Library, Harvard University Press.

Wittgenstein, L. (1969) *On Certainty*, ed. G. E. M. Anscombe and G. H. von Wright, trans. D. Paul and G. E. M. Anscombe, New York: Harper.

RECENT WORKS

Adler, J. (1994) "Testimony, trust, knowing," *Journal of Philosophy* 91: 264-275.

Agassi, J., ed. (1987) *Rationality*, Dordrecht: Nijhoff.

Airaksinen, T. (1982) "Contextualism: A new theory of epistemic justification," *Philosophia* 12: 37-50.

Akerlof, G. (1970) "The market for lemons: Qualitative uncertainty and the market mechanism," *Quarterly Journal of Economics* 84: 488-500.

Alcoff, L. and Potter, E., eds (1993) *Feminist Epistemologies*, London: Routledge.

Alston, W. (1989a) *Epistemic Justification*, Ithaca: Cornell University Press.

——— (1989b) "A 'doxastic practice' approach to epistemology," in Clay and Lehrer (1989).

——— (1989c) "Internalism and externalism in epistemology," in Alston (1989a).

——— (1991) *Perceiving God*, Ithaca: Cornell University Press.

——— (1993a) "Epistemic desiderata," *Philosophy and Phenomenological Research*.

——— (1993b) *The Reliability of Sense Perception*, Ithaca: Cornell University Press.

Annis, D. (1978) "A contextualist theory of justification," *American Philosophical Quarterly* 15: 213-29.

——— (1982) "The social and cultural component of epistemic justification: A reply," *Philosophia* 12: 51-55.

Anscombe, G. E. M. (1981a) *The Collected Philosophical Papers of G. E. M. Anscombe*, vol. 1, *From Parmenides to Wittgenstein*, Oxford: Oxford University Press.

——— (1981b) "Hume and Julius Caesar," in Anscombe (1981a).

Asquith, P. and Hacking, I., eds (1978) *PSA 1978, vol.* 2, East Lansing, Mich.: Philosophy of Science Association, 227-239.

Baird, D. (1985) "Lehrer-Wagner consensual probabilities do not adequately summarize the available information," *Synthese* 62: 47-62.

Baker, J. (1987) "Trust and rationality," *Pacific Philosophical Quarterly* 68: 1-13.

Barnes, B. (1974) *Scientific Knowledge and Sociological Theory*, London: Routledge.

——— (1977) *Interests and the Growth of Knowledge*, London: Routledge.

Barnes, B. and Bloor, D. (1982) "Relativism, rationalism and the sociology of knowledge," in Hollis and Lukes (1982).

Barth, E. (1991) "Argumentation—distributed or monological?" *Communications and cognition* 24: 15-24.

Belensky, M. F., Clinchy, B. M., Goldberger, N. R., and Tarule, J. M., eds (1986) *Women's Ways of Knowing*, New York: Basic Books.

Bennett, W. L. (1983) *The News: The Politics of Illusion*, New York: Longmans.

Berger, R. L. (1981) "A necessary and sufficient condition for reaching a consensus by De Groot's method," *Journal of the American Statistical Association* 76: 415-418.

Bernardo, J. M., DeGroot, M. H., Lindley, D. H., and Smith, S. F. M., eds (1985) *Bayesian Statistics*, Elsevier: North-Holland.

Blair, A. and Johnson, R. (1987) "Argumentation as dialectical," *Argumentation* 1: 41-56.

Blais, M. (1987) "Epistemic tit for tat," *Journal of Philosophy* 84: 363-375.

Bloor, D. (1976) *Knowledge and Social Imagery*, London: Routledge; (1991) 2nd edn, Chicago: University of Chicago Press.

——— (1983) *Wittgenstein: A Social Theory of Knowledge*, New York: Columbia University Press.

——— (1984) "A sociological theory of objectivity," *Philosophy* supp. 17: 229-246.

Bogdan, R., ed. (1976) *Local Induction*, Dordrecht: Reidel.

——— (1991a) "Common sense naturalized: The practical stance," in (Bogdan 1991b).

——— (1991b) *Mind and Common Sense*, Cambridge: Cambridge University Press.

BonJour, L. (1985) *The Structure of Empirical Knowledge*, Cambridge, Mass.: Harvard University Press.

Bowler, P. (1989) *The Mendelian Revolution: The Emergence of Hereditarian Concepts in Modern Science and Society*, Baltimore: The Johns Hopkins University Press.

Boyd, R. (1988) "How to be a moral realist," in Sayre-McCord (1988).

——— (1991) "Realism, anti-foundationalism and the enthusiasm for natural kinds," *Philosophical Studies* 61: 127-148.

Brinton, A. (1985) "A rhetorical view of the *ad hominem*," *Australasian Journal of Philosophy* 63: 50-63.

Brislin, R., Bochner, S., and Lonner, W., eds (1975) *Cross-cultural Perspectives on Learning*, New York: Wiley.

Broad, C. D. (1953a) "Henry Sidgwick and psychical research," in Broad (1953b).

——— (1953b) *Religion, Philosophy and Psychical Research —Selected Essays*, London: Routledge and Kegan Paul.

Brooks, D. (1986) "Group minds and indeterminacy," *Australasian Journal of Philosophy* 64: 456-470.

Brown, H. (1989) *Rationality*, London: Routledge.

——— (1992) "Response to Matheson," *Social Epistemology* 6: 45-55.

Brown, J. R., ed. (1984) *Scientific Rationality: The Sociological Turn*, Dordrecht: Reidel.

——— (1989) *The Rational and the Social*, London: Routledge.

Buckhout, R. (1974) "Eyewitness testimony," *Scientific American* 231: 23-31.

Buczkowski, P., ed. (1991) *The Social Horizon of Knowledge*, Amsterdam: Rodopi.

Burge, T. (1983) "Intellectual norms and the foundations of mind," *Journal of Philosophy* 83: 697-720.

——— (forthcoming) "Content Preservation."

Burian, R. (1986) "Lillie's paradox—Or, some hazards of cellular geography," typescript.

Burian, R., Gayon, J., and Zallen, D. (1988) "The singular fate of genetics in the history of French biology, 1900-1940," *Journal of the History of Biology* 21: 357-402.

Campbell, D. (1986) "Science's social system of validity-enhancing collective belief change and the problem of the social sciences," in Fiske and Shweder (1986).

Carnap, R. (1958) "The methodological character of theoretical concepts," in *Minnesota Studies in the Philosophy of Science*, vol. 1, Minneapolis: University of Minnesota Press.

——— (1967) *The Logical Structure of the World*, trans. R. A. George, Berkeley: University of California Press.

Cartwright, N. (1983) *How the Laws of Physics Lie*, New York: Oxford.

——— (1991) "Replicability, reproducibility, and robustness: Comments on Harry Collins," *History of Political Economy* 23: 143-155.

Cerf, C. and Navasky, V. (1984) *The Experts Speak*, New York: Pantheon.

Chomsky, N. (1980) *Rules and Representations*, New York: Columbia University Press.

Clarke, D. S. (1988) *Rational Acceptance and Purpose*, Totowa, N.J.: Rowman and Littlefield.

——— (1991) "Knowledge, information exchange, and responsibility," *Southern Journal of Philosophy* 29: 445-463.

Clay, M. and Lehrer, K., eds (1989) *Knowledge and Skepticism*, Boulder: Westview.

Clifford, B. R. (1978) "A critique of eyewitness research," in Gruenberg et al. (1978).

Coady, C. A. J. (1973) "Testimony and observation," *American Philosophical Quarterly* 10: 149-155.

——— (1975) "Collingwood and historical testimony," *Philosophy* 50: 409-424.

——— (1981) "Mathematical knowledge and reliable testimony," *Mind* 90: 542-556.

——— (1989) "Reid on testimony," in Dalgarno and Matthews (1989).

——— (1992) *Testimony: A Philosophical Study*, Oxford: Oxford University Press.

Code, L. (1989) "Collingwood's epistemological individualism," *Monist* 72: 542-567.

Cohen, G. A. (1967) "Beliefs and roles," *Proceedings of the Aristotelian Society* 67: 17-34.

Cohen, L. J. (1977) *The Probable and the Provable*, Oxford: Oxford University Press.

Cohen, S. (1986) "Knowledge and context," *Journal of Philosophy* 83: 574-583.

——— (1987) "Knowledge, context, and social standards," *Synthese* 73: 3-26.

Cohen, S. and Young, J. (1981) *The Manufacture of News*, 2nd edn, Beverly Hills: Sage.

Cole, M. (1975) "An ethnographic psychology of cognition," in Brislin, Bochner, and Lonner (1975).

Collingwood, R. G. (1970) *The Idea of History*, Oxford: Oxford University Press.

Collins, H. (1983) "An empirical relativist program in the sociology of science," in Knorr-Cetina and Mulkay (1983).

——— (1985) *Changing Order*, London: Sage.

——— (1991) "The meaning of replication and the science of economics," *History of Political Economy* 23, 1.

Cooke, R. (1991) *Experts in Uncertainty: Expert Opinion and Subjective Probability in Science*, Oxford: Oxford University Press.

Cooper, D. (1987) "The epistemology of testimony: Assertion, phenomenology and essence," *Aristotelian Society Supplement* 61: 85-106.

Corlett, J. A. (1991a) "Epistemology, psychology, and Goldman," *Social Epistemology* 5: 91-100.

——— (1991b) "Social epistemology and social cognition," *Social Epistemology* 5: 135-149.

——— (forthcoming a) "Goldman and the foundations of social epistemology," *Argumentation*.

——— (forthcoming b) *Analyzing Social Knowledge*.

Craig, E. (1990) *Knowledge and the State of Nature: An Essay in Conceptual Synthesis*, Oxford: Clarendon Press.

Dalgarno, M. and Matthews, E., eds (1989) *The Philosophy of Thomas Reid*, Dordrecht: Kluwer.

Davidson, D. (1986) "A coherence theory of knowledge and truth," in LePore (1986).

Dawes, R. (1988) *Rational Choice in an Uncertain World*, Orlando, Fla: Harcourt Brace Jovanovich.

De Groot, M. H. (1974) "Reaching a consensus," *Journal of the American Statistical Association* 69: 118-212.

Delaney, C. F. (1991) "Peirce on the Social and Historical Dimensions of Science," in McMullin (1992b).

Dostoevsky, F. M. (1943) *The Brothers Karamazov*, tr. Constance Garnett, New York: Random House.

Dretske, F. (1982) "A cognitive cul de sac," *Mind* 91: 109-111.

Duran, J. (1986) "A contextualist modification of Cornman," *Philosophia* 16: 377-388.

——— (1990) *Toward a Feminist Epistemology*, Savage, Md.: Rowman and Littlefield.

——— (1991) "I know what I know, if you know what I mean," *Social Epistemology* 5: 151-159.

——— (1993) *Knowledge in Context: Naturalized Epistemology and Sociolinguistics*, Lanham, Md.: Rowman and Littlefield.

Egeth, H. E. and McCloskey, M. (1984) "Expert testimony about eyewitness behaviour: Is it safe and effective?" in Wells and Loftus (1984).

Entman, R. M. (1989) *Democracy without Citizens: Media and the Decay of American Politics*, New York: Oxford University Press.

Feher, M. (1984) "Epistemology naturalized vs. epistemology socialized," in Hronszky et al. (1984).

Feldman, R. (forthcoming) "Deductivism."

Feldman, R. and Conee, E. (1985) "Evidentialism," *Philosophical Studies* 48: 15-34.

Ferejohn, J. A. and Kuklinski, J. H., eds *(1990) Information and Democratic Processes*, Urbana: University of Illinois Press.

Feyerabend, P. (1978) *Science in a Free Society*, London: New Left Books.

Field, H. (1986) "The deflationary conception of truth," in MacDonald and Wright (1986).

Fine, A. (1986) *The Shaky Game*, Chicago: University of Chicago Press.

Fine, A. and Machamer, P., eds (1987) *PSA* 1986, vol. 2, East Lansing, Mich.: Philosophy of Science Association.

Fiske, D. and Shweder, R. (1986) *Metatheory in Social Science*, Chicago: University of Chicago.

Fiske, S. T. and Taylor, S. E. (1984) *Social Cognition*, Reading, Mass.: Addison-Wesley.

Fodor, J. (1974) "Special sciences, or the disunity of science as a working hypothesis," *Synthese* 28: 77-115.

Foley, R. (1987) *The Theory of Epistemic Rationality*, Cambridge, Mass.: Harvard University Press.

——— (1993) *Working without a Net*, New York: Oxford University Press.

Forgus, J. P., ed. (1982) *Social Cognition*, London: Academic Press.

Forrest, Peter (1985) "The Lehrer-Wagner theory of consensus and the zero weight problem," *Synthese* 62: 73-78.

French, P., Uehling, T., and Wettstein, H. (1980) *Midwest Studies in Philosophy*, vol. 5, Minneapolis: University of Minnesota Press.

French, S. (1985) "Group consensus probability distributions: A critical survey," in Bernardo et al. (1985).

Fricker, E. (1987) "The epistemology of testimony," *Aristotelian Society Supplement* 61: 57-83.

Fuller, S. (1988a) *Social Epistemology*, Bloomington: Indiana University Press.

——— (1988b) "Social epistemology: From the Republic beyond Edinburgh and toward the New Atlantic," *Explorations in Knowledge* 5: 1-10.

——— (1991) "Social epistemology: Basic principles and prospects," *Kennis en Methode* 15: 251-266.

Galison, P. and Stump, D., eds (forthcoming) *Disunity and Contextualism in the Philosophy of Science Studies*, Stanford: Stanford University Press.

Gauker, C. (1991) "Mental content and the division of epistemic labour," *Australasian Journal of Philosophy* 69: 302-318.

Gauld, A. (1992) *A History of Hypnotism*, Cambridge: Cambridge University Press.

Gellatly, A. G., Rogers, D. and Sloboda, J. A., eds (1989) *Cognition and Social Worlds*, Oxford: Clarendon Press.

Gelman, R. (1978) "Cognitive development," *Annual Review of Psychology* 29: 297-332.

Gettier, E. (1963) "Is justified true belief knowledge?" *Analysis* 23: 121-123.

Gibbard, A. (1990) *Wise Choices, Apt Feelings*, Cambridge, Mass.: Harvard University Press.

Giere, R. (1988) *Explaining Science: A Cognitive Approach*, Chicago: University of Chicago Press.

Gilbert, M. (1987) "Modelling collective belief," *Synthese* 73: 185-204.

——— (1989) *On Social Facts*, London: Routledge.

——— (1993a) "Agreements, coercion, and obligation," *Ethics* 103.

——— (1993b) "Is an agreement an exchange of promises?" *Journal of Philosophy*.

——— (1993c) "Shared intentions," American Philosophical Association Symposium.

——— (1994) "Durkheim and social facts," in Pickering and Martins (1994).

Goldman, A. I. (1980) "The internalist conception of justification," in French et al. (1980).

——— (1986) *Epistemology and Cognition*, Cambridge, Mass.: Harvard University Press.

——— (1987a) "The cognitive and social sides of epistemology," in (Fine and Machamer 1987).

——— (1987b) "Foundations of social epistemics," *Synthese* 73: 109-144.

——— (1991a) "Epistemic paternalism: Communication control in law and society," *Journal of Philosophy* 88: 113-131.

——— (1991b) "Social epistemics and social psychology," *Social Epistemology* 5: 121-126.

——— (1992) *Liaisons: Philosophy Meets the Cognitive and Social Sciences*, Cambridge, Mass.: MIT Press.

——— (1994) "Argumentation and social epistemology," *Journal of Philosophy* 91: 27-49.

Goldman, A. I. and Shaked, M. (1991) "An economic model of scientific activity and truth acquisition," *Philosophical Studies* 63: 31-55.

Goldstein, T. (1985) *The News at Any Cost: How Journalists Compromise Their Ethics to Shape the News*, New York: Simon and Schuster.

Goodman, N. (1955) *Fact, Fiction and Forecast*, Cambridge, Mass.: Harvard University Press.

Gould, S. J. (1981) *The Mismeasure of Man*, New York: Norton.

Govier, T. (1987) *Problems in Argument Analysis and Evaluation*, Dordrecht: Foris Press.

——— (1992) "What is a good argument?" *Metaphilosophy* 23: 393-409.

Gruenberg, M., Morris, P., and Sykes, R., eds (1978) *Practical Aspects of Memory*, London.

Hacking, I. (1983) *Representing and Intervening*, Cambridge: Cambridge University Press.

——— (1988) "On the stability of the laboratory sciences," *Journal of Philosophy* 85: 507-514.

——— (1992) "Statistical language, statistical truth, and statistical reason: The self-authentication of a style of scientific reasoning," in (McMullin 1992b).

Hallin, D. C. (1986) *The "Uncensored War": The Media and Vietnam*, New York: Oxford University Press.

Haraway, D. (1990) *Primate Visions*, London: Routledge.

——— (1991) *Simians, Cyborgs and Women: The Reinvention of Nature*, New York: Routledge.

Harding, S. (1986) *The Science Question in Feminism*, Ithaca: Cornell University Press.

——— (1993) "Rethinking standpoint epistemology: What is 'strong objectivity'?" in Alcoffs and Potter (1993).

Harding, S. and Hintikka, M., eds (1983) *Discovering Reality*, Dordrecht: Reidel.

Hardwig, J. (1985) "Epistemic dependence," *Journal of Philosophy* 82: 335-349.

——— (1988) "Evidence, testimony, and the problem of individualism: A response to Schmitt," *Social Epistemology*, 2: 308-322.

——— (1991) "The role of trust in knowledge," *Journal of Philosophy* 88: 693-708.

Harman, G. (1974) *Thought*, Princeton: Princeton University Press.

Heal, J. (1978) "Common knowledge," *Philosophical Quarterly* 28: 116-131.

Heil, J., ed. (1993) *Rationality, Morality, and Self-interest*, Savage, Md.: Rowman and Littlefield.

Hesse, M. (1980) *Revolutions and Reconstructions in the Philosophy of Science*, Bloomington: Indiana University Press.

——— (1984) "Socializing epistemology," in Hronzsky et al. (1984).

Heyes, Cecilia (1991) "Who's the horse? A response to Corlett," *Social Epistemology* 5: 127-134.

Hinman, L. (1982) "The case for *ad hominem* arguments," *Australasian Journal of Philosophy* 60: 338-345.

Hollis, M. (1992) "Social thought and social action," in McMullin (1992b).

Hollis, M. and Lukes, S., eds (1982) *Rationality and Relativism*, Cambridge, Mass.: MIT Press.

Horowitz, Gregg (1991) "Avoiding the subject," *Social Epistemology* 5: 187-192.

Horwich, P. (1990) *Truth*, Oxford: Basil Blackwell.

Hronszky, I., Feher, M., and Dajka, B., eds (1984) *Scientific Knowledge Socialized*, Dordrecht: Kluwer.

Hull, D. (1988) *Science as a Process*, Chicago: University of Chicago Press.

Hutchins, E. (1980) *Culture and Inference: A Trobriand Case Study*, Cambridge, Mass.: Harvard University Press.

Kahneman, D., Slovic, P., and Tversky, A., eds (1982) *Judgments under Uncertainty: Heuristics and Biases*, Cambridge: Cambridge University Press.

Kaplan, M. (1991) "Epistemology on holiday," *Journal of Philosophy* 3: 132-154.

Katz, J. (1989) "Rational common ground in the sociology of knowledge," *Philosophy of the Social Sciences* 19: 257-271.

Keller, E. F. (1985) *Reflections on Gender and Science*, New Haven: Yale University Press.

King, R. (1991) "Keeping ideology political," *Social Epistemology* 5: 177-186.

Kitchener, R. (1989) "Genetic epistemology and the prospects for a cognitive sociology of science: A critical synthesis," *Social Epistemology* 3: 153-169.

Kitcher, P. (1983) *The Nature of Mathematical Knowledge*, Oxford: Oxford University Press.

——— (1984) "1953 and all that: A tale of two sciences," *Philosophical Review* 93: 335-373.

——— (1990) "The division of cognitive labor," *Journal of Philosophy* 87: 5-22.

——— (1991) "Socializing knowledge," *Journal of Philosophy* 88: 675-676.

——— (1992) "Authority, deference, and the role of individual reasoning in science," in McMullin (1992b).

——— (1993) *The Advancement of Science*, Oxford: Oxford University Press.

——— (forthcoming a) "Knowledge, society, and history," *Canadian Journal of Philosophy*.

——— (forthcoming b) "Real realism."

Knorr-Cetina, K. (1981) *The Manufacture of Knowledge*, Oxford: Pergamon Press.

——— (1983) "The ethnographic study of scientific work," in Knorr-Cetina and Mulkay (1983).

Knorr-Cetina, K. and Amann, K. (1990) "The fixation of (visual) evidence," in Lynch and Woolgar (1990).

Knorr-Cetina, K. and Mulkay, M. (1983) *Science Observed: Perspectives on Social Studies of Science*, London: Sage.

Kornblith, H. (1987) "Some social features of cognition," *Synthese* 73: 27-42.

——— (1988) "How internal can you get?" *Synthese* 74: 313-327.

——— (1989) "Introspection and misdirection," *Australasian Journal of Philosophy* 67:410-422.

——— (1993) *Inductive Inference and Its Natural Ground: An Essay in Naturalistic Epistemology*, Cambridge, Mass.: MIT Press.

——— ed. (1994) *Naturalizing Epistemology*, Cambridge, Mass.: MIT Press.

Kronn, W. (1984) "Social change and epistemic thought," in Hronszky et al. (1984).

Kuhn, T. (1970) *The Structure of Scientific Revolutions*, 2nd edn, Chicago: University of Chicago Press.

Kvanvig, J. (1986) "Is there an 'us' in justification?" *Synthese* 62: 63-73.

Laboratory of Comparative Human Cognition (1979) "Cross-cultural psychology's challenges to our ideas of children and development," *American Psychologist* 34: 827-833.

Laddaga, R. (1977) "Lehrer and the consensus proposal," *Synthese* 36: 473-477.

Latour, B. (1987) *Science in Action*, Cambridge, Mass.: Harvard University Press.

——— (1992) "One more turn after the social turn," in McMullin (1992b).

Latour, B. and Woolgar, S. (1979) *Laboratory Life*, London: Sage.

Laudan, L. (1977) *Progress and Its Problems*, Berkeley: University of California Press.

——— (1984) "The pseudoscience of science?" in Brown (1984).

Laudan, L. and Leplin, J. (1991) "Empirical equivalence and underdetermination," *Journal of Philosophy* 88: 449-472.

Laudan, R. (1978) "The recent revolution in geology and Kuhn's theory of scientific change," in Asquith and Hacking (1978).

Laudan, R. and Laudan, L. (1989) "Dominance and the disunity of method: Solving the problems of innovation and consensus," *Philosophy of Science* 5: 221-237.

LeGrand, H. E. (1988) *Drifting Continents and Shifting Theories*, Cambridge: Cambridge University Press.

Lehrer, K. (1975a) *Analysis and Metaphysics: Essays in Honor of R. M. Chisholm*, Dordrecht: Reidel.

——— (1975b) "Social consensus and rational agnoiology," *Synthese* 31: 141-160.

——— (1976a) "Induction, consensus, and catastrophe," in Bogdan (1976).

——— (1976b) "When rational disagreement is impossible," *Nous* 10: 327-332.

——— (1977) "Social information," *The Monist* 60: 473-487.

——— (1985) "Consensus and the ideal observer," *Synthese* 62: 109-120.

——— (1987) "Personal and social knowledge," *Synthese* 73: 87-108.

——— (1990) *Theory of Knowledge*, Boulder: Westview.

Lehrer, K. and Smith, J. (1985) "Reid on testimony and perception," *Canadian Journal of Philosophy*, supp. vol. 11.

Lehrer, K. and Wagner, C. (1981) *Rational Consensus in Science and Society*, Dordrecht: Reidel.

LePore, E., ed. (1986) *The Philosophy of Donald Davidson: Perspectives on Truth and Interpretation*, London: Basil Blackwell.

Levi, I. (1985) "Consensus as shared agreement and outcome of inquiry," *Synthese* 62:3-12.

Lewis, D. (1969) *Convention: A Philosophical Study*, Cambridge, Mass.: Harvard University Press.

——— (1983a) *Philosophical Papers*, vol. 1, Oxford: Oxford University Press.

——— (1983b) "Scorekeeping in a language game," in Lewis (1983a).

Linstone, H. and Turoff, M., eds (1975) *The Delphi Method: Techniques and Applications*, Reading, Mass.: Addison-Wesley.

Loewer, B., ed. (1985) *Synthese* 62, Special Issue: Consensus.

Loewer, B. and Laddaga, R. (1985) "Destroying the consensus," *Synthese* 62: 79-96.

Longino, H. (1990) *Science as Social Knowledge: Values and Objectivity in Scientific Inquiry*, Princeton: Princeton University Press.

——— (1991) "Multiplying subjects and the diffusion of power," *Journal of Philosophy* 88: 666-674.

——— (1992) "Essential Tensions—Phase Two: Feminist, Philosophical, and Social Studies of Science," in McMullin (1991b).

——— (1993) "Science, power, knowledge: Description and prescription in feminist philosophy of science," in Alcoff and Potter (1993).

Lyddon, W. J. (1991) "Socially constituted knowledge: Philosophical, psychological, and feminist contributions," *Journal of Mind and Behavior* 12: 263-279.

Lynch, M. (1983) "Temporal order in laboratory work," in Knorr-Cetina and Mulkay (1983).

Lynch, M. and Edgerton, S. (1988) "Preparatory practice and closure: A case study of image processing in astronomy," *British Society for the History of Science Proceedings*, Manchester.

Lynch, M. and Woolgar, S., eds (1990) *Representation in Scientific Practice*, Cambridge, Mass.: MIT Press.

MacDonald, G. and Wright, C., eds (1986) *Fact, Science, and Morality*, Oxford: Basil Blackwell.

MacKuen, M. (1990) "Speaking of politics: Individual conversational choice, public opinion, and the prospects for deliberative democracy," in Ferejohn and Kuklinski (1990).

Maffie, James (1991) "What is social about social epistemics?" *Social Epistemology* 5:101-110.

Manicas, P. and Rosenberg, A. (1985) "Naturalism, epistemological individualism and 'the Strong Programme' in the sociology of knowledge," *Journal for the Theory of Social Behavior* 15: 76-101.

——— (1988) "The sociology of scientific knowledge: Can we ever get it straight?" *Journal for the Theory of Social Behavior* 18: 51-76.

Marr, D. (1982) *Vision*, San Francisco: Freeman.

Martin, M. (1982) "Impersonal Knowledge," *Dialogos* 17: 123-130.

Matheson, C. (1992) "Review of Brown's *Rationality*," *Social Epistemology* 6: 35-44.

McDowell, J. (1980) "Meaning, communications and knowledge," in Van Straaten (1980).

McLaughlin, B. and Rorty, A. (1988) *Perspectives on Self-deception*, Berkeley: University of California Press.

McMullin, E. (1992a) "Introduction: The Social Dimensions of Science," in McMullin (1991b).

——— (1992b) *The Social Dimensions of Science*, South Bend, Ind.: Notre Dame University Press.

Medin, D. and Ortony, A. (1989) "Comments on part I: Psychological essentialism," in Vosniadu and Ortony (1989).

Meiland, J. (1989) "Argument as inquiry and persuasion," *Argumentation* 3: 185-196.

Menard, H. W. (1986) *The Ocean of Truth: A Personal History of Global Tectonics*, Princeton: Princeton University Press.

Milgrom, P. (1981) "Good news and bad news: Representation theorems and applications," *Bell Journal of Economics* 13: 380-391.

Mokrzycki, E. (1989) "The problem of going to: Between epistemology and the sociology of knowledge," *Social Epistemology* 3: 203-216.

Moore, J. A. (1991) "Knowledge, society, power, and the promise of epistemological externalism," *Synthese* 88: 379-398.

Mulkay, M. (1982) "Sociology of science in the West," *Current Sociology* 28: 1-116.

Munitz, M. and Unger, P., eds (1974) *Semantics and Philosophy*, New York: New York University Press.

Nickles, T. (1992) "Good science as bad history: From order of knowing to order of being," in McMullin (1992b).

Nisbett, R. and Ross, L. (1980) *Human Inference: Strategies and Shortcomings of Social Judgment*, Englewood Cliffs, N.J.: Prentice Hall.

Nola, R. (1990) "The strong programme for the sociology of science, reflexivity and relativism," *Inquiry* 33: 273-296.

Nurmi, Hannu (1985) "Some properties of the Lehrer-Wagner method for reaching rational consensus," *Synthese* 62: 13-24.

Olby, R. (1974) *The Path to the Double Helix*, Seattle: University of Washington Press.

Paletz, D. L. and Entman, R. M. (1981) *Media, Power, Politics*, New York: Free Press.

Papineau, D. (1979) *For Science in the Social Sciences*, New York: St. Martin's Press.

Parenti, M. (1985) *Inventing Reality: The Politics of the Mass Media*, New York: St. Martin's Press.

Pels, D. (1991) "Values, Facts, and the Social Theory of Knowledge," *Kennis en Methode* 15: 274-284.

Pickering, A. (1984) *Constructing Quarks*, Chicago: University of Chicago Press.

Pickering, W. and Martins, H. (1994) *Debating Durkheim*, London: Routledge.

Pinch, T. J. (1986) *Confronting Nature: The Sociology of Solar-Neutrino Detection*, Dordrecht: Reidel.

Plantinga, A. (1993) *Warrant and Proper Function*, Oxford: Oxford University Press.

Polanyi, M. (1958) *Personal Knowledge*, Chicago: University of Chicago Press.

Pollock, J. (1986) *Contemporary Theories of Knowledge*, Savage, Md.: Rowman and Littlefield.

Popper, K. (1968) *Conjectures and Refutations: The Growth of Scientific Knowledge*, 2nd edn, New York: Harper and Row.

Putnam, H. (1978) *Meaning and the Moral Sciences*, London: Routledge.

——— (1981) *Reason, Truth, and History*, Cambridge: Cambridge University Press.

——— (1983) *Realism and Reason*, Cambridge: Cambridge University Press.

Quine, W. V. (1969a) "Epistemology naturalized," in Quine (1969b).

——— (1969b) *Ontological Relativity and Other Essays*, New York: Columbia University Press.

Quinton, A. (1971) "Authority and Autonomy in Knowledge," *Proceedings of the Education Society of Great Britain*, supp. issue 5: 201-215.

——— (1975-76) "Social Objects," *Proceedings of the Aristotelian Society* 76: 1-27.

Radford, C. (1985) "Must knowledge—or 'knowledge'—be socially constructed?" *Philosophy of the Social Sciences* 15: 15-34.

Ravetz, J. (1970) *Science and Its Social Problems*, New York: Oxford.

Reardon, K. K. (1981) *Persuasion: Theory and Conduct*, London: Sage.
Riegel, K. and Meacham, J. (1976) *The Developing Individual in a Changing World*, vol. 1, Chicago: Aldine.
Ringer, F. (1991) "The Origins of Mannheim's Sociology of Knowledge," in McMullin (1991a).
Rogers, E. M. (1983) *Diffusion of Innovation*, New York: Free Press.
Rogers, E. M. and Kincaid, D. L. (1981) *Communication Networks: Toward a New Paradigm for Research*, New York: Free Press.
Rogoff, B. and Lave, J. (1984) *Everyday Cognition: Its Development in Social Context*, Cambridge, Mass.: Harvard University Press.
Rorty, R. (1980) *Consequences of Pragmatism*, Minneapolis: University of Minnesota Press.
Ross, A. (1986) "Why do we believe what we are told?" Ratio 28: 69-88.
Ross, J. (1975) "Testimonial evidence," in Lehrer (1975a).
Roth, P. (1987) *Meaning and Method in the Social Sciences: A Case for Methodological Pluralism*, Ithaca: Cornell University Press.
Rouse, J. (1987) *Knowledge and Power: Toward a Political Philosophy of Science*, Ithaca: Cornell University Press.
——— (1991) "The dynamics of power and knowledge in science," *Journal of Philosophy* 88: 658-665.
——— (forthcoming a) "What are cultural studies of scientific knowledge?" *Configurations*.
——— (forthcoming b) "Beyond epistemic sovereignty," in Galison and Stump (forthcoming).
Ryle, G. (1948) *The Concept of Mind*, London: Hutchinson.
Sapp, J. (1987) *Beyond the Gene: Cytoplasmic Inheritance and the Struggle for Authority in Genetics*, Oxford: Oxford University Press.
Sarkar, H. (1983) *A Theory of Method*, Berkeley: University of California Press.
Sayers, S. (1989) "Knowledge as a social phenomenon," *Radical Philosophy* 52: 34-37.
Sayre-McCord, G., ed. (1988) *Essays on Moral Realism*, Ithaca: Cornell University Press.
Schick, F. (1984) *Having Reasons: An Essay on Rationality and Sociality*, Princeton: Princeton University Press.
Schiffer, S. (1972) *Meaning*, Oxford: Oxford University Press.
Schmaus, W., Segerstrale, U., and Jesseph, D. (1992) "A manifesto," *Social Epistemology* 6: 243-265.

Schmitt, F. (1985) "Consensus, Respect, and Weighted Averaging," *Synthese* 62: 25-46.

——— (1987a) "Justification, sociality, and autonomy," *Synthese* 73: 43-86.

——— (1987b) *Synthese* 62, Special Issue: Social Epistemology.

——— (1988a) "Epistemic Dimensions of Self-deception," in McLaughlin and Rorty (1988).

——— (1988b) "On the road to social epistemic interdependence," *Social Epistemology* 2: 297-307.

——— (1988c) "Testimony and Evidence," *Social Epistemology* 2: 323-326.

——— (1991) "Social epistemology and social cognitive psychology," *Social Epistemology* 5: 111-120.

——— (1992a) *Knowledge and Belief*, London: Routledge.

——— (1992b) "Review of Edward Craig, *Knowledge and the State of Nature: An Essay in Conceptual Synthesis*," *Mind* 101: 555-559.

——— (1993) "Epistemic perspectivism," in Heil (1993).

Scribner, S. (1976) "Situating the experiment in cross-cultural research," in (Riegel and Meacham 1976).

Sellars, W. (1963a) "Empiricism and the philosophy of mind," in (Sellars 1963b).

——— (1963b) *Science, Perception, and Reality*, London: Routledge.

Semin, G. R. and Gergen, K. J., eds (1990) *Everyday Understanding*, London: Sage.

Shakespeare, N. (1993) "Diary," *Telegraph Magazine*, July 10, 10.

Shapin, S. (1982) "History of science and its social reconstructions," *History of Science* 20: 157-211.

Shapin, S. and Schaffer, S. (1985) *Leviathan and the Air-pump*, Princeton: Princeton University Press.

Shapley, L. S. and Grofman, B. (1984) "Optimizing group judgmental accuracy in the presence of interdependence," *Public Choice* 43: 329-343.

Shope, R. (1983) *The Analysis of Knowing*, Princeton: Princeton University Press.

Siegel, H. (1988) "Rationality and epistemic dependence," *Educational Philosophy and Theory* 20: 1-6.

——— (1989) "Epistemology and critical thinking pedagogy," *Argumentation* 3: 127-140.

Sigal, L. V. (1973) *Reporters and Officials: The Organization and Politics of Newsmaking*, Lexington, Mass.: D. C. Heath.

Smith, J. W. (1983) "Rationalism and the Strong Programme of the sociology of knowledge: Reconciliation without tears," *Philosophical Papers* 12: 1-31.

Smith, N. V., ed. (1982) *Mutual Knowledge*, New York: Academic Press.

Sniezek, J. and Henry, R. (1989) "Accuracy and confidence in group judgment," *Organizational Behavior and Human Decision Processes* 43: 1-28.

Sobel, J. H. (1987) "On the evidence of testimony for miracles: A Bayesian interpretation of David Hume's analysis," *Philosophical Quarterly* 73: 166-186.

Solomon, M. (1992) "Scientific rationality and human reasoning," *Philosophy of Science* 59: 439-455.

——— (1994) "Social empiricism," *Nous* 28.

——— (forthcoming) "Is there an invisible hand of reason?"

Sosa, E. (1991a) *Knowledge in Perspective: Selected Essays in Epistemology*, Cambridge: Cambridge University Press.

——— (1991b) "Testimony and coherence," in Sosa (1991a).

Spence, M. (1974) *Market Signaling*, Cambridge, Mass.: Harvard University Press.

Stalnaker, R. (1973) "Presuppositions," *Journal of Philosophical Logic*.

——— (1974) "Pragmatic presuppositions," in Munitz and Unger (1974).

——— (1984) *Inquiry*, Cambridge, Mass.: MIT Press.

Stevenson, L. (1993) "Why believe what people say?" Synthese 94: 429-451.

Stewart, J. (1990) *Drifting Continents and Colliding Paradigms*, Bloomington: Indiana University Press.

Stich, S. (1985) "Could man be an irrational animal?" in Kornblith (1994).

——— (1990) *The Fragmentation of Reason*, Cambridge, Mass.: MIT Press.

Stich, S. and Nisbett, R. (1980) "Justification and the psychology of human reasoning," *Philosophy of Science* 47: 188-202.

Sturgeon, N. (1992) "Nonmoral Explanation," *Philosophical Perspectives* 6: 97-117.

Susser, B. (1989) "Sociology of science and its enemies," *Inquiry* 32: 245-260.

Taubes, Gary (1993) *Bad Science: The Short Life and Weird Times of Cold Fusion*, New York: Random House.

Thagard, P. (1991) "Societies of minds: Science as distributed computing," typescript.

——— (1992) *Conceptual Revolutions*, Princeton: Princeton University Press.

Tibbetts, P. (1986) "The sociology of scientific knowledge: The constructivist thesis and relativism," *Philosophy of the Social Sciences* 16, 39-57.

Traiger, S. (forthcoming) "Humean testimony," *Pacific Philosophical Quarterly*.

Traweek, S. (1988) *Beamtimes and Lifetimes*, Cambridge, Mass.: Harvard University Press.

Triplett, T. (1986) "Relativism and the sociology of mathematics: Remarks on Bloor, Flew and Frege," *Inquiry* 29: 439-450.

——— (1988) "Azande logic versus Western logic," *British Journal for the Philosophy of Science* 39: 361-366.

——— (forthcoming) "Is there anthropological evidence that logic is culturally relative?: Remarks on Bloor, Jennings, and Evans-Prichard."

Tuchman, G. (1978) *Making News: A Study in the Construction of Reality*, New York: Free Press.

Tuomela, R. (1992) "Group beliefs," *Synthese* 91: 285-318.

Unwin, N. (1987) "Beyond truth: Towards a new conception of knowledge and communication," *Mind* 76: 299-317.

Vallicella, W. (1984) "Relativism, truth and the symmetry thesis," *Monist* 67: 452-466.

Van Fraassen, B. (1980) *The Scientific Image*, New York: Oxford University Press.

Van Straaten, Z., ed. (1980) *Philosophical Subjects: Essays Presented to P. F. Strawson*, Oxford: Clarendon Press.

von Wright, G. H., ed. (1972) *Problems in the Theory of Knowledge*, The Hague: Nijhoff.

Vosniadu, S. and Ortony, A., eds (1989) *Similarity and Analogical Reasoning*, Cambridge: Cambridge University Press.

Wagner, C. (1985) "On the formal properties of weighted averaging as a method of aggregation," *Synthese* 62: 97-108.

Wagner, S. (1983) "Cartesian epistemology," typescript.

Walton, D. (1980) "Why is the *ad populum* a fallacy?" *Philosophy and Rhetoric* 13: 264-78.

——— (1990) "What is reasoning? What is an argument?" 87: 399-419.

Watkins, J. W. N. (1987) "Epistemology and politics," in Agassi (1987).

Webb, M. O. (1993) "Why I know about as much as you: A reply to Hardwig," *Journal of Philosophy* 90: 260-70.

Welbourne, M. (1979) "The transmission of knowledge," *Philosophical Quarterly* 29: 1-9.

——— (1981) "The community of knowledge," *Philosophical Quarterly* 31: 302-314.

——— (1986) *The Community of Knowledge*, Aberdeen: Aberdeen University Press.

Wells, G. and Loftus, E., eds (1984) *Eyewitness Testimony: Psychological Perspectives*, Cambridge: Cambridge University Press.

Welshon, Robert (1991) "Ideology, first person authority and self-deception," *Social Epistemology* 5: 163-176.

——— "General response," *Social Epistemology* 5: 207-219.

Wettersten, J. (1983) "The sociology of knowledge vs. the sociology of science: A conundrum and an alternative," *Philosophy of the Social Sciences* 13: 325-334.

White, M. 1989. "The politics of epistemology," *Ethics* 100: 77-92.

Willard, C. (1990) "Authority," *Informal Logic* 12: 11-22.

Williams, B. (1972) "Knowledge and reasons," in von Wright (1972).

Wilson, I. (1987) *The After-death Experience: The Physics of the Non-physical*, New York: William Morrow.

Woods, J. (1989) "The maladroitness of epistemic Tit for Tat," *Journal of Philosophy* 86: 324-331.

Woods, J. and Walton, D. (1974) "*Argumentum ad verecundiam*," *Philosophy and Rhetoric* 7: 135-153.

Woolgar, S., ed. (1988) *Knowledge and Reflexivity: New Frontiers in the Sociology of Knowledge*, London: Sage.

Yearley, S. (1982) "The relationship between epistemological and sociological cognitive interest," *Studies in the History and Philosophy of Science* 13: 353-388.

Ziman, J. (1978) *Reliable Knowledge*, Cambridge: Cambridge University Press.

Index

a priori knowledge 11-14, 25, 38, 191, 226
Alston, W. P. 4
Annis, D. 269, 270
Aquinas, T. 2, 5
Aristotle 2, 181
authority 1, 2, 15, 54-61, 63,-65, 67, 68, 70-73, 86, 104, 106, 107, 114, 145, 152, 153, 221, 229
autonomy 72, 77, 78
Bacon, F. 1, 2
Barnes, B. 135, 137
Berkeley, G. 79
bias 19, 115, 125, 138, 139, 145, 221, 228-230
Blair, A. 173-176, 180, 185
Bradley, F. H. 75-86, 89-91
certainty 2, 5, 190
Chisholm, R. 15
circularity 37-44, 46, 175, 183, 184, 265, 285
Coady, C. A. J. 2, 4, 12, 15, 22
coherence 7, 13-15, 78, 144
coherentism 7, 14, 19, 78, 277, 280-282
collective knowledge and belief 4, 19, 114, 116, 167, 180, 235, 236, 241-245, 248, 251-253, 259, 260
Collins, H. 140, 141, 217, 229
common sense 1, 2, 4
communal knowledge 19, 27, 78, 87, 257, 283-285
consensus 1, 3, 4, 20, 26, 114, 115, 125, 140, 142, 144-146, 221, 222-225, 227, 228, 284
Cox, J. 18
Craig, E. 18
criteria 25, 32, 36, 137, 138, 144, 145, 149, 150, 155, 167, 181, 195, 267, 269
deduction 32, 38, 39, 41, 162, 177
deductivism 159, 161-163
defeasibility 13, 14, 67, 70, 107, 137, 138, 281
Descartes, R. 1, 2, 5, 6, 9, 111, 112, 189, 217
Duhem, P. 126, 127
Durkheim, E. 116
egocentric 6, 7
egoism 53, 55, 57-61, 70-72
expertise 1, 12, 45, 56, 58, 66, 68-71, 81-83, 85, 97-100, 102-104, 174, 191, 212, 218-220
Feldman, R. 18
feminist epistemology 3, 124, 138, 155
Foley, R. 4, 13
Foucault, M. 217
foundationalist 19, 78
Gibbard, A. 54
Gilbert, M. 20, 259-262, 286
Goldman, A. I. 18, 31, 167-170, 173, 174, 189, 192, 217, 218
Harding, S. 3
Hesse, M. 136
Hull, D. 143
Hume, D. 1-3, 5, 6, 16, 57, 77
induction 5, 9-12, 14, 25, 38, 94, 95, 98, 112, 136, 161, 162, 166, 177
inference to the best explanation 12
innate 30, 95
internalism
  accessibility 8, 9, 16, 100
  perspectival 278-280
Johnson, R. 173-175, 180, 185
Kahneman, D. 10, 220
Kitcher, P. 19, 25, 56, 135, 138,

149-152, 155, 217, 218, 229, 284
Kornblith, H. 4, 217, 218
Knorr-Cetina, K. 137, 138, 217
Kuhn, T. 3
Latour, B. 24, 137, 141, 143, 218
Laudan, L. 136, 217
Locke, J. 1, 5, 57, 90
logic 41, 83, 159, 178, 247
Longino, H. 26, 135, 138, 139, 146, 148, 218, 219, 280
Lynch, M. 139-141
Mannheim, K. 1
meaning 1, 20, 23, 79, 251, 252
Medin, D. 95
methodological individualism 116, 120
Mill, J. S. 235
naturalistic epistemology 4, 94, 97, 100
Nietzsche, F. 3
ontological holism 259, 260
ontological individualism 259, 260
Ortony, A. 95
Peirce, C. S. 3, 20, 217
perspectivism 277-283
Pinch, T. 229
Plantinga, A. 11, 15
Plato 1, 2, 217
plural subject 244, 245, 246, 248-251, 259
Pollock, J. 15, 277
Popper, K. 75
psychologism 260
Putnam, H. 22, 218
Quine, W. V. 4, 35, 126, 127
realism 123-125, 128
reflective equilibrium 6, 7, 25, 281
Reid, T. 3, 11, 13, 15, 57
relativism 47, 117-119, 120, 122, 125, 128, 135, 136, 139, 181-183
reliabilism 16, 113, 277, 282, 283
Rorty, R. 111, 218
Rouse, J. 20-24
Schmitt, F. 218
Sextus Empiricus 13
Shaked, M. 18
Shapin, S. 1
Sidgwick, H. 76, 83, 84, 89, 90
skepticism 7, 8, 26, 57, 80, 185, 186, 214, 279
social constructivism 4, 23, 24, 27, 218
social empiricism 219, 226-230
social interests 3, 18, 136, 156
social relations 1-3, 22, 23, 114
social roles 115, 269, 270, 272
sociology of knowledge 1, 93, 104, 120
sociology of science 3, 24, 25, 105, 106, 126, 135
Solomon, M. 19, 20, 27, 217, 220, 221, 283
strong program in the sociology of knowledge 3, 24, 120, 135-137
symmetry principle 14, 120, 122, 212
testimony 1, 2, 4-17, 32, 53, 57, 61, 63, 76-88, 91, 98, 270
trust 13, 14, 55-67, 70, 72, 78, 79, 81-83, 85-89
Tversky, A. 10, 220
Wittgenstein, L. 30, 32, 136, 217
Woolgar, S. 24, 218, 229

Contributors

WILLIAM P. ALSTON is Professor of Philosophy Emeritus at Syracuse University. His main areas of research are epistemology, philosophy of religion, philosophy of language, philosophical psychology, and metaphysics. Recent publications include *Epistemic Justification (1989), Divine Nature and Human Language (1989), Perceiving God (1991)*, and *The Reliability of Sense Perception (1993)*, all from Cornell University Press.

C. A. J. COADY is Professor of Philosophy at the University of Melbourne. His areas of specialization are philosophy of language, epistemology, and political philosophy. He is the author of *Testimony: A Philosophical Study* (Oxford University Press, 1992).

JAMES C. COX is Professor of Economics and Senior Associate of the Economic Science Laboratory at the University of Arizona. His research includes papers in experimental economics on auction markets, search models, and incentive mechanisms. He has also written on public policy toward the oil industry and minimum wage legislation.

RICHARD FELDMAN is Professor and Chair, Department of Philosophy, University of Rochester. His areas of specialization are: epistemology and metaphysics. Publications include *Reason and Argument* (Prentice-Hall, 1993); "Reliability and Justification," *The Monist* 68 (1985): 159-174; "Evidentialism" (co-authored with Earl Conee), *Philosophical Studies* 48 (1985): 15-34; "Epistemic Obligations," in *Philosophical Perspectives* vol. 2, *Epistemology*, ed. James Tomberlin (Ridgeview, 1988, 235-256); "Proper Functionalism," *Nous* (1993).

RICHARD FOLEY is Professor of Philosophy and Dean of the Faculty of Arts and Sciences at Rutgers University. He is the author of *The Theory of Epistemic Rationality* (Harvard University Press, 1987) and *Working without a Net* (Oxford University Press, 1993).

MARGARET GILBERT is Professor of Philosophy at the University of Connecticut, Storrs, where she has taught since 1983. Her areas of specialization include philosophical social theory, philosophy of social science, and philosophical foundations of game theory. Her major publications include *On Social Facts* (Routledge, 1989), and articles including, most recently, "Agreements, Coercion, and Obligation," *Ethics* (1993), and "Is an Agreement an Exchange of Promises?" *Journal of Philosophy* (1993). She is at work on a monograph on political obligation.

ALVIN I. GOLDMAN is Professor of Philosophy and Research Scientist in Cognitive Science at the University of Arizona. He does research on epistemology, philosophy of mind, and philosophy of the cognitive and social sciences. His books include *A Theory of Human Action (Prenctice-Hall, 1970), Epistemology and Cognition (Harvard University Press, 1986)*, and *Liaisons: Philosophy Meets the Cognitive and Social Sciences* (MIT Press, 1992).

PHILIP KITCHER is Presidential Professor of Philosophy at the University of California at San Diego. He is the author of *Abusing Science: The Case against Creationism* (MIT Press, 1982), *The Nature of Mathematical Knowledge* (Oxford University Press, 1983), *Vaulting Ambition: Sociobiology and the Quest for Human Nature* (MIT Press, 1985), and *The Advancement of Science* (Oxford University Press, 1993). He is also the author of numerous articles on topics in epistemology and the philosophy of science.

HILARY KORNBLITH is Professor of Philosophy at the University of Vermont. He has written on topics in epistemology, metaphysics, and philosophy of language. He is the author of *Inductive Inference and Its Natural Ground* (MIT Press, 1993) and editor of *Naturalizing Epistemology (MIT Press, 1994).*

HELEN E. LONGINO is Professor of Philosophy at Rice University and Winton Visiting Professor for 1993-1995 at the University of Minnesota. She is the author of *Science as Social Knowledge: Values and Objectivity in Scientific Inquiry* (Princeton, 1990) and of numerous articles in philosophy of science and feminist philosophy.

FREDERICK F. SCHMITT is Professor of Philosophy at the University of Illinois at Urbana-Champaign. His areas of specialization are epistemology and the history of epistemology. He is the author of *Knowledge and Belief* (Routledge, 1992) and *Truth—A Primer* (Westview, forthcoming).

MIRIAM SOLOMON is Assistant Professor at Temple University. Her areas of specialization are philosophy of science and epistemology. Her publications include "Quine's Point of View," *Journal of Philosophy 86* (1989): 113-136; "Scientific Rationality and Human Reasoning," *Philosophy of Science 59* (1992): 439-455; and "Social Empiricism," *Nous* (1994). She is currently working on a book entitled *Social Empiricism.*

JAMES SPELLMAN is a research and teaching assistant in the Philosophy Department of the University of Illinois at Urbana-Champaign. His interests are primarily in metaphysics and the philosophy of mind. He is the author (with F. Schmitt) of "Naturalizing Epistemology—A Bibliography," in Hilary Kornblith, ed., *Naturalizing Epistemology* (MIT Press, 1994).